The new left and the Jews

THE
NEW LEFT
AND
THE JEWS

EDITED BY

Mordecai S. Chertoff

PITMAN PUBLISHING CORPORATION

New York   Toronto   London   Tel Aviv

ACKNOWLEDGMENTS

This volume had its genesis in a weekend conference on Israel, America, and the New Left, held at Arden House in February, 1970, under the auspices of the American Histadrut Cultural Exchange Institute. Seven of the papers included — those by Robert Alter, Noam Chomsky, Leonard Fein, Saadia Gelb, Nathan Glazer, Tom Kahn, and Nathan Rotenstreich — were prepared for presentation at the conference. The articles by Menachem S. Arnoni, Tom Milstein, and myself were written especially for this volume. The balance have been reprinted as follows:

Irving Howe, "Political Terrorism: Hysteria on the Left." Copyright © 1970 by the New York Times Company. Reprinted by permission.

Amos Kenan, "New Left Go Home." This article first appeared in *Yediot Achronot* (Israel). Reprinted by permission.

Walter Laqueur, "Reflections on Youth Movements." Copyright © 1961 by the American Jewish Committee. Reprinted by permission.

Seymour Martin Lipset, "'The Socialism of Fools': The Left, the Jews, and Israel." This is a revised version of an article which first appeared in *Encounter* (1969 December). Reprinted by permission of the author.

Robert A. Nisbet, "The Twilight of Authority." Copyright (in part) © 1969 by National Affairs, Inc.; (in part) © 1970 by the New York Times Company. Reprinted by permission.

Marie Syrkin, "The Claim of the Palestinian Arabs." Much of this article first appeared in *Midstream* (1970 January). Reprinted by permission of the author.

The author would also like to acknowledge the kindness of Philip Horn, director of the University Department of the American Zionist Youth Foundation, for information on and materials from the various new groups of young Jewish radicals.

THE NEW LEFT AND THE JEWS

71-44

CONTENTS

IN GENERAL . . .

1   *Revolt and the democratic society*   3
    ROBERT ALTER

2   *The twilight of authority*   24
    ROBERT A. NISBET

3   *Political terrorism:*
    hysteria on the left   38
    IRVING HOWE

4   *Reflections on youth movements*   54
    WALTER LAQUEUR

5   *From the ashes of the new left:*
    toward a new student movement   77
    TOM KAHN

IN PARTICULAR

6   *"The socialism of fools":*
    the left, the Jews, and Israel   103
    SEYMOUR MARTIN LIPSET

7 *The new left and Israel* 132
LEONARD FEIN

8 *Jewish interests and the new left* 152
NATHAN GLAZER

9 *The new left and the newer leftists* 166
MORDECAI S. CHERTOFF

10 *Israel and the new left* 197
NOAM CHOMSKY

11 *The new left and the right to exist* 229
NATHAN ROTENSTREICH

12 *The claim of the Palestinian Arabs* 246
MARIE SYRKIN

13 *Why the new left needs Israel* 270
MENACHEM S. ARNONI

14 *The new left: areas of Jewish concern* 289
TOM MILSTEIN

15 *New left go home* 306
AMOS KENAN

16 *The kibbutz as a revolutionary society* 312
SAADIA GELB

In general . . .

1   *Revolt and the democratic society*

ROBERT ALTER

In striking contrast to what it became in the late sixties, the American college campus was traditionally remote from political—let alone revolutionary—activism. Whereas European students were quick to mount the barricades, their American counterparts were more apt to be concerned with the relative strengths of their respective football teams or competitively swallowing goldfish. There were politically oriented clubs on many campuses, but their following and influence were small. For all its digging, the Rapp-Coudert Committee of the early forties found very few radicals even in the New York City colleges.

What little political activity there was in the forties seemed to fade away completely in the decade that followed—so much so that it might fairly be characterized as the "apathetic fifties." It seemed as though students were turning away completely from any but their own narrow interests and were concerned, above all else, with how to make it into the Establishment.

Then came the sixties and the New Left. Almost overnight, students seemed to turn radical with a vengeance; the talk was of "revolution," of overthrowing the Establishment and thereby uprooting primordial evil. American society was moribund, and the under-thirty generation, the new revolutionaries, were totally disillusioned with what they were inheriting. They had the solution to America's ills, however: dismantle the old, destroy what there was, and a brave new world would emerge. The first step—and their blueprint seemed to go no further—was revolt.

The first group of essays in this volume deals with the nature of that revolt—its premises and its promises—and provides a perspective for those who would

ROBERT ALTER *is Professor of Hebrew and Comparative Literature, University of California, Berkeley.*

3

*like to understand it better. Dr. Robert Alter, who
opened the Arden House Conference on which this
symposium is based, addresses himself to the American
scene and to the question of the impact of the New Left
on our American society—the role of revolt and the
permissible limits of revolt in a democracy. Drawing
on the writings of Herbert Marcuse and other leftist
theoreticians, he points out the confusion which results
from identifying all authority with a monolithic Establishment and seeing all authority as reflecting the views
of that monolith. He discusses the dangers implicit
in the careless use of terms—the tendency to dehu-
manize those with whom one disagrees by applying
crude nicknames to them and the danger inherent in
the leftist confusion of messianism and reformism.*

I shall address myself to some large, abstract political problems,
although I am not a student of political theory, social movements, or social structures. I come from Berkeley, but I claim
no special lines of communication to what is going on "out
there." Like you, I read the *New York Times,* and, beyond that,
I observe what happens in Sproul Plaza and elsewhere on my
own campus. Because I do not pretend to any kind of professional expertise outside my field, I approach the whole complex
of issues related to my theme—the role of revolt and the limits
of revolt in a democratic society—as a humble humanist who,
at best, can offer one humanist's limited perspective on some
of the things that have been going on. As I talk about protest,
by the way, I'll be drawing all my examples from student protest, because I've observed at least some of it firsthand. I think,
however, that most of my generalizations would probably apply
to other types of protest as well.

Let me add this: there may be some advantage in avowing
one's ignorance, for I think that the worst thing one can do on
this subject is to pretend to know exactly what has happened,
why it has happened, and what will happen in the future. A
very recent and, I think, rather embarrassing example of such

presumptuousness is an essay that appeared in the February 1970 issue of *Encounter,* Robert Nisbet's "What Killed the Student Revolution?" Robert Nisbet—I don't know him personally—has been a senior member of the Department of Sociology at Berkeley. Although I would not discount everything Nisbet says, it seems to me that it's very ill advised at this point, six or eight months after the last really violent disruptions, for anyone to talk about what killed the student revolution. That is, if my colleagues and I who have been involved in this from the faculty side have learned anything over the last three or four years, it's to make no predictions.

Last year some of the "savviest" people I know on the Berkeley campus, who have been around the academic scene a long time and are not inclined to alarmism, were talking about a period of perhaps ten or twenty years, during which we would have to live in a state of guerrilla warfare on our campuses. This year there doesn't seem to be much sign of that, but I think we would be foolhardy to talk at the moment about the future. As I reread these words now [in May, 1970] events have already exposed the foolhardiness of premature "autopsies." Windows are again smashed all over the Berkeley campus, exploded tear-gas cannisters are scattered everywhere, and there have been major disturbances at half a dozen major universities, involving rock throwing, arson, and even shootings.

My own purpose here is not to give a definitive scientific explanation of what the protest has been, what protest should be in a democratic society, or what can be expected in the near future. What I shall try to describe instead is a certain climate of thought—and I think we have ample evidence that such a climate exists at least locally and sporadically—where protest can become harmful to a democratic society. This of course doesn't mean that the protests we have had are in fact going to become radically harmful. Since, in describing harmful trends out of context, I may sound like an alarmist, I would like to emphasize that I'm not terribly alarmed personally, and I think that we have all tended too much to alarmism about this whole phenomenon that we've been witnessing in this country.

It seems to me that all of us, even if we're quite sophisticated intellectually, find ourselves in the McLuhan situation of being surrounded by the news media, and as a result we tend to think in images more than we should—isolated visual images, images torn from their complicated context of explanation. And to the degree that we summon language to help us, there is a tendency to use either not very helpful, subversively misleading abstractions or certain kinds of obfuscating epithets and slogans. I'll come back to this use of language a little bit later, because it seems to me one of the essentially troubling things that has been happening in our climate of protest.

To illustrate briefly what I mean about our tendency to think in terms of images, let me take two counterposed images. In one variation or another we've all seen each of these images, either in photographic reproduction or on the television screen. One image is of a cop and a student, and, for good measure, let's say the student is black. The cop is wearing one of those blue crash helmets with a plastic visor, so that he looks a little like a man from Mars, less like a human being. He has a nightstick in his hand, and, ideally, he's already used it once, so that you can see blood streaming down the head of the student, who may be having his arm twisted or the scruff of his neck held at the same time. Well, that picture says a great deal. The trouble is, it can also say a great deal that's misleading, if you don't know what has led up to that moment—what the student has done and what the cop has done—and what the respective motives of the cop and the student are. Photographs like this one, blown up to poster size, have been displayed very effectively in various kinds of store windows and public bulletin boards in Berkeley. If it is nothing else, this is surely a great age of propaganda.

Let me remind you, on the other hand, of an image which we all saw on the front page of the *New York Times* and other newspapers throughout the country in the spring of 1969, a picture of a group of Negro students standing in front of a university building on the Cornell campus with guns in their hands. If the mere fact is worrisome, the image itself has a kind of violent immediacy, an unsubtlety that may misrepresent the actual circumstances. The key concept here is a total lack of context, which leads one to draw what may be very erroneous and, for the most part, alarmist inferences that the situation itself may not warrant.

Let me add to this intrinsically unsubtle directness of the image another fact that we're all aware of, which is simply that news media are attracted to what is most spectacular, not necessarily to what is most representative, in any particular phenomenon, political or otherwise. For that reason, whether your politics are left, right, or center, there can often be a big gap between what you think is happening on the basis of what you encounter in the media and what in fact is happening.

Recently a Chicago-based organization called the Urban Research Corporation published a detailed study of last year's student disruptions. Using their findings, I would like to run through a few salient figures here to illustrate the difference between the way most of us conceived that last year's protest was going and the way it actually was going.

In 75 percent of the campus protests across the country last year, there was no destruction or violence of any kind. Not that I think we need dismiss the other quarter in which there was destruction and, at times, violence of a serious kind. But, again, I think our image of what happened is rather different.

In 60 percent of the protests there was no interruption of college routine. In only 6 percent of the protests were nonnegotiable demands made. In only 13 percent of the protests were ultimatums of various kinds made.

New Left participation, which I assume to mean observable New Left participation, counted for about 28 percent of the protests. That is, of course, an appreciable number, somewhere between a quarter and a third, but considerably less than many people would have supposed.

LOCAL ISSUES PREDOMINATE

On 59 percent of the affected campuses the issues were racial. On 42 percent of the affected campuses, the issues involved student power in one way or another, and antiwar or antimilitary issues occurred on 25 percent of the affected campuses. In other words, on the decisive majority of campuses where there were disruptions last year, the issues turned out to be local issues in the final analysis.

Finally, what happened with these protests last year? At the end of the six-month period of the study, 69 percent of all demands were still unsatisfied.

Although I think these figures speak for themselves, let me spell out a few inferences I would draw from them before I go on to consider the intrinsic dangers in the climate of protest that has been created.

It seems obvious that, on the whole, the protests that took place last year did not have the kind of apocalyptic extremism that was often attributed to them. And, as I have said, they tended to occur as a response to local irritants. In any case, they certainly did not occur on any great scale as part of a national revolutionary movement concerned with larger ideological issues.

EFFECTIVENESS OF PROTESTS

The protests had a very modest degree of effectiveness. The figures seem to indicate that they were more effective where black students were involved, and that makes obvious sense. That is, administrators responded to protest on issues where the administration itself had a bad conscience or was nervous, politically nervous. But I think this must be added: the administrators responded where the response didn't cost them too much—where it didn't effect any very radical change in the constitution of the institution. Even considering the nervousness about black protest and all the talk about minority groups in the New York city colleges last year, it is a long step between talking and acting to offer unqualified open admissions for disadvantaged groups, if such a step is going to completely change the constitution of the institution. There is, then, a certain obvious but limited utility to protest, and if we talk about the danger of protest, I think we should also keep in mind that protest has its uses in overcoming the inertia of entrenched institutions within a democratic society.

Now, I'm not going to talk about what *kinds* of protests are admissible and what kinds inadmissible. To some extent, no comment is needed because many of these differentiations are self-evident. Clearly, burning down buildings and tossing bombs are acts that none of us would want to accept as admissible forms of protest in a democratic society, whereas nondisruptive picketing or perhaps even boycotts would not be objectionable as a matter of principle. There are, of course, many cases that are going to fall on a debatable middle ground, but I don't think that such debate would be very fruitful here.

What I would like to talk about, as I said, is the climate of thought in which protest can become potentially dangerous for the survival of a democratic society. Let me begin with Herbert Marcuse, who both expresses and reflects such a climate of thought. I will quote from his last book, *An Essay on Liberation*,[1] with a certain degree of bad conscience because it is, admittedly, Marcuse at his weakest. However, I think it is a justified example to cite here. Reading it, I cannot escape the impression that

1. Herbert Marcuse, *An Essay on Liberation* (Boston: Beacon Press, 1969).

this Grand Old Man of the New Left (as some would have him) has nothing more to give us than a wilting combination of Marxist infrastructure and utopian naiveté.

MARCUSE'S PECULIAR USE OF LANGUAGE

An Essay on Liberation is, nevertheless, an important symptom of certain patterns of thought and action of the left, both because it tries to articulate an ideological rationale for what is going on and because it is clearly a self-conscious response to what is going on. George Kateb, in a recent *Commentary* article, "The Political Thought of Herbert Marcuse," called it Marcuse's "love letter" to the young generation.[2] Even on the basis of the passages I'm going to quote here, perhaps you will see the justice of that description: "Never perhaps since the Middle Ages has accumulated repression erupted on such global scale in organized aggression against those outside the repressive system—'outsiders' within and without." (That is, the North Vietnamese and the Third World people on the one hand, and hippies, American blacks, and American dissidents of all sorts on the other hand.)

I would suggest that there is a kind of shady game going on even in regard to historical comparisons. "Never perhaps since the Middle Ages" may point to the Crusades, but if such repression hasn't been manifest since the Middle Ages on the same global scale, it is simply because subsequent historical events have not, until now, taken place on the same global scale. And furthermore, before the intervention of modern communications media, people could not be aware of what was happening all over the world as they are aware today. In any case, the notion that exactly the same energy of aggression, with the same psychological mechanism, is being directed against hippies on the one hand and against oppressed Third World people on the

2. George Kateb, "The Political Thought of Herbert Marcuse," *Commentary* (January 1970), pp. 48–63.

other seems to me extremely dubious. But let me go on to the heart of Marcuse's argument, which really brings us to the central node of justification for the kinds of disruptive protest we've seen.

> In the face of the scope and intensity of this sanctioned aggression [this aggression occurring on a global scale], the traditional distinction between legitimate and illegitimate violence becomes questionable. If legitimate violence includes, in the daily routine of "pacification" and "liberation," wholesale burning, poisoning, bombing, [then] the actions of the radical opposition, no matter how illegitimate, can hardly be called by the same name: violence.

Something that Marcuse does here with language begins to be very unsettling. He denies that we should use the term *violence* to describe the overt actions of people who oppose, let's say, the bombing of North Vietnam by beating people up or trying to burn down buildings or disrupt university activities. (Marcuse's own examples of such opposition tactics are rather toned down.) This is a little bit like saying that, after Auschwitz, an individual murder no longer deserves to be called murder. This can lead to developing language rules which enable one to say that A is not A or that B is not B. But Marcuse continues:

> Can there by any meaningful comparison, in magnitude and criminality, between the unlawful acts committed by the rebels in the ghettos, on the campuses, on the city streets on the one side, and the deeds perpetrated by the forces of order in Vietnam, in Bolivia, in Indonesia, in Guatemala on the other? Can one meaningfully call it an offense when demonstrators disrupt the business of the university, the draft board, the supermarket, the flow of traffic, to protest against the far more efficient disruption of the business of life of untold numbers of human beings by the armed forces of law and order? Here, too, the brute reality requires a redefinition of terms: the established vocabulary discriminates a priori against the opposition—it protects the Establishment.

I am very troubled by what happens with language here, in the hands of a man who we can assume has a great deal more intellectual sophistication than the students out at the barricades. In this paragraph, Marcuse uses two heavily loaded phrases: "the forces of order" and "the armed forces of law and order." Then, in his next paragraph, he goes on to say, "Law and Order: these words have always had an ominous sound." In purely historical terms, I would tend to doubt that myself. In any case, Marcuse assumes a monolithic entity, the forces of law and order, universally and homogeneously repressive, acting in exactly the same way in Vietnam, in Bolivia, in Indonesia. Without going into the historical details of each of these examples, it is sufficient to observe that the arbitrary lumping together of such different political phenomena is either the reflex of a simple mind or the trick of a demagogue.

In Marcuse's usage, all these forces of law and order are subsumed under that great capitalized term *the Establishment.* Now, it seems to me that we'd all breathe a little more freely and think a little more clearly if we could have, let's say, a ten-year moratorium on the use of the word *Establishment.* In the *New Yorker* of October 19, 1968, there appeared an article by Henry Fairlie, the British journalist, called "The Evolution of a Term." Fairlie claims to have introduced the term *Establishment* more or less in its present usage back in the mid-fifties. He is absolutely appalled at the way it is now misused, overused, and abused in so many ways, especially in America. He quotes, for example, one Sunday issue of the *New York Times,* in which he finds half a dozen different uses of the term, all of them vaguely negative and many of them mutually contradictory.

What happens in Marcuse's usage is a kind of elevation of the unexamined term to a level of mythic existence. After all, it is only in the realm of myth that perfectly fixed, unchanging powers are found, whereas institutions are multifaceted, internally complex, ambiguous, and susceptible to change. The Sun God is unchanging. Jupiter is always Jupiter. In like manner, this big, vague obstruction, the Establishment, is imagined as being always the same, working out one eternal plan of repression on the streets of Berkeley, in Vietnam, in Indonesia, in Bolivia, wherever.

Toward the end of his article, Fairlie quotes from the great French Jewish historian, Marc Bloch, who was murdered by the Nazis. A few months before his death, Bloch made this self-critical observation in a kind of personal spiritual legacy entitled *Strange Defeat*:

> I referred a while back to the "High Command." But scarcely had my pen written the words than the historian in me was shocked by their use. For the ABC of my trade consists in avoiding the big-sounding abstract terms. Those who teach history should be continually concerned with the task of seeking the solid and the concrete behind the empty and the abstract. In other words, it is on men rather than functions that they should concentrate their attention. The errors of the High Command were, fundamentally, the errors of a specific group of human beings.

ATMOSPHERE OF VIOLENCE

It is partly because so many people have used such abstractions in this obfuscating way that we have begun to create at least the potential for an atmosphere of murderous violence. I can't blame eighteen-year-olds for this as much as some thirty- and fifty-year-olds, and even seventy-year-olds like Marcuse. I am not, of course, suggesting that we eschew abstractions altogether; without them thought would be impossible. Certainly, one can speak of power and the exercise of power as a relational quality present in many different situations. The danger is in equating this relational quality with a Power Structure or an Establishment, a monolithic *agency* equally present in all power situations.

Let me say this, parathentically, while I'm talking about the use of facile abstractions. In spite of all the shouting about relevance—and, again, I hear it less this year at Berkeley—as a humanist committed to the careful analysis of literary texts, some of them going back many centuries, I find that the relevance of my own professional activity is precisely in trying to preserve for myself and my students some sense that words have to be used and interpreted with care, and that sloganizing leads to a form of intellectual paralysis.

What has happened, as I intimated before, is that we are plagued by two kinds of language abuse. One is insulting expletive, as, for example, *pigs* for police or *honkey* for white, which are, of course, merely counter-terms for the abusive language of majority prejudice. The other kind of abuse is the use of large formulaic or even mythicized abstractions such as *the Establishment* and *the forces of law and order.*

What results can be expected when language is used this way and combined with the violent immediacy of the image-out-of-context that I talked about earlier?

A few days before the outbreak of the first serious disruptions in the Third World strike in the winter of 1969, Berkeley radicals were writing in the student newspaper in the following manner: Just as our brothers, the Viet Cong, are putting their lives on the line out in the jungles of Southeast Asia, we have got to get out there in the streets and put our lives on the line for the freedom of humanity. In this case, I am not quoting directly, but my paraphrase, I think, is not a parody, but rather a fairly accurate imitation of the way such people use language. That is, by invoking emotive clichés, the writer would have you imagine, as Marcuse has already pointed out, that you and the Vietnamese face exactly the same enemy, embodied here in the campus security staff and the Berkeley police force; he would also have you remember that just as the Vietnamese are faced with nothing less than the threat of *genocide* (another word used with promiscuous freedom in the most surprising contexts these days) so you are fighting for your life, and therefore *anything* you do is really justified.

Some of the things that, in fact, were done by protesters were rather scary. Fire bombs were thrown into buildings on the Berkeley campus, both when the buildings were empty and when they were filled with students and staff. (It's never been fully established that student activists carried out the one successful act of arson among several separate attempts—the burning of Wheeler Hall, with damage of over half a million dollars—but the facts, in any case, look suspicious.) Attempts were made to plant a bomb in the office of a liberal professor at San Francisco State College across the Bay. In the same institution, a poor, mixed-up black youngster blew off most of his fingers when he tried to plant a bomb in a locker room, where, if the bomb had worked as intended, it could have killed or maimed perhaps a dozen students at once. Again in Berkeley, tear-gas bombs were thrown into crowded lecture halls. As a point of historical fact, for all the hideousness and stupidity of the action of Sheriff Madigan and the National Guard in attacking the campus with tear gas in May 1969, it must be said that the first tear-gas bomb thrown on our campus was thrown by student activists into 155 Dwinelle Hall, a large lecture hall full of students, during the Third World Liberation disturbances in early 1969.

I don't mean in any way to exculpate the "forces of repression," to use the kind of mind-numbing language that has unfortunately been brought into play. What emerges is a mutually reinforcing cycle of role playing. That is, if the students imagine themselves as the Viet Cong, the police forces, especially when under the command of such an enlightened figure as Sheriff Madigan of Alameda County, California, eagerly respond by imagining themselves as the spearhead of a search-and-destroy operation. Having been present at the first general invasion of the campus by police and the National Guard, equipped with fixed bayonets and chemical agents, I can attest that there was no disruptive protest of any kind going on when the order to attack was given. However, the police and the guardsmen knew they had an enemy to subdue, they possessed all the implements for warfare against revolutionary hordes—gas masks and protective helmets, pepper foggers, tear-gas grenade launchers, riot guns, bayonets and clubs—and they carried out their pincer operations by surrounding the scattered groups on campus and undertaking exercises in assault that included pouring tear gas into class buildings. Clearly, then, there is a powerful self-fulfilling element in this whole atmosphere of violence: people on both sides of the barriers are being propagandized into believing in a situation that really does not exist and are then converting their conviction into brutal fact.

The danger of the promiscuous use of vilifying epithets is even clearer. At this point in history, such a familiar fact should hardly need much emphasis. But to cite a recent, painful example, let me recall the participant in the Songmy massacre who, when interviewed on television, quite unreflectingly kept talking about "the gooks": "Well, there were these gooks there," and so forth. It's all too clear that the ability to label people as "gooks" makes it easier to think of them as other than human beings, whose lives are not to be taken seriously. To take a current example from the other end of the political spectrum, calling police "pigs" can very easily have precisely the same effect.

THE PORNOGRAPHY OF VIOLENCE

I'd like to share with you a rather startling illustration of how one begins to view people, human life, and violence when one thinks in these terms and these images. The following letter appeared about a month ago in the *Daily Californian,* the student newspaper in Berkeley. It is signed by Daniel Andler, a student of mathematics, who clearly considers himself a revolutionary, but, as will become apparent, a revolutionary of a moderate, civilized sort. The letter is dated January 18, 1970.

> Last Friday, as *The Battle of Algiers* was being shown in Pauley Ballroom, a strong minority in the audience ap-

plauded and even laughed each time a policeman was shot in the back or a bomb exploded in a cafe or a club. This behavior, a standard reaction to World War II pictures, would have no doubt surprised Pontecorvo, who directed *The Battle,* and calls for reflection.

In an ethical perspective, one finds it hard to applaud the applauders. It could be asserted, for instance, that the death of a man can in no case be, as such, a matter for applause: "Any man's death diminishes me, because I am involved in mankind." More specifically, policemen and civilians who were killed during the first attacks in 1954 and 1955 had committed no more atrocities than, say, their American counterparts before the outburst of violence: do the applauders really believe they themselves deserve death? Had a bomb exploded in Pauley Ballroom that evening, would the survivors have rejoiced and, supposing they were still capable of recognizing the political necessity of their friends' deaths, would they have considered them just? Even within the minimal ethical framework of self-interest, applause seems hardly appropriate; for if indeed man is a wolf to man (and this was at stake in the very tense ballroom when a girl ran out during the showing, crying, begging us to stop, to stop the applause and the killing, screaming that we were all brothers), then our own fate is our sole concern, and little doubt as to theirs is left to the applauders in the picture.

The entire scene is troubling enough, but what is especially poignant and painful is that image of the girl getting up and running out, with a plea to the audience to stop the applause and the killing. The kind of atmosphere one senses here has been precisely characterized by the film critic Stanley Kauffmann in a phrase he used to describe this picture: "The pornography of violence." This atmosphere of violence is almost palpable in the letter writer's description of the screening, and clearly there's often no more than a step between experiencing this sort of thing ritually, as in a film, and acting it out on the streets or elsewhere.

In line with my earlier remarks about Marcuse, I might interject here that in *An Essay on Liberation* he has a great deal to say about the redemptive function of using violent language, including, of course, vilifying epithets. This strikes me as a particularly good example of how blind he is to what is happening right now. By invoking such an inane form of utopianism, he is really encouraging tendencies that are subversive not of an Establishment but rather of the possibilities of civilized life. Clearly, I do not want to relate violent language to the kind of violence that uses all the implements of technology to try to bomb a Southeast Asian people into the Stone Age. Moreover, the claims of those who argue that only disruption can stir institutions from their criminal inertia are not to be easily dismissed. But the scene at *The Battle of Algiers* is symptomatic of a hard truth too easily forgotten—that violence has its own dynamics and its own powerful inner momentum. The movement from violent words and images to bombings in banks and other public buildings and perhaps to bloodier kinds of destructiveness is not inevitable, but it is perilously easy.

NEOBARBARISM

As I stated at the outset, I find little ground for apocalyptic alarmism. Nevertheless, we should not ignore inherent dangers which could become very grave dangers if given sufficient encouragement. In this connection, I sense that there is a kind of neobarbarism which finds an outlet in the protests at their worst.

Certain manifestations of protest deserve to be called neobarbarism because they ultimately represent not a rebellion for a political purpose, no matter how much Che, Mao, Frantz Fanon, or any other ideological guide is cited, but rather a rebellion against restriction, against the disciplines of culture and the mutual restraints that are necessary if men are to live their lives together.

The attitude towards technology in this regard seems to me particularly suggestive and troubling. True, Marcuse, in his unflagging utopian vision, places a great deal of—probably too much—faith in the redemptive power of technology. Ironically, the New Left includes a strong antitechnological undercurrent, as can be seen, for example, in the films of Jean Luc Godard. A number of observers have noted the neo-Luddite desire to smash the hated and threatening machines of the age of automation as well as the latter-day mills of industry. The spectacular shambles made of the computer center at Montreal's Sir George Williams University last year and the abortive attempts on other computer centers in major universities surely reveal an underlying impulse in some of the protesters to destroy the new technology itself.

THE WAR ON CULTURE

In certain crucial protests, moreover, protesters have tried to get to university card catalogs or to the books themselves. I find this especially disturbing and, at the same time, very revealing of the kind of destruction possible in this atmosphere of violence. At Berkeley, several hundred cards were ripped from the files but were quickly rescued; in at least one major university library, a large part of the central card catalog was destroyed. Let me remind you that if the card catalog of a major library is destroyed, the library itself becomes essentially unusable for a period of perhaps five years or longer. Surely not all protesters secretly dream of razing civilization to the ground. However, at least this much can be said: through constant exposure to vicious, propagandistic rhetoric, students have become addicted to thinking in unqualified images to such a degree that some of them are now expressing violent resentment against the whole superstructure of culture with which they have to live.

ORIGINS OF MESSIANISM

As a final observation about different kinds of protest, I would like to make a working distinction between messianism and reformism. In terms of the history of ideas, the word *messianism* has been both overused and misused. It is commonly held that the Jews first conceived the messianic idea, from which ultimately are derived Freudian messianism, Marxist messianism, and, of course, Zionism. According to this view, almost any messianic movement must derive from the biblical messianic idea.

I think this view is partly wrong because I suspect that, in the history of ideas, Plato's *Republic* may have more to do with what in the modern age is generally called political messianism than does Isaiah, Jeremiah, or Ezekiel. For the biblical Prophets, redemption is expected to come from without. Man remains imperfect, trying somehow to lessen his imperfection, but it is the power of God working through history that ultimately is going to redeem man; it is God, at best only calling on man to be his partner, who is going to send his annointed one, his Messiah, to bring about the redemption. In Plato, on the other hand, we encounter the notion of human reason *planning* the redemption, planning the perfect society, and bringing it about through a ruthlessly systematic political translation of an intellectual scheme. Plato's Republic, to be sure, was conceived not to redeem the whole world, but rather only an enclosed society. Nevertheless, it remains the first model for all rationalistically redemptionist—which in practice usually means totalitarian—states.

For my purposes, the essential difference between messianic redemptionism and reformism is simply the assumption about the perfectability of man. That is, the messianist assumes that man is totally perfectable; somehow, he can absolutely transcend the nature of human existence and make himself into a kind of god. (I am referring, of course, not to messianism as it was actually articulated in the Prophets, but rather to the more recent movements usually called messianic, though perhaps better described as varieties of political Platonism.) This is a grand, ennobling idea. But it can also be absolutely pernicious, because if you believe that you have the key to make things utterly different and utterly better, then in order to realize your program you may do whatever you want. You may massacre millions of people and toss them on the garbage heap of history. You may be as ruthless as you want or as your plan requires, because you have a clear knowledge of the perfect good that you are in the process of realizing through political action.

REFORMISM AND MAN'S IMPERFECTION

The reformist, on the other hand, has a sense that man is an imperfect, ambiguous creature and that human societies are a very mixed business necessarily. This doesn't by any means suggest that the reformist acquiesces in imperfection and injustice. It means rather that he is very vigorous in continually struggling to make social institutions and individual human beings better and more just, even though he is finally aware of the enormous resistance and limitation of human nature itself. There is, I should think, something empirical and patiently tentative in the reformist that sets him apart from the messianist. The reformist does not assume that he has a sure grip on absolute truth.

In this connection and by way of conclusion, I would like to quote and comment on one of the really disquieting passages in Nietzsche's *The Birth of Tragedy* which may have some bearing on our own cultural predicament:

> Now we must not hide from ourselves what is concealed in the womb of this Socratic culture: optimism with its delusion of limitless power.[3] We must not be alarmed if the fruits

3. *Socratic culture* is precisely the culture that assumes that reason is the fulfillment of man and that builds on knowledge and its endless accumulation. Nietzsche alternatively describes it as *Alexandrian culture*, derived, of course, from ancient Alexandria. Everything works in terms of knowledge, implemented, to some extent, in action. Nietzsche at this early point in his career sees his own nineteenth-century Germany in this light.

of this optimism ripen—if society, leavened to the very lowest strata by this kind of culture, gradually begins to tremble with wants and agitations and desires, if the belief in the earthly happiness of all, if the belief in the possibility of such a general intellectual culture changes into the threatening demand for such an Alexandrian earthly happiness, into the conjuring up of an Euripidean *deus ex machina.*

Let us mark this well. The Alexandrian culture, to be able to exist permanently, requires a slave class, but with its optimistic view of life, it denies the necessity of such a class.[4] And consequently when its beautifully seductive and tranquillizing utterances about the "dignity of man" and the "dignity of labor" are no longer effective, it gradually drifts toward a dreadful destruction. There is nothing more terrible than a class of barbaric slaves who have learned to regard their existence as an injustice and now prepare to avenge not only themselves but all generations.

DELUSION OF LIMITLESS POWER

After beginning in moderation, I do not want to end with this grim note from Nietzsche intoning dire prophesies of doom. It would be too simplistic to say that, in the protests we have seen in this country, in France, and in Germany, we can identify a barbaric slave class ready "to avenge not only themselves but all generations." However, I do think that, along with all the other factors that charge and confuse our atmosphere, something of that cataclysmic potential has also been present and is beginning to be exploited through the kind of ideological and verbal promiscuity I've tried to describe. Nietzsche's telling description of the delusion of limitless power deriving from the optimism of the Socratic society is precisely suited to the phe-

4. Clearly, Nietzsche is not being absolutely literal, because he also has nineteenth-century Germany in mind. It seems that his term *slave* also denotes what we would call the disadvantaged classes. Not everybody is equally privileged in a society based on the power of knowledge; not everybody can be an equal member of the elite.

nomenon reflected in so embarrassingly naive a way in Marcuse's notion of liberation, as, indeed, it is reflected in other ways in most socialist visions. This is not to discount the very real human value of socialism, but simply to say that socialism and other kinds of political messianism have not fully confronted the darker complexities and ambiguities of human nature.

Robert Heilbroner, in his fine essay "Socialism and the Future," recently published in *Commentary*, points out with great effectiveness what others have also observed, that one of the chief deficiencies of socialism as a world view is that it lacks an adequate theory of man.[5] It doesn't have a sufficient notion either of the contradictions, the stubborn perversities, and the complexities of human nature or of the peculiarities of man as a volitional, rather than a rational, animal. If there is one thing we can learn from the serious study of our literature and our history, it is surely that without an adequate theory of man we can get ourselves into a great deal of trouble. We can begin by participating in that Pauley Ballroom screening, where the students applaud each time a cop is shot in the back or a bomb explodes in a cafe, and we can go on from there to things much worse.

5. Robert Heilbroner, "Socialism and the Future," *Commentary* (December 1969), pp. 35-45.

2   *The twilight of authority*

ROBERT A. NISBET

The current revolt against the Establishment is not simply a revolt against the powers that be. It is that, to be sure—a revolt against parents, teachers, and administrators, collegiate and governmental—but it is even more a revolt against the authority of reason and a rejection of all discipline and responsibility, even revolutionary responsibility.

Robert A. Nisbet traces the nature of authority in its various manifestations and indicates what its decline presages both for society at large and for its prime transmitter of values—the university.

The most striking fact in the present period of revolutionary change is the quickened erosion of the traditional institutional authorities that for nearly a millennium have been Western man's principal sources of order and liberty. I am referring to the manifest decline of influence of the legal system, the church, family, local community, and, most recently and perhaps most ominously, of school and the university.

There are some who see in the accelerating erosion of these authorities the beginning of a new and higher freedom of the individual. The fetters of constraint, it is said, are being struck off, leaving creative imagination free, as it has never been free before, to build a truly legitimate society. Far greater, however, is the number of those persons who see in this erosion, not the new shape of freedom, but the specters of social anarchy and moral chaos.

I would be happy if I could join either of these groups in their perceptions. But I cannot. Nothing in history suggests to me the likelihood of either creative liberty or destructive license

ROBERT A. NISBET *is Professor of Sociology at the University of California, Riverside.*

for very long in a population witnessing the dissolution of the social and moral authorities it has been accustomed to. I should say, rather, that what is inevitable in such circumstances is the rise of *power:* power that invades the vacuum left by receding social authority; power that tends to usurp even those areas of traditional authority that have been left inviolate; power that becomes indistinguishable in a short time from organized and violent forces, whether of the police, the military, or the paramilitary.

The human mind cannot support moral chaos for very long. As more and more of the traditional authorities seem to come crashing down, or to be sapped and subverted, it begins to seek the security of organized power. The ordinary dependence on order becomes transformed into a relentless demand for order. And it is power, however ugly its occasional manifestations, that then takes over, that comes to seem to more and more persons the only refuge from anxiety and apprehension and perpetual disorder.

So was it in ancient Athens when, after the brilliant fifth century had ended in the disastrous Peloponnesian Wars and intimations of dissolution were rife, the Athenians turned to despots, generals, and tyrants who could, it was thought, restore the fabric of authority. So was it in Rome after the deadly civil conflicts of the first century. So was it in Western Europe after the French Revolution had mobilized itself into the Terror — the better, it was thought by Jacobins and others, to destroy the final remnants of corrupt, traditional authority, thus freeing forever the natural virtue in man. What France got, as we know, was neither freedom nor virtue, but the police state of Napoleon; and what Western Europe got was an age of political reaction in which governments took on powers over human life never dreamed of by absolute monarchs of earlier centuries. And so was it in the Germany of a generation ago when, after a decade of spiritual, cultural, and material debauchery, of more and more aggressive assaults on the civil order by the political left,

Germany got Nazism and Hitler—to the open satisfaction at the time of a large part of the German people, the secret satisfaction of many others, and, in due course, the total satisfaction of nearly all.

AUTHORITY VERSUS POWER

To see the eruption of organized power and violence as the consequence of a diminishing desire for liberty is easy. What requires more intelligence or knowledge or wisdom is to see such power as the consequence of loss of *authority* in a social order. Authority and power: are these not the same, or but variations of the same, thing?

They are not, and no greater mistake could be made than to suppose they are. Throughout human history, when the traditional authorities have been in dissolution, or have seemed to be, it is power—in the sense of naked coercion—that has sprung up. What Aristotle called *stasis,* "perpetual civil strife," is at bottom no more than the fragmentation of authority in society. It is *stasis,* warned Aristotle, that democratic societies have to fear above all else. It is the fateful prelude to despotism.

Authority, unlike power, is not rooted in force alone, whether latent or actual. It is built into the very fabric of human association. Civil society is a tissue of authorities. Authority has no reality save in the memberships and allegiances of the members of an organization, be this the family, a political association, the church, or the university. Authority, function, membership: these form a seamless web in traditional society. The authority of the family follows from its indispensable function. So does that of the church, the guild, the local community, and the school. When the function has become displaced or weakened, when allegiances have been transferred to other entities, there can be no other consequence but a decline of authority.

Culture too, as Matthew Arnold wrote memorably a century

ago, is inseparable from authority. There is the authority of learning and taste; of syntax and grammar in language; of scholarship, of science, and of the arts. In traditional culture there is an authority attaching to the names of Shakespeare, Montaigne, Newton, and Pasteur in just as sure a sense of the word as though we were speaking of the law. There is the authority of logic, reason, and genius. Above all, there is the residual authority of the core of values around which Western culture has been formed. This core of values—justice, reason, equity, liberty, charity—was brought into being through the union of the Greek and Judaic traditions 2000 years ago.

Until the present age, it has managed to withstand all assaults upon it. In the eighteenth and nineteenth centuries, conservatives, liberals, and radicals, however passionately they may have fought each other, nevertheless recognized, all of them, the authority of such values. It was culture and its authority, not their destruction, on which minds as diverse as Newman, Spencer, Marx, and even Proudhon rested their causes. Proudhon, let us emphasize immediately, was an anarchist and is today the subject of youthful lip service. But no one could have surpassed Proudhon in his recognition of the necessity of authority in the social order: the authority of the family, the community, the guild; above all the authority of morality that he, as a member of the European community, recognized as the indispensable framework of culture and of social justice.

THE REVOLT AGAINST RATIONALITY

Of all current manifestations of the decline of authority, none is more menacing to the possibility of civilized life than decline in the authority of reason. One sees this most vividly in attacks upon the ideal of objectivity that have begun to come in rising frequency from the New Left. It is easy, of course, to treat objectivity as an illusory goal, one incapable of full attainment, given the diversity of needs and interests in human society. Our search for forms of logic, for ever more trustworthy scientific methods and techniques, is indication enough of how fallible reason can be that is unattended by strict regard for the ways in which reason becomes manifest. Nevertheless, whatever authority reason has had in the West since the time of the pre-Socratic philosophers in ancient Greece has come from rising confidence among human beings in knowledge that springs, not from self-interest alone, not from greed, aggression, fear, or even piety, but from desire to know: to know as dispassionately and objectively as reason and method permit.

It is this form of authority, the authority of reason itself, that is under such relentless attack at the present time. And the attack comes, not from the political right primarily, not from those areas of personal, economic, military, or political interest one might have expected such attack to come from once, but rather from among those who are themselves supposedly engaged in the search for knowledge. The locus of attack upon the very ideal of objectivity in the study of society is to be found in the social sciences, and overwhelmingly in that sector of the social sciences occupied by youthful partisans of the New Left.

What are the prime manifestations of this revolt against objectivity, this scuttling of the ideal of dispassionate reason in the study of man and society? I will limit myself to two or three of the more striking ones.

First, self-styled *radical* social scientists declare that objectivity of inquiry is not even a proper end of the social sciences. From radical sociologist to radical political scientist to radical anthropologist, all across the spectrum of the social sciences, the refrain is the same: "Social scientists have heretofore sought to understand society. The point, however, is to destroy and then remake society." It is not, obviously, the mature Marx, who was capable of devoting himself for many years in the British Museum to the study of capitalism and society, but the youthful romantic Marx that these voices choose to echo.

If anyone thinks I exaggerate the impact at the present time of the self-styled radical social scientist, I invite him to any annual meeting of one of the learned societies.

Let us look briefly at the second symptom. It is for me somewhat more chilling inasmuch as it makes inevitable a recollection of the Nazi Rosenberg and his efforts in the 1930s to demonstrate differences between German or Aryan science on the one hand and Jewish or plutocratic science on the other. I refer here to widening belief at the present time in what can only be called *the necessary ethnic roots of science.*

It is being said, by white and black alike, though chiefly with respect to studies of blacks, chicanos, and other ethnic minorities, that it is not possible by any stretch of one's dedication to objectivity for the white to understand the black or the black to understand the white. There is black science and there is white science, and the twain shall never meet. More recently, there have been manifestations of a women's social science. As though one were dealing with public rest rooms.

How the gods must be laughing. We had no sooner started to erase (admittedly, *just* started) some of the more preposterous kinds of ethnic segregation in American society when there began to be manifest—and began, let it be emphasized, among those forming the vanguard of reform—a far more deadly type of segregation, deadly because it deals with the epistemological roots of the scientific study of man.

Let us concede immediately that one must be a Negro to understand what it is like being a Negro. The same is exactly true of being a Wasp, a Puerto Rican, a mountain climber, a college professor. It is impossible for men to understand women, and women men. All of this has been said for a long time, and in the sense that is usually meant I am willing to stipulate that it will always be true; just as I am willing to trumpet the imperishable truth that no one—not my wife, children, lawyer, physician, least of all, friends—will ever understand me. No one to my knowledge has ever challenged the existence in each of us, in each ethnic or cultural strain, of some doubtless forever unreachable essence. And, as the immortal Charlie Brown has concluded, it is probably good, all things considered, that this essence is unreachable.

But we are talking about science, not the metaphysics of identity or being. The movement I refer to among younger social scientists today is directed to the nature of science, *social science*. What used to be said by engineers, chemists, and the lay public is now being said by an ever-widening group of social scientists themselves, particularly the younger ones. An objective understanding of social behavior is impossible; such understanding will always be limited by the political, or ethnic, or social and economic position one occupies in the social order. Its embedded values must become the values of the investigator and, hence, the bias of his conclusions. There is nothing that can be done about this.

Therefore it behooves us to abandon the vain pursuit of objective knowledge and to throw ourselves into action oriented toward values we can cherish. The remarkable study of conditions of classroom achievement in the schools, completed a year or two ago by James Coleman, sociologist at Johns Hopkins University, cannot be believed because, first, Coleman is white and, second, his massive study was financed by the federal government. So runs the argument of what I can only think of as the most unbelieveable development today in the social sciences.

That it is hard to achieve objectivity, especially in the social sciences, admits of no doubt. The philosophical literature of the West is filled with notations of the idols of the mind—as they were called by Francis Bacon—that incessantly seek to engage our attention. I assume that the most dedicated practitioner of science, even physical science, would not cavil at this. In all scientific work, however good, there is no doubt some lingering element of personal predilection, some thrust that is rooted in bias.

But with this said, is there, then, no significant difference between the gathering and interpreting of ethnic data by an Otto Klineberg or a James Coleman and the gathering and interpreting of such data by a George Wallace? I assume all but the most hopelessly fanatical would say, yes, there is a difference. But, given the crisis of the times—the roles into which we are being forced by history and by the impending revolution—the difference is not worth emphasizing. Better, it is said, for the Klinebergs and the Colemans to abandon the idle conceit of a value-free science and to join directly the fight against George Wallace. It is quicker that way.

That it is also suicidal, on the evidence of history, seems not to enter the minds of the radical social scientists. Or if it does, it seems not to matter greatly. Without wanting to put too fine a point on the matter it is sometimes hard to resist the conclusion that this generation of the left has a rendezvous with suicide. Retreat to drugs, to sensitivity sessions, to illusory communitarianism, and to the calculatedly clownish behavior of the Chicago 7 would suggest it.

THE IMPORTANCE OF BEING BORED

Boredom is one of the most dangerous accompaniments of the loss of authority in a social order. Between boredom and brute violence there is as close an affinity historically as there is between boredom and inanity, boredom and cruelty, boredom and nihilism. Yet boredom is one of the least understood, least appreciated forces in human history. A few years ago, the scientist Harlow Shapley listed boredom as third among the five principal potential causes of world destruction. Today it might seriously be considered first.

Nothing so engenders boredom in the human species as the sense of material fulfillment, of goals accomplished, of affluence possessed. It is such boredom, born of what Eric Hoffer has called the effluvia of affluence, that goes furthest, I think, toward explaining the peculiar character of the contemporary New Left. I do not deny that youth brings idealism in some degree to this movement, that disenchantment with the more corrupt manifestations of middle-class society plays its part. Youth is beyond question idealistic. But in our present society, youth is also bored. And it is from boredom, more than from idealism, that so much of the intellectual character of radical political action today is derived. I should more accurately say *non*intellectual character, for it is the consecration of the *act,* the cold contempt for philosophy and program, and the increasingly ruthless behavior toward even the most intellectual parts of traditional culture that give to the New Left its most distinctive character at the present time.

It is not idealism but boredom—boredom born of natural authority dissolved, of too long exposure to the void; boredom inherited from parents uneasy in their middle-class affluence and who mistake failure of parental nerve for liberality of rearing; boredom acquired from university teachers grown intellectually impotent and contemptuous of calling—that explains the mindless, purposeless depredations today by the young on that most precious and distinctive of Western institutions, the university.

We do well to take seriously the university and what happens to its authority in our culture. For among its prime functions traditionally has been that of serving as arbiter to that age group that has, at least temporarily, outgrown the authorities of family, church, and neighborhood. Potentially, this age group is the most revolutionary of all groups in society, far more revolutionary than, say, the workers, the unemployed, the impoverished. High in intelligence, emotionally buoyant, at full physical tide, this is the age group that is channeled by the university into the several areas of the professions, that provides the intellectual leaders of society. In the university is acquired lasting motivations toward learning, toward profession, toward high culture, toward membership in the social order. But, by the same token, it is this age group in the university that has largely furnished the West with its steady supply of revolutionaries. Not out of slavery, the peasantry, or the sweatshop have our revolutionaries come, for the most part. They have been bred, especially during the past century and a half, by the university. Who is to say that our society does not require its occasional infusion of revolutionaries? But in the present age the revolutionaries have turned on the university itself, and this is not only destructive but totally self-destructive.

The university is the institution that is, by its delicate balance of function, authority, and liberty, and by its normal absence of power, the least able of all institutions to withstand the fury of revolutionary force and violence. Through some kind of perverted historical wisdom the nihilism of the New Left has correctly understood the strategic position of the university in modern culture and also its constitutional fragility. Normally there are no walls, no locked gates and doors, no guards to repulse attacks on classroom, office, and academic study. Who, before the present age, would have thought it necessary to protect precious manuscripts from the hands of revolutionary marauders? Above the din of the New Left's incessant and juvenile cry for immediate amnesty can be heard Voltaire's "Ecrasez l'infâme," directed, however, not at a corrupt feudalism, but at the most liberal and humane of all Western institutions.

"Il dit tout ce qu'il veut"—so runs a French critic's harsh indictment in the last century—"mais malheureusement il n'a rien à dire." This is perhaps the New Left's most vivid mark of distinction from all previous lefts in Western society. It is free to say all that it wishes, but it has nothing to say. Its program is the act of destruction, its philosophy the obscene word or gesture, its objective the academic rubble. One need but read the recently published *Obsolete Communism: The Left-Wing*

Alternative[1] by Daniel and Gabriel Cohn-Bendit, present philosopher-heroes of the New Left, to see the truth of this. Nowhere in its 250 pages is there to be found so much as a paragraph that a Robespierre, a Marx, a Proudhon, even—save the mark—an American Communist would not have thrown in the wastebasket as juvenile and inane.

It does not matter. A philosophy and program are not needed. Boredom suffices to win the New Left its constant flow of recruits. *Credo quia absurdum* could be their motto. *Alienation* is the popular and prestigious word to explain the behavior of the New Left. But the word is as ill-fitting as would be a surplice or academic hood on the shoulders of a clown. Alienation is a noble state of the human spirit, one compounded of idealism and suffering and rejection. Alienation compares with boredom as tragedy does with farce. There is no real alienation in the New Left, only the boredom that is itself the result of erosion of cultural authority, of failure of nerve in middle-class society, and of adult fear of youth.

TOWARD A NEW SOCIAL CONTRACT

It would all be a transitory charade, a tale told by an idiot, were it not for one thing: the fears aroused in this same middle-class society that has lost its anchoring in natural authority. Fear of the void is for human beings a terrible fear, one that will not long be contained. That state of nature that Thomas Hobbes described as one of "continual fear, and danger of violent death," with "the life of man solitary, poor, nasty, brutish, and short" seems always to the anxious and apprehensive to be about to break through the social order, even as it seemed to Hobbes. And in this state of mind, it is only *power* that can seem redemptive, however stained with blood and violence it may be.

The modern media, and especially television, have the

1. Daniel and Gabriel Cohn-Bendit, *Obsolete Communism: The Left-Wing Alternative* (New York: McGraw-Hill, 1969).

capacity for widening and deepening apprehensions beyond anything known before. We are told that a majority of the French people did not know about the storming of the Bastille for months. The entire country watched last summer's confrontation between New Left and police in Chicago. It was violent and ugly and could only have aroused the chill of fear in those who had chanced to see the rise of Nazism in Germany, the burning of the Reichstag, and the beginnings of a police system that was in time to enclothe German society like a straitjacket. But I know of no national poll or study that has shown other than approval of police actions by a large majority. The size of this majority will grow. People, we say, should know better, should not let civilized restraint be undermined by demons of fear. But, as the great Bishop Butler wrote, "Things and actions are what they are, and the consequences of them will be what they will be; why, then, should we desire to be deceived?"

Human beings, I repeat, will tolerate almost anything but the threatened loss of authority in the social order: the authority of law, of custom, of convention. The void does not have to be great, or seem great, for the fears it arouses to become sweeping and for sanity in politics to disintegrate. We are told by the polls that a large number of people watching their television screens that night in Chicago found even the berserk actions of police and pseudopolice gratifying, reassuring, healing to their sense of security. Let us not forget that there is also a strong upswell of boredom in affluent middle-class society. And power, as history tells us, is as often the antidote to boredom in society as it is to anxiety.

As Max Lerner recently wrote in a thoughtful and moving column, we need a new social contract in our society, one that will do for our violence-torn social order what the doctrine of the social contract sought to do in the seventeenth century, fresh as it was from the horrors of the religious wars. But the task will be far more difficult. The institutions of Western society are less solid and encompassing than they were then. Two cen-

turies of convulsive social change and of remorseless increase
in centralized political and economic power have seen to that.
We are plagued even by our achievements, for material progress
has inevitably taken its toll of traditional culture.

There are, as the recent flights of the Apollo project have
made clear, great events taking place in our society. But they
are events of the technological, not the social, order. If the life
of society is to be saved from boredom that only great technological events can relieve—if it is to be saved from armed power,
from depredations on traditional culture, from mass movements
in which exhilaration produced by power is man's substitute
for accustomed liberties—ways must be found, and found
shortly, to restore the sense of initiative in the social as well as
the technological order. Above all, at this moment we need a
liberalism that is able to distinguish between legitimate authority—the authority resident in university, church, local
community, family, and language and culture—and mere power.
Failure to make this distinction between authority and power
can only result in the ever-wider replacement of the former
by the latter. If our liberalism can see no profound difference
between the authority of an academic dean, however fallible
he may sometimes be, and the power of the police riot squad,
we shall find ourselves getting ever greater dosages of the latter.
History, surely, is unmistakable in its testimony on this point.

At the present time, the nearest approach to a philosophy
and program in the political left is its incantatory phrases about
the Establishment, bureaucracy, and technology. But with every
fresh assault on the traditional authorities of the social order,
the day of those whom Burckhardt called the "terrible simpli-
fiers," the new men of power drawn precisely from technology
in the service of armed force, comes nearer. The impulse to
liberty can survive everything but the destruction of its contexts; and these are contexts of authority—a legitimate authority
that is inseparable from institutions.

"Men are qualified for civil liberty," wrote Edmund Burke,

"in exact proportion to their disposition to put moral chains upon their own appetites." There is nothing extraordinary or mysterious about the fact that all the great renascences of the human spirit—the great efflorescences of the mind—which are the truest measure of real freedom, have had their roots in communities that knew well the difference between liberty and license and were well acquainted with the limits set by authority upon human appetite. The pouring forth of multifarious genius among the Greeks of the fifth century B.C., the Italians in Renaissance Florence, the English in the Age of Elizabeth, and the Jews in the twentieth century must be viewed in contexts of the very marked authority present in each of these communities.

I do not say that authority and individual liberty are the same thing. I am mindful that there is a degree of authority in civil society, however benign in character, that even the minds of greatest genius cannot break through. I know only that, without the preservation of authority in substantial degree—the authority of culture, of reason, of civility—there can be no genius or creative expression whatever. Without authority, there can be only license and anarchy, surmounted by power that will, in time, destroy everything beneath it.

There are, alas, those of a romantic and sentimental turn of mind who believe that what Burke called "moral chains" are, in fact, a part of man's biological nature and that there is consequently no need to fear they will weaken. What blind folly! In our own century, the horrors perpetrated by Hitler and Stalin should have taught us forever the precariousness of either moral virtue or of intellect that depends upon what lies in the individual alone. In truth, man's virtue, freedom, and creativity are inseparable from, and as precarious as, the tissue of authorities of which his culture is made.

3 Political terrorism: hysteria on the left

IRVING HOWE

The idealism of the young is an awesome thing. It is extolled as the hope of the future, the antidote to the fatigue and the cynicism of the old. But when that idealism turns to violence, when the young angrily proclaim that they "have tried everything else" and that there is no other way left to them, that idealism becomes more awful than awesome.

Bombings have destroyed banks, college buildings, ROTC buildings, and Army induction centers during the past months, and it is barely short of miraculous that the death toll has not skyrocketed as the number of incidents increases.

The young have no sense of history, no awareness of the consequences of violence in other societies, and, therefore, no intimation of what it can lead to in ours. Irving Howe explores the political terrorism which has become so frightening a part of the American scene and reflects on its consequences for both the terrorist and his victim: American society.

The life of the political terrorist is overwhelmed by loneliness, not merely because he can no longer trust completely friend or comrade, but because he cuts himself off from all movements and communities in which choices can be weighed. Staking everything on the act, he blocks off all that comes before it and all that comes after. Deciding whom to smite, he replaces God. Choosing whom to punish, he replaces the justice (be it good or bad) of society. And since the conflicts of social classes must be bent to his will, he replaces history, too. The terrorist carries a

IRVING HOWE *is a member of the faculty of the City University of New York and is the editor of* Dissent.

moral burden only saints or fanatics would undertake—at worst, fanatics mistaking themselves for saints.

Greater still is his political loneliness. The terrorist surrenders the possibility of sharing the experiences of a mass political movement, be that movement democratic or authoritarian. He discards responsibility to his people, his class, his generation. For he cannot hold an open discussion on where to throw the next bomb, and, although he may keep mumbling "power to the people," he denies in effect whatever power the people may have over his behavior. In a hallucinatory transaction he "becomes" the people.

We have had plenty of terrorism in the United States, mostly by far-right lunatics and racists; lynching is an American contribution to the repertoire of death. But the far right, shrewder than its symbiotic opposite on the far left, has never articulated an ideology of the rope and the bomb; it has done its dirty business and kept its mouth shut.

A few years ago it would have seemed—it would have *been* —a gross slander for anyone to ask whether terrorism might become a weapon of the dissident young, so hopeful did many of them seem in their idealism and fraternity. Today, that question must be asked about a fringe of the New Left. Serge Nechayev,[1] heroic and ruthless terrorist of nineteenth-century Russia, would until recently have seemed a creature alien to our national experience; now it is possible that his spirit has migrated to our shores.

I say this not because I accept the scatter-shot malevolence

1. Serge Nechayev (1847–1882), a Russian revolutionary fanatic, who, scorning the Marxist idea of "going to the masses," advocated the use of terror, arson, robbery, and spying on comrades. His *Catechism of the Revolutionist*, a classical exposition of political amorality, begins with the sentence: "The revolutionist is a doomed man." In 1869, while forming underground groups, Nechayev arranged for the murder of Ivanov, a comrade who had begun to doubt Nechayev's grandiose claims to being the leader of a vast movement. Three years later, Nechayev was captured by the police and sentenced to solitary confinement, where he spent the remainder of his life.

that men in authority direct against students, but because I have witnessed the conduct and read the journals of the New Left grouplets. The great majority of the young, dissident or not, still seem to believe in democratic norms and nonviolent methods, though they are sadly unable to reach coherent articulation. But fragments of the New Left, by now fractured to the point of jungle warfare, are inflamed with the rhetoric of violence. Some flirt with sabotage and terror; others inflict minor physical brutalities on intraleft opponents. Perhaps there have also been a few ventures in actual bombings. We don't yet know.

About the recent incidents I have no revelations. All I propose to do here is to look into the rationales developed by the far-out wings of the New Left, the responses these get from half-sympathetic students, and the likely repercussions of terrorism. I confess at the outset that I have no comprehensive theory to account for everything.

There is a standard liberal explanation for the growth of terrorist moods in or near the New Left, and like all standard liberal explanations it is neither entirely right nor wrong. The young rebels, we are told, tried every method of peaceful persuasion; they protested and picketed; they marched and electioneered. But the country, choosing Nixon and Agnew, turned its back on their outcry. As a result, they have become desperate and see no solution but guerrilla warfare. At this point, usually over a drink or in a faculty lunchroom, the more chuckleheaded kind of liberal will add, "Of course I don't approve of such methods, *but still* . . ."

Though it contains a good portion of the truth, perhaps even a decisive portion, this analysis strikes me as too simple, and the "but still" as a proviso that could lead us to disaster.

There is plenty of reason for dismay and disgust at the state of American society. Every sensible person knows the list of our troubles. The thought of three, or seven, or more years of an administration that regards Judge G. Harrold Carswell as a fit candidate for the Supreme Court and the barbaric regime in Athens as an appropriate ally fills many of us with bitterness. But—and I want to emphasize this point—there is no necessary political, logical, or moral connection between this response to our present condition and the methods the *kamikaze* segments of the New Left are turning to.

If you feel the country to be in a desperate condition, it does not follow that you should necessarily start throwing bombs. First, you ought to do some thinking. You must take into account the sentiments of millions of middle- and working-class Americans; you must reckon the power of the state; you must ask whether the consequences of terrorism, whether "successful" or not, would be worse than the problems we already have. (All this is on the prudential level; I will come to the moral issues later.) If you do consider such matters, the only rational conclusion is, I believe, to continue political activity—the creation of movements and alliances—so that, through elections, public programs, and militant protest we can turn this country onto the path of social reconstruction.

To say that all means of peaceful action have been exhausted is nonsense; they have barely begun to be employed. To say that nothing has been achieved by opponents of the war is a masochistic delusion; the results of protest have been notable. True, some of the New Left young have by now devoted as much as five or six years to politics and appear shocked that the centuries-long struggle for social justice did not come to instant triumph in 1969. It is not callous, it is merely humane, to suggest that this struggle seems likely to continue a while longer, and that among the requirements for it are the maturity needed for speaking with patience and decency to the unconverted. No one has ever been convinced by a bomb.

I am impatient with the maudlin claim that the young "have tried everything." For those who wish to change society there is no shortage of tasks: help Sam Brown organize the Moratorium against the war; join Cesar Chavez in unionizing grape pickers and Leon Davis in unionizing hospital workers; campaign for Allard K. Lowenstein's reelection to Congress; work with Ralph Nader for consumer rights and Philip Stern for tax reforms. There are a thousand and one other things crying to be done and far more useful, *far more radical,* than the posture of bomb throwing. What's more, if you don't like my list, make up your own.

Now, I do not mean to say that the despair felt by thousands of young Americans has nothing to do with the turn a few of them seem to have taken toward terrorism. Obviously, there is a strong connection, but mainly as an encompassing condition rather than as a direct and immediate cause. For since the despair is widespread and the terrorism very limited, there must also be other sentiments and convictions behind the throwing of bombs.

The despair felt by the extremist segments of the New Left is given an explosive or, if you prefer, hysterical quality by their having yielded to ideologies such as Maoism and Castroism, an act which has cut them off from both American realities and democratic norms. And the severe internal disintegration of the New Left seems also to have driven some of its adherents to the thought of desperado tactics.

The two main wings of Students for a Democratic Society — the Maoists chained to a totalitarian ideology and the anarcho-authoritarians running wild in search of another ideology — analyze precisely the dilemmas of one another. The Maoist cadre, hair cut and contemptuous of drugs, make devastating criticisms of the dilettantism and political *Custerism* (last-ditch bravado) of their factional opponents, especially the Weathermen. But it is precisely the unreality of Maoist dogma, with its faith in a proletarian revolution in the United States, that leads many young radicals to the scatter of opposing groups. In turn, the increasingly suicidal and pathological character of groups like the Weathermen, to say nothing of their political incoherence, creates a strong revulsion among the more rational young leftists. All are trapped. To be profoundly caught up in the fevers of ideology, to be unable to settle upon one that has a touch of realism, to drive oneself through rituals of "discussion" and then to exhaust one's body and imperil one's skin in hopeless street battles—all this must lead to desperation.

Though its sympathizers may have increased in number, the New Left meanwhile is incapable of reaching organizational or political stability. Its inner life is befouled by dreary factionalism and, sometimes, plain hoodlumism. It remains a sect, even if a large one, that cannot gain acceptance from any major segment of the population beyond the campus. To have grown and then to fracture, to know wild hopes and yet to be unable to suppress intimations of futility—this, too, must lead to despair.

Such, I wish to suggest, is the immediate or triggering factor in the outbreak of desperado moods. There are others. American radicalism, alas, has almost always looked abroad for its models. Today, none of the traditional wings of the European left, neither Social Democracy nor Bolshevism, command much authority among the young, since, for all their differences, they are both too rational and disciplined to satisfy the moods of youth. Brezhnev—who but a bureaucrat could identify with him? Mao—a warlord of the left. The style that captures romantic imaginations is that of Guevara, who was personally heroic, dashing, and free-lance; at the same time, he was also a mediocre thinker and a scandalously inept revolutionist (he did not even know the language of the Bolivian peasants he meant to "liberate," any more than his local admirers know the language of the American workers). Guevara signifies to the radical young a vision of instant revolution, personal risk, guerrilla exposure— the old Hemingway notion of discovering one's manhood through physical risk, but now in the context of political exaltation.

Let us also remember that a large percentage of the New Left young are the children of the middle class and the rich. (It is curious that a movement calling itself Marxist does not perform a class analysis on itself. Why does New Leftism appeal

mostly to upper-class youth and not to young proletarians?)
The affluent young leftists have little experience in doing significant work, work either that is socially useful or that could
give them a sense of personal independence. They are riddled
with guilt, they have no clear awareness of their place in the
world, they have been raised to expect instant gratification.
And, therefore, they often debase the admirable impulse to
social involvement and sympathy with which they begin.

In the past I have avoided the view that the desperado
wings of the New Left show symptoms of being the spoiled children of affluence, but it becomes hard to resist precisely that
impression. A significant proportion of the young desperadoes —
we have no statistics — comes from the upper bourgeoisie. Un-
trained at persisting in behalf of personal or public ends; unwilling to dig in at the job of persuading the American people
to accept their ideas; and perhaps afraid that even making that
effort would create the risk of being influenced by the very
masses they have yet to meet — at least a few of these children of
the rich, at once idealistic, disturbed and very bright, abandon
themselves to the delirium of terrorist fantasy.

In utterly American style, it is a delirium with a large portion of innocence. They talk about and may even take a crack at
violence, but deep down they seem still to expect that the society
will treat them with the indulgence they have come to expect
from at least some of their liberal teachers. They are innocent
of history and innocent of social reality. A Columbia student
is quoted in justification of terrorism: "If we don't take an active
part in the revolution, the workers won't listen to us." Poor
deluded boy. Does he have any idea what the American workers
think of him, his politics, and his methods?

Tragedy in comedy, comedy in tragedy. Identities shuffled,
costumes tried on, the revolution as theater. Nobody knows who
he is, everyone plays parts. Abbie Hoffman, accredited clown of
the movement, chants praise to the bombs — "Boom!" — and his
educated admirers chant back, "Boom, boom!" Jewish boys and

girls, children of the generation that saw Auschwitz, hate democratic Israel and celebrate as revolutionary the Egyptian dictatorship. Some of them pretend to be indifferent to the anti-Jewish insinuations of the Black Panthers; a few go so far as to collect money for Al Fatah, which pledges to take Tel Aviv. About this I cannot say more; it is simply too painful.

Meanwhile, the ideology of the New Left itself creates strong inducements to political desperation. That ideology runs along these lines: There is a worldwide class war between imperialism, led by the United States, and the third world of revolutionary nations; in this international class war it is *our* job to weaken, disrupt, and help destroy the main enemy, which is the American government. In this view, which might be called the politics of Dean Rusk stood on its head, there is a tiny plausibility and a mountain of errors.

The third world does not exist as any sort of unified, let alone revolutionary, force; the underdeveloped countries have enormous differences in political character, social progress, and economic need. Some, like India and Venezuela, are democratic, and to propose "revolution" in these countries is to favor imposing elitist dictatorships. Others require modest beginnings in both industrialization and democracy. The "revolutionists" celebrated by our New Left are often tiny bands of deracinated intellectuals and students who have no contact with the people of their countries. And, finally, the relation between the United States and the third-world nations, while requiring radical correction, is far more complicated than the New Left picture allows. Yet, even if one does accept the Guevarist analysis, Weathermen tactics don't necessarily follow—unless, perhaps, a "final conflict" is expected within the next year or two.

To all of these factors contributing to terrorism, I would add two, not as direct causes but as aggravating conditions: the mass media and the intellectuals.

That the mass media, especially TV, have been irresponsible in their coverage of youth rebellion and black upsurge seems to me beyond question. (Living in California last year, I sometimes felt that the SDS was a creation of TV and provided it with an unfailing flow of usable items; on reflection, I concluded it was a phantom dreamed up by Ronald Reagan to insure his reelection.)

The irresponsibility of the mass media takes the form of a raging thirst for sensation, and this, I am inclined to think, is built into the very nature of modern communications. If the medium is the message, then the message is bad news, gross simplification, and exploitation. There is no time for qualifying nuances, no appetite for complex reflection; the idiot box processes the life of man into polarities of mindlessness. If a Roy Wilkins spends a lifetime fighting Jim Crow and a Bayard Rustin comes up with a program for training ghetto youngsters for jobs, that hardly constitutes news by the standards that allow fly-by-night loudmouths to scream "Burn, baby, burn!"at audiences of wide-eyed or dull-eyed suburbanites. Television seems inherently melodramatic and thereby made to order for farceurs like Abbie Hoffman. It encourages New Leftists, born to the corruptions of publicity, to act out an endless serial: *Which building will be liberated today?*

More serious is the role of the intellectuals, too many of whom have proved susceptible to the delights of being 90-day campus heroes. I think of the distinguished movie critic, yesterday an absolute pacifist, who helped raise money for SDS after the Columbia events; the brilliant novelist who told his admirers they must prove their courage by feats of bravado and speculated on the moral propriety of beating up fifty-year-old candy-store keepers; the erudite Hegelian philosopher who taught the young that tolerance is bourgeois deception and liberal values are a mask for repression; the fierce sociologist who kept reminding us that "violence is as American as apple pie," without troubling to ask whether such a pie might give one a bad case of food poisoning; the bright young journalist who announced that "morality comes out of the barrel of a gun"; the editor of a stylish literary paper who ran a diagram on its cover, perhaps as part of an adult-education program, to show how to make a Molotov cocktail.

Of course, none of these people favor terrorism; their only violence is of the phrase. But at some point sorcerers must take a bit of responsibility for their strayed apprentices. For it's not as if everything leading up to the present debacle on the New Left—the elitism, the authoritarianism, the contempt for democracy, the worship of charismatic dictators, the mystique of violence—hadn't already been visible two or three years ago, when such intellectuals began offering the New Left an aura of intellectual responsibility. What the young radicals needed from the intellectuals was sober criticism; what they got too often was a surrender of critical faculties. And it did no one any good.

As for the sympathetic young, unhappy with the idea of terrorism yet inclined to murmur "but still . . . ," let me print a little dialogue, all too true to life, between one of them, whom I'll call *He,* and an interlocutor, whom I'll call *I.* No illusions need be entertained that *I* persuades *He:*

HE: If this country can drop endless numbers of bombs on defenseless Vietnamese, why get so outraged when these fellows, whoever they are, drop some here?

I: If I thought that dropping them here could speed up the end of dropping them there, I'd still be against doing it, but at least I'd admit there's something to argue about. But you know as well as I do that dropping bombs here isn't going to help end the Vietnam war; if anything, quite the contrary. Besides, why can't we be indignant toward both?

HE: Well, I don't like terrorism any more than you, but nothing else has worked.

I: Does that mean that if bombing emptied buildings doesn't "work," they'll take the next step?

HE: And bomb buildings with people in them? I don't know. So far they've only bombed buildings, but not hurt people.

I: Sorry, that won't do—for three reasons:

First, I don't trust their aim.

Second, I don't share your faith in the efficiency of the police. Suppose the cops hadn't proved fast enough in responding to one of those phone calls that give them twenty minutes to empty out a building. Or suppose they'd been distracted from a "revolutionary" phone call about a real bomb by a nut's phone call about an imaginary bomb.

Third, they already have, it seems, killed some people: themselves.

About the political consequences of continued terrorism there can be no doubt. The first and mildest consequence would be Reaganism. "The one indispensable element in Reagan's political survival," says Jesse Unruh, who ought to know, "is campus unrest." The Reagan backlash, suave in manner and graced with a Hollywood smile, depends more on police than street mobs, and it rests upon the assurance of winning elections. Ultimately, Reaganism might be the least of it, for this country can produce for worse. It has.

For most New Leftists, the argument concerning backlash in particular and consequences in general has little persuasive power. They affect to see little or no difference between Reagan and a liberal Democrat, and some even prefer a victory for Reagan out of the suicidal expectation that after apocalypse their turn will come. A good portion of the SDS campus guerrillas can retreat, if necessary, to their parents' town and country houses or quickly find the money to flee the country. But no such luxury of choice is open to the residents of Watts, the patients in California's hospitals, the teachers and students in its colleges; they must suffer the consequences of Reagan's policies.

Now, in a country with an atomized population, weak military forces, widespread illiteracy, feeble structure of government, and no tradition of national unity, terrorist methods might prove effective. But it is really a sign of political dementia to suppose that a few hundred people could terrorize a country with unprecedented wealth and power, enormously vigorous agencies of government, and a population with a large conservative segment. All terrorism might do in the United States is to frighten or enrage authority, which now acts with a measure of restraint but could brutally smash its opponents.

Some New Leftists, however, are enchanted by their clever tactics. They don't have a centralized organization that can be infiltrated on top, so, they reason, they are not as vulnerable as were past radical groups. Another delusion! For while it's true that confrontationist tactics have been shrewd and, at first, have caught authorities unprepared, radicals ought to recognize that there are intelligent and determined people on the other side too. Each time confrontation has brought into play student ingenuity, it has resulted in an escalation of retaliatory measures. Nevertheless, it speaks rather well for the people of this country that, despite what they consider to be provocations and outrages, they have thus far refrained from letting themselves be stampeded into hysterical and repressive moods.

Terrorism by small groups is admittedly hard to detect, but one consequence of this could be that, if limited responses don't cope with bank burners and bomb throwers, men in authority will be driven to employ total measures, e.g., large-scale preventive detention. Those of us who believe in civil liberties would fight as hard as we could against such proposals, just as Norman Thomas fought for the rights of Communists who had steadily abused him. But who is prepared to say that in the kind of social atmosphere created by terrorism we would have much chance of success? Every state, whether good or bad, must react against terrorism; otherwise, it ceases to exist.

What for the government might be an intermittent nuisance could, for American radicals, be a complete disaster. It is hard enough for the American left to gain a hearing, hard enough to convince our fellow citizens that we wish an extension of democracy into all areas of social and political life and that we share their loathing for all varieties of dictatorship.

But now, if that amorphous entity called *the left* is in the slightest degree to be identified with terrorist methods, we will be thrown back one hundred years—literally one hundred years—to the point where, in both Europe and America, the left movements had to spend decades disassociating themselves from a handful of anarchist bomb throwers. How one despairs of the indifference to history shown by the radical young! If only they would read, say, the second volume of G. D. H. Cole's authoritative *History of Socialist Thought,* in which he shows with crushing detail the way the terrorists hurt the socialist movements of Europe and America by exposing them to provocation and smear. Cole goes still further by remarking of the bomb throwers: "In the twentieth century they would have become Fascists or Nazis; and some of them got as near to this as they could by joining the special anti-Anarchist police after a spell of Anarchist activity."

For civil libertarians, the consequences of terrorism will be equally disastrous. In the past, people of the liberal-left community could usually assume that charges of "plotting to overthrow the government," when brought by prosecuting attorneys against radicals, were politically motivated and false in substance. When communist leaders were so charged in the nineteen-fifties, those of us on the left who had long been anti-Stalinist could nevertheless react immediately in opposition to such prosecution. We knew that people like Eugene Dennis and Gus Hall weren't manufacturing dynamite or planning a coup. They *were* trying to strengthen their position in the unions and other institutions. But whatever else, they were not fools.

In the future, however, how will we know? By its reckless talk and mindless acts, the far-out fringe of the New Left lays itself open—but also lays open all other sections of the left, old or new—to endless legal harassment and, to be blunt, to a maze of provocations and frame-ups. Yet, such provocations and frame-ups will be greatly helped if there is at least a smidgin of reality behind them, if there are in fact sticks of dynamite as well

as the rhetoric of dynamite. Given that possibility, civil libertarians will be hard pressed to distinguish between victims of
persecution and candidates for prosecution.

Lest anyone think I am exaggerating, here is a statement put
out by a committee in defense of three persons charged in New
York City with bombings:

> Either the accused did strike a magnificent blow against
> those who make profit through the destruction of our lives
> and our world and they are our most courageous and be-
> loved comrades; or they are being framed by a government
> bent on destroying our movement. . . . In both cases, they
> deserve our total support.

In short, hurrah if they threw bombs and hurrah if they
did not. But what about those people who choose to be more
discriminating with their hurrahs?

It would be a grave error to argue against terrorism mainly
on grounds of expediency. To throw bombs is wrong. It is wrong
because it is inhumane, because it creates an atmosphere in
which brute force settles all disputes, because even if the bomb
throwers could win power through such methods they would
no longer be (if they ever had been) the kind of people who
could build a good society. Above all, it is wrong because minorities in a democratic society, as long as their right to dissent
and protest is largely protected, do not have the right to impose
their will upon the majority through violence or terror. This
has always been a central argument of democratic socialism,
an argument that classical liberalism also accepts.

I would extend this argument to property. In a democratic
society minorities have no right to inflict damage on property
simply because they oppose the arrangements of capitalism.
The aim of socialists is to socialize the control of property, not
to vandalize or destroy it. Toward this end we must first achieve
a certain minor victory: we must persuade millions of our coun-
trymen that our goal is a desirable one. Until and unless we do
that, we must abide, no matter with what pain, by the judgments

of the majority, so long as our rights of criticism and dissent are protected. There is the still more essential point that, as the history of our century shows, any effort to establish socialism through terror ends, and must end, as a ghastly caricature of our hope.

There remains one issue concerning the consequences of terror, and I wish to stress it more strongly than all the others. *What kind of people are you going to become if you turn to such methods?* "Those who set out to kill monsters should take care not to turn into monsters themselves." These words were spoken by Nietzsche before the experience of totalitarianism, and all the blood and pain of our century confirms their wisdom. Ironically, some seven or eight years ago, when the then-young radicals were turning away from Leninism, it was precisely such perceptions that struck them as central.

The moral consequences for the lives of the young terrorists are already clear. Bernadine Dohrn, a Weatherman leader, is quoted by a New Left paper, the *Guardian,* as saying that the Weathermen "dig" Charlie Manson, accused leader of the gang that allegedly murdered several people in Beverly Hills. "Dig it, first they killed the pigs, then they ate dinner in the same room with them, then they even shoved a fork into a victim's stomach! Wild!" is how the *Guardian* quotes Miss Dohrn. Other New Leftists have expressed their admiration for Sirhan Sirhan, killer of Robert Kennedy. Some have even toyed with the notion that fascism is a necessary prelude to the introduction of utopia: first arsenic and then strawberries and cream. Are these the kind of people who are going to create a bright new world and to whom we are to entrust the future of our children?

But a youthful voice answers me: "Our moral integrity will be protected by our revolutionary commitment, by our fight against injustice, by our sacrifice and ideology."

Alas, too slender a reed! Do you suppose that some of the GPU men who tortured innocent victims in Stalin's prisons had not once told themselves the same thing? Do you suppose that some of them might not have imagined that their maiming and murdering was in behalf of the revolution, and that in the end history would vindicate them? No, what matters is the quality and discipline of the life one leads at a given moment, and what one sees at the outer edges of the New Left—I do not speak of it as a whole—is at least as discouraging as what one sees in American society at large.

The bomb thrower and the jailer are brothers under the skin. Is it not possible to revitalize in America the politics of democratic norm and radical change? Our traditions, our best impulses, our most humane energies, our needs all speak for it. Do that, and terror will die.

4 Reflections on youth movements

WALTER LAQUEUR

American college students talk fondly of each person doing "his own thing," whatever it may be, and would be appalled to learn that the particular thing each of them is doing is neither original nor new. Youth movements in France, Germany, and Russia traveled the same road, and some historians would have it that, were it not for student terrorism in Europe, the world would have been spared the horrors of fascism and the Second World War.

Walter Laqueur describes some of these youth movements and explores the ways in which they parallel the American New Left today. The questions that remain unanswered are: to what extent these parallels will hold, and whether the Russian, German, or French movement proves to be the prototype for the American.

I can well imagine that on Saturday nights across this country, at hundreds of faculty parties where a year and a half ago the main subject of discussion was the war in Vietnam, thousands of professors and their wives now passionately debate the pros and cons of the student movement, the tactics of the SDS, and the significance of the generational conflict. I myself have attended several such gatherings and have been struck not so much by the intensity with which the actions of the students are either approved of or condemned by their elders, as by the baffled consensus among those elders that the movement is both unprecedented and totally inexplicable in terms of what the university has historically represented. When I am asked, as I invariably am, for the European view on these matters, I rarely

---

WALTER LAQUEUR *is director of the Institute of Contemporary History in London and a professor in the History of Ideas Department at Brandeis University.*

manage more than a few words, to the effect that the American situation is unique and that anyway history never repeats itself—which, needless to say, is of no great help to anyone. And yet, I believe there *is* something to be learned from the European experience, even if the lesson is an ambiguous one. Not the least thing to be learned is that the Western university has by no means always represented that tranquil meeting ground, so fondly misremembered now by American professors, of those who would gladly learn with those who would gladly teach.

Quite the contrary. Organized youth revolt has for a long time been an integral part of European history. That, on the one hand. On the other, the idea of the university as a quiet place, devoted to the pursuit of learning and unaffected by the turbulence of the outside world, is of comparatively recent date. The medieval university certainly was no such place. As Nathan Schachner has pointed out, it was a place characterized more by bloody affrays, pitched battles, mayhem, rape, and homicide: "Indeed by the frequency of riots one may trace the rise of the University to power and privilege."

In his monumental study, *Universities of Europe in the Middle Ages,* Hastings Rashdall relates the violence of the medieval university to the violence of medieval times in general, when the slitting of a throat was not regarded even by the Church as the worst of mortal sins. Thus, a master of arts at the University of Prague who had cut the throat of a friar bishop was merely expelled, while in the case of other offenders punishment consisted in the confiscation of scholastic effects and garments. The police were openly ridiculed by students, and the universities did nothing to exact discipline from their own scholars. In dealing with the subject of students' morals, Rashdall is constrained to write in Latin. According to Charles Thurot's history of Paris University in the Middle Ages, masters frolicked with their pupils and even took part in their disorders. The university was a great concourse of men and boys freed from all parental restrictions; morality, as Schachner notes, was a private affair, as were the comings and goings of the students. Nor was the trouble localized; the same complaints were to be heard from Oxford to Vienna and Salamanca.

As for the professor, his position in the medieval university was not what it became in later days. He was, first of all, paid by the students. A professor at Bologna needed his students' permission if he wanted to leave town even for a single day; he had to pay a fine if he arrived late in class or if he ended his lecture before the chiming of the church bells; should his lectures not meet with favor, there was a good chance that he would be interrupted, hissed, or even stoned. Supported by king and church, medieval students enjoyed almost unlimited freedom. It was an unwritten rule, for instance, that they were always in the right in their clashes with townspeople.

Of course, from time to time the citizenry would get even by killing a few students; the Oxford town-and-gown riots of 1354 were one such response, if a major one, to student provocation— provocation that took the form, in the words of a contemporary chronicler, of "atrociously wounding and slaying many, carrying off women, ravishing virgins, committing robberies and many other enormities hateful to God." To be sure, the real troublemakers were a minority, some of them not even students but rather young vagabonds enjoying the immunities of the scholar, drifting from master to master and from university to university. For every scholar involved in felonious offenses there were dozens whose stories are unknown. As Schachner notes,

> They studied conscientiously, attended lectures and disputations, worked hard, ate frugally, drank their modest stoup of wine, and had no time for the delights of tavern and brothel. The annals of the virtuous, like the annals of a happy people, are short and barren.

Nevertheless, it is a fact that only in later ages did the university begin to impose stricter discipline on its students.

If student violence in the Middle Ages can be ascribed mainly to the high spirits of youth, by the eighteenth century a new figure had appeared on the scene: the student as freedom fighter. *Die Raeuber* ("The Robbers"), the play that made Schiller famous, tells the story of a group of students who, disgusted by society and its inequities, take to the mountains to lead partisan warfare against the oppressors. (In the 1920s when Piscator staged the play in Berlin, he had Spiegelberg, one of the leaders of the gang and incidentally a Jew, appear in the mask of Trotsky.)

Sturm und Drang, the first real literary movement of youth revolt, combined opposition to social conventions with a style of life that is familiar enough today: wild language, long hair, and strange attire. Within a few decades after its inception, the romantics had made this movement fashionable, if not respectable, all over Europe. Suddenly there was Young England and Young Germany, Young Italy, Young Hungary, and Young Russia—all up in arms against the tyranny of convention, tradition, and outworn beliefs. One of the very few places untouched by the cult of youth at that time was America, itself a young country, unencumbered by the dead weight of tradition. "America," Goethe apostrophized, "du hast es besser. . . ."

Some youth groups in the modern period have done much good, while others have caused a great deal of harm. It has been the custom in writing about them to divide them into the progressive and the reactionary, the wholesome and the decadent, so that, for example, the revolutionary Russian student movement of the nineteenth century, the Italian Risorgimento, and the Chinese May 1919 movement fall in one camp, and the fascist youth movements fall in the other. But this scheme is at best an oversimplification, since almost all movements of youthful revolt have contained in themselves both elements at once. The historical role a movement finally played depended in each case on political conditions in the society at large, the gravity of the problems the movement faced, the degree of its cultural development, and the quality of the guidance it received from its mentors.

The dual character of youth movements is illustrated with

particular clarity by the example of the early German student circles, the *Burschenschaften*. In his recent book, Lewis Feuer characterizes the members of these circles as "historicists, terrorists, totalitarians and anti-Semites"—all of which is perfectly true.[1] But they were also genuine patriots who dreamed of German unity and set out to combat the tyranny and oppression of the Holy Alliance. Most of them, in addition, were democrats of sorts and their movement was regarded by the liberals of the day as one of great promise. Their story is briefly told. The leader of the group was Karl Follen, a lecturer at Jena, of whom a contemporary wrote that "no one could be compared with him for purity and chastity of manners and morals. He seemed to concentrate all his energies upon one great aim—the revolution." In 1818, a certain Karl Sand, an idealistic and highly unstable student of theology who had come under Follen's influence, assassinated a minor playwright by the name of August Kotzebue who was suspected of being a Russian agent. Sand genuinely expected that this action, undertaken in the service of a holy cause, would trigger a revolution. But the choice of victim was haphazard, and the consequences regrettable: the government seized the opportunity to suppress the *Burschenschaft* as well as the whole democratic movement. Follen escaped to America, where he became professor of German literature and preacher at Harvard (he later drowned at sea in a shipwreck). It took almost thirty years for the movement he had led to recover from the blow dealt it by the authorities.

The idealism, spirit of sacrifice, devotion to one's people, and revolutionary fervor that marked the *Burschenschaft* have been an inherent part of all youth movements over the last hundred years. It is a mistake to assume that the fascist youth movements were an exception to this rule, that their members were mainly sadistic, blindly destructive young thugs. To be sure, they preached a doctrine of violence, but as Mussolini

1. Lewis S. Feuer, *The Conflict of Generations* (New York: Basic Books, 1969).

said, "There is a violence that liberates, and there is a violence that enslaves; there is moral violence and stupid, immoral violence" (compare Marcuse: "In terms of historical function, there is a difference between revolutionary and reactionary violence, between violence practiced by the oppressed and by the oppressors").

The ideological forerunners of Italian fascism, men like Corradini and Federzoni, were second to none in their condemnation of capitalism and imperialism and in their defense of the rights of the "proletarian nations." Early fascist programs demanded a republic, the abolition of all titles, a unified education, the control and taxation of all private income, and the confiscation of unproductive capital. They also placed great stress on youth. Giovanni Gentile, the philosopher of fascism, considered the sole aim of the new movement to be the "spiritual liberation of the young Italians." The very anthem of the fascist regime was an appeal to the young generation: "Giovinezza, Giovinezza, primavera di bellezza."

Similarly in Germany, where the student movement after World War I was strongly nationalist, the Nazi student association emerged as the leading force in the German universities (and in Austria) in 1930, well before Hitler had become the leader of the strongest German party. With 4,000 registered members out of a total of 132,000 students, the Nazis easily took control of the chief organization of German students several years before the party's seizure of national power. The declared aim of the Nazi student association was to destroy liberalism and international capitalism; point two on its program was to "purge the university of the influence of private capital"; point nine called on students to join the ranks of the workers.

The slogan of "student power" made its first appearance at the *Goettingen Studententag* in 1920. Later on it was linked to the demand that the university be made political, a real "people's university," and that all the academic cobwebs and so-called objective sciences be cleaned out. Even before Hitler came to power, leading German professors attacked the "idea of false tolerance" of the humanist university. Invoking Fichte, Hegel, and Schleiermacher, they held that liberal democracy was the main enemy of the true scientific spirit, and demanded that henceforth only one political philosophy be taught.

The Nazis, needless to say, were still more radical: academic life, they said, had largely become an end in itself; located outside the sphere of real life, the university educated two types of students—the only-expert and the only-philosopher. These two types produced a great many books and much clever and refined table talk, but neither they nor the universities which sustained them were in a position to give clear answers to the burning questions of the day.

Criticisms like these were common at the time all over Europe. An observer of the French scene wrote in 1931 that the main characteristic of the young generation was its total rejection of the existing order: "Almost no one defends the present state of affairs." One of the most interesting French youth groups was *L'Ordre Nouveau,* whose manifesto, written by Dandieu and Robert Aron, had the title *La Révolution Nécessaire. Ordre Nouveau* stood for the liberation of man from capitalist tyranny and materialistic slavery; bolshevism, fascism, and national socialism, it declared, had assumed the leadership of the young generation and for that reason would prevail everywhere. The young in France were deeply affected—to quote yet another contemporary witness—by a "tremendous wave of revolutionary enthusiasm, of holy frenzy and disgust." When several prominent young socialists seceded from the SFIO *(Section Française de L'Internationale Ouvrière)* in opposition to the rule of the old gang and established a movement of their own, this too was welcomed as one more manifestation of the rebellion of the young generation. All these people were deeply troubled by the existing state of affairs and no doubt well meaning in their intentions; together with Jean Luchaire, the leader of *Ordre Nouveau,* many of them ended up as Nazi collaborators during World War II.

The tactics adopted by these youth groups vis-à-vis the universities were the tactics of agitation. Even before World War I, members of the *Action Française* had made it a custom to disrupt systematically the lectures of professors at the Sorbonne who had provoked their ire for political reasons. Nazi students perfected the system, forcing universities to dismiss Jewish professors and even one Christian pacifist, well before 1933. But the question must be asked again: was this rowdyism, or an action undertaken in the genuine conviction that one's country was in grave danger and that the professors were enemies of the people who had to be removed? Among the fascist youth movements in the late twenties, one of the most sinister was the Rumanian terrorist band, the *Archangel Michael,* which later became the Iron Guard. Yet even the members of this group were not devoid of sincerity and idealism; Eugen Weber recently wrote of their leader:

> From a mendacious people he demanded honesty, in a lazy country he demanded work, in an easy-going society he demanded self-discipline and persistence, from an exuberant and windy folk he demanded brevity and self-control.

Whoever describes a youth movement as idealistic only states the obvious. Youth movements have never been out for personal gain; what motivates them is different from what motivates an association for the protection of the interests of small shopkeepers. The fascist experience has shown that the immense potential which inheres in every youth movement can be exploited in the most disastrous way; but the potential itself must be seen as neutral.

Almost everything that is great has been done by youth, as Benjamin Disraeli observed, who was himself at one time a fighter in the ranks of generational revolt. Professor Feuer would counter: many disasters in modern European politics have been caused by students and youth movements. The exploits of the *Burschenschaften,* he argues, set back the cause of German freedom thirty years. Russian student terrorism in the

1880s put an end to progress toward constitutionalism in that country. But for the terror and stress of World War I (inaugurated by a bomb thrown by yet another student hero, Gavrilo Princip), Russia would have evolved in a liberal capitalist direction, and European civilization would not have been maimed by fascism and a second world war. According to Professor Feuer, the qualities needed to bring about peaceful social and political change are not those usually found in youth movements, and he accuses students of almost always acting irrationally in pursuing their objectives.

Unfortunately, however, peaceful change is not always possible in history, nor are patience and prudence invariably the best counsel. Take the Munich students who revolted against Hitler in 1943 and the student rebels who were recently sentenced in the Soviet Union; had they acted entirely rationally, they might well have convinced themselves that, as a consequence of long-term political and social processes, the dictatorship would disappear anyway or at least be mitigated in its ferocity. Why therefore endanger their lives? To their eternal credit, such rational considerations did not enter the students' minds. The impetuosity, the impatience, and sometimes the madness of youth movements have been a liberating force in the struggle against tyranny and dictatorship. Tyranny cannot be overthrown unless at least some people are willing to sacrifice their lives, and those willing to do so usually do not come from the ranks of the senior citizens. It is only when youth movements have launched a total attack against democratic regimes and societies—in Germany, France, and Italy in the twenties and in other countries later on—that they have come to play by necessity a reactionary and destructive role.

Most of the basic beliefs and even the outward fashions of the present world youth movements can be traced back to the period in Europe just before and after World War I. The German *Neue Schar* of 1919 were the original hippies; long-haired, sandaled, unwashed, they castigated urban civilization, read Hermann Hesse and Indian philosophy, practiced free love, and distributed in their meetings thousands of asters and chrysanthemums. They danced, sang to the music of the guitar, and attended lectures on the "Revolution of the Soul."

The modern happening was born in 1910 in Trieste, Parma, Milan, and other Italian cities where the Futurists arranged public meetings to recite their poems, read their manifestoes, and exhibit their ultramodern paintings. No one over thirty, they demanded, should in future be active in politics. The public participated actively at these gatherings, shouting, joking, and showering the performers with rotten eggs.

In other places, things were not so harmless. "Motiveless terror" formed part of the program of a group of young Russian anarchists, the *Bezmotivniki,* in their general struggle against society. The *Bezmotivniki* threatened to burn down whole cities, and their news sheets featured diagrams for the production of homemade bombs. Drug taking as a social phenomenon, touted as a way of gaining new experience and a heightened sensibility, can be traced back to nineteenth-century France and Britain.

The idea of a specific youth culture was first developed in 1913 and 1914 by the German educator Gustav Wyneken and a young man named Walter Benjamin who later attained literary fame. In 1915, Friedrich Bauermeister, an otherwise unknown member of the youth movement, developed the idea of the *class struggle of youth.* Bauermeister regarded the working class and the socialist movement (including Marx and Engels) as *eudaimonistic*; the socialists, he admitted, stood for a just order and higher living standards, but he feared that once their goals were achieved they would part ways with the youth movement. Bauermeister questioned whether even the social revolution could create a better type of man, or release human beings from their "bourgeois and proletarian distortions."

The ideas of this circle were developed in a little magazine called *Der Anfang* in 1913 and 1914. Youth, the argument ran (in anticipation of Professor Kenneth Keniston), was *milieulos,* not yet integrated into society. Unencumbered by the ties of family or professional careers, young people were freer than other elements of society. As for their lack of experience, for which they were constantly criticized by their elders, this, far from being a drawback, was in fact a great advantage. Walter Benjamin called experience the "mask of the adult." For what did the adult wish above all to prove? That he, too, had once been young, had disbelieved his parents, and had harbored revolutionary thoughts. Life, however, had taught the adult that his parents had been right after all, and now he in turn smiled with condescending superiority and said to the younger generation, "This will be your fate too."

For the historian of ideas, the back issues of the periodicals of the youth movement, turned yellow with age, make fascinating reading. The great favorites of 1918 and 1919 were Hermann Hesse, Spengler's *Decline of the West,* Zen Buddhism and Siddharta, Tagore's gospel of spiritual unity *Love not Power,* and Lenin. It is indeed uncanny how despite all the historical differences, the German movement preempted so many of the issues agitating the American movement of today, as well as its literary fashions.

Some youth movements in the last hundred years have been unpolitical in character. Most, however, have had definite political aims. Of this latter group, some have belonged to the extreme left, others have gravitated to the extreme right; some have sought absolute freedom in anarchy, others have found fulfillment in subordinating themselves to a leader. To find a common denominator seems therefore very nearly hopeless. But the contradictions are often more apparent than real, not only because many of those who originally opted for the extreme left later moved to the right, or vice versa, or because the extremes sometimes found common ground as in the National Bolshevik movement which gained some prominence in various countries in the 1920s. Whether a certain movement became political or unpolitical, whether it opted for the left or the right, depended on the historical context. It hardly needs to be explained in detail why youth movements were preponderantly right-wing after World War I, whereas more recently most have tended toward the left. But beyond the particular political orientation there are underlying motives which have remained remarkably consistent throughout.

Youth movements have always been extreme, emotional, enthusiastic; they have never been moderate or rational (again, no major excursion into the psychology of youth is needed to explain this). Underlying their beliefs has always been a common anticapitalist, antibourgeois denominator, a conviction that the established order is corrupt to the bones and beyond redemption by parliamentary means of reform. The ideologies of democracy and liberalism have always been seen as an irretrievable part of the whole rotten system; all politicians, of course, are crooks. Equally common to all youth groups is a profound pessimism about the future of present-day culture and an assumption that traditional enlightened concepts like tolerance are out of date. The older generation has landed the world in a mess, and a radical new beginning, a revolution, is needed. Youth movements have never been willing to accept the lessons of the past; each generation is always regarded as the first (and the last) in history. And the young have always found admiring adults to confirm them in their beliefs.

This leads us to the wider issue of *Kulturpessimismus*. The idea that the world is in decline—an idea that is about as old as the world itself—had an impact on modern youth movements through the mediating influence of neoromanticism. The themes of decadence and impending doom can be traced like a bright thread through the nineteenth century from Alfred de Musset ("Je suis venu trop tard dans un monde trop vieux"), to Carlyle, Ruskin, and Arnold with their strictures against the universal preoccupation with material gain. So widespread a fashion did *Kulturpessimismus* enjoy that one can scarcely find a single self-respecting nineteenth-century author who did not complain about the disjunction between mankind and the world and between idea and reality, or about the spiritual bankruptcy and moral consumption of his age.

In Germany, as *mal du siècle* turned into *fin de siècle,* a whole phalanx of Cassandras raised their voices, denouncing mass culture, crass materialism, and the lack of a sense of purpose in modern life. *Kulturpessimismus* induced in some a sense of resignation and gave rise to decadent moods in literature and the arts; at the same time, however, it acted as a powerful stimulus to movements of regeneration. Whereas dissatisfaction led some to ennui and perversions (*La jeune France,* an all-out revolt against social conventions, was decadent and wholly unpolitical in character), elsewhere and in other periods boredom gave birth to activism.

Thus, on the eve of World War I, a whole generation of young Europeans, having pronounced themselves culturally suffocated, welcomed the outbreak of hostilities as heralding a great purge, a liberation that would somehow put things right. The close connection between *Kulturpessimismus* and boredom deserves more study than it has received so far, as does the connection between boredom and prosperity. Max Eyth, the German popular writer, astutely diagnosed the illness of his age in the autobiography he wrote during the Wilhelminian era: "Es is uns seit einer Reihe von Jahren zu gut gegangen" (We had it too good for a number of years).

One of the main problems facing the decadents was that of combining their hatred of modern civilization with their love of the refinements that civilization had made possible. (This is still very much of a problem, although some of today's revolutionaries seem to have solved it on the personal if not on the ideological level.)

The decadents also faced the dilemma of squaring their *langueur*—Verlaine wrote, "Je suis l'Empire à la fin de la décadence"—with their fascination with violence and revolutionary action. The indiscriminate assassinations and bombings carried out by the French anarchists found many admirers among both the decadents and the right-wing futurists. "What matter the victims, provided the gesture is beautiful," Laurent Tailhade wrote.

D'Annunzio's writings progressed from descriptions of courtesans in modish clothes, luminous landscapes, and villas by the sea, to the most lavish praise of the freshness and joy of war. Having begun by calling on youth to "abolish all moral restrictions," he ended as the prophet of moral regeneration and the poet laureate of fascism.

The list could be lengthened: Maurice Barrès made his way from the decadent movement to the *Action Française;* Johannes R. Becher, who in the early twenties was known in Germany as the mad expressionist poet who had killed his girl friend, was to become in later life minister of culture in Walter Ulbricht's East Germany.

If the youth movements of the early twentieth century arose, then, in a milieu in which the sense of decadence was widespread, they represented at the same time an attempt to overcome it. Their leaders were moralists, forever complaining about the evils of corporate guilt. Like all moralists, they exaggerated those evils, speaking out of the antihistorical perspective which is a hallmark of the moralist. For the study of history teaches that other periods have, broadly speaking, not been much better than one's own. This is why the moralist and the revolutionary regard history as a reactionary discipline, the story of big failures and small successes. The study of history is a breeding ground of skepticism; the less the moralist knows of it, the more effectively will he pursue his mission with an untroubled conscience. Thomas Mann, pleading in a famous speech to German students in the 1920s for "aristocratic skepticism in a world of frenetic fools," was sadly out of touch with the mood of an audience longing for firm belief and certain truths.

If in what I have said up till now my remarks have indicated a certain ambivalence of feeling toward youth movements in general, it is because I have been trying to distinguish between the various ideas which they have espoused—ideas which are certainly deserving of criticism—and, what I take to be of even greater significance, the depth of emotional experience which they have provided their members.[2] (I say this as one who shared that experience at one stage in his life.) The politics and culture of youth movements have always been a reflection of the Zeitgeist, a hodgepodge, often, of mutually exclusive ideas. A proto-Nazi wrote about the unending and fruitless discussions of German youth movements in 1920:

> Look at those *Freideutsche* leaders and their intellectual leap-frogging from Dostoevsky to Chuang-tse, Count Keyserling, Spengler, Buddha, Jesus, Landauer, Lenin, and whichever literary Jew happens to be fashionable to the moment. Of their own substance they have little or nothing.

There was, let's face it, more than a grain of truth in this criticism; a list of the main formative intellectual influences on the American movement would look even more incongruous.

But what was essential about the German youth movement, at least in its first phase, was not its "intellectual leap-frogging" and confused politics but something else entirely. The movement represented an *un*political form of opposition to a civilization that had little to offer the young generation, a protest against the lack of vitality, warmth, emotion, and ideals in German society. Hoelderlin had this observation to make:

> I can conceive of no people more dismembered. . . . You see workmen but no human beings, thinkers but no human beings, priests but no human beings, masters and servants, youth and staid people, but no human beings. . . .

2. Although I originally intended this as a statement about youth movements of the past, I now read in Martin Duberman's review of Christopher Lasch's new book *The Agony of the American Left:* "I think what is most impressive about the radical young people is not their politics or their social theories, but the cultural revolution they have inaugurated—the change in life style."

The movement wanted to develop qualities of sincerity, decency, open-mindedness, to free its members from petty egoism and careerism, to oppose artificial conventions, snobbery, and affectation. Its basic character was formless and intangible, its authentic and deepest experience difficult to describe and perhaps impossible to analyze: the experience of marching together, of participating in common struggles, of forming lasting friendships. There was, of course, much romantic exaltation as well, but although it is easier to ridicule the extravagances of this state of mind than to do it justice, the temptation should be resisted; experiences of such depth are very serious matters indeed.

The nonpolitical phase of the German youth movement ended roughly speaking with World War I. Summarizing that early phase, I wrote several years ago that "if lack of interest in politics could provide an alibi from history, the youth movement would then leave the court without a stain on its character."[3] In retrospect, this judgment seems a trifle misplaced; the truth is that the movement was simply not equipped to deal with politics. Being romantic and opposed to "arid intellectualism," its thought was confused and its outlook illiberal. Oriented toward a mythic past and an equally mythic future, it was darkly suspicious of the values of the Enlightenment—an attitude that did not have much to commend it in a country where the Enlightenment had not met with conspicuous success anyway—and it was easily swayed in different directions by philosophical charlatans and political demagogues preaching all kinds of eccentric doctrines.

All this appeared very clearly in the second, political phase of the German youth movement after World War I. By 1930, the youth movement was displaying an incontinent eagerness to rid Germany of democracy. Almost all its members shared the assumption that anything at all would be better than the detested

3. Walter Laqueur, *Young Germany: A History of the German Youth Movement* (New York: Basic Books, 1962).

old regime. Lacking experience and imagination, they clearly misjudged the major political forces of their time. One of their leaders wrote much later:

> We had no real principles. We thought everything possible. The ideas of natural law, of the inalienable rights of man, were strange to us. As far as our ideas were concerned we were in midair, without a real basis for our artificial constructions.

It was, in brief, not an intellectual movement, and any attempt to evaluate it on the cultural and political level alone will not do it justice; it moved on a different plane. The movement arose in response to a certain malaise; it attempted, without success, to solve the conflicts facing it; and it was, in retrospect, a splendid failure. With all its imperfections, it did succeed in inspiring loyalties and a deep sense of commitment among its members.

I am not sure whether today's youth movements can achieve even this much. "People who screw together, glue together," claims the Berkeley SDS, but if that were true, the Roman Empire would still be in existence. Some time ago, I happened to meet with members of a radical pacifist communal settlement in upstate New York. This settlement had had its origins in the early German youth movement; its members were believing Christians who took their cue from the New Testament: "Ye cannot serve God and Mammon" and "The love of money is the root of all evil." Setting out to realize the ideal of social justice in their own lives, they established two settlements in Germany, moved to England in 1934, then to Paraguay, and finally to New York State. Still convinced that their way of life is the best of all possible ways, the surviving members have recently been trying to find supporters and active followers. On their tours of college campuses they are invariably met with tremendous enthusiasm and a great show of willingness to join. Then, a few days after each appearance, they send a bus around to take prospective candidates for a tour of the settlement. No one shows up.

One could argue that it is unfair to compare the depth of commitment and the ardor of present-day revolutionaries with that shown by those who challenged less permissive societies in bygone days. Where the nineteenth-century revolutionary risked the gallows or a lifetime in Siberia, the rebel of the sixties risks a warning from a disciplinary committee. In these adverse circumstances a breed of devoted revolutionaries is unlikely to arise. That may be finally all to the good, but I for one confess to a certain nostalgia for the breed.

It has been said of youth movements: blessed is the land that has no need of them. For a long time, America was such a land. In the nineteenth and early twentieth centuries, it alone among the major Western countries did not experience a widespread movement of generational conflict. The reasons for this are not particularly obscure. For one thing, the burden of the past was not felt as heavily in America as it was in Europe. Less distance separated parents and children, teachers and students; adventurous young men went West, the country was forever expanding; society as a whole was far less rigid. Then in the twentieth century, when these factors had ceased to be quite so important, America was spared a movement of youth revolt by a series of economic and foreign political crises. For it is a rule of youth movements that, like *Kulturpessimismus,* they prosper only against a background of rising affluence. Another rule appears to be that they cannot strike deep roots in a country whose general mood is basically optimistic.

America in the sixties is a prosperous society, but it is no longer optimistic; the American dream has been lost on the way to affluence. It was thus in a sense inevitable that, when the worldwide wave of youth revolt broke earlier in this decade, American youth should assume a leading role. (I am not speaking here of the black student revolt, because this is not a generational conflict but part of a wider movement for full political

and social emancipation, and the success or failure of this movement will depend ultimately on the blacks themselves.)

But the American situation is a complicated one, not only
because it is accompanied by such factors as a general breakdown
of authority, a crisis in the universities, and a widespread sense
of cultural malaise, but also because of the response it has elicited
in the society at large. Youth movements have come and gone,
but never before has one been taken so seriously. Never in the
past has an older generation been so disconcerted by the on-
slaught of the young. Previous generations of adults, more certain of their traditions and values, less ridden by feelings of
guilt, have shown little patience with their rebellious sons and
daughters. The middle-aged, middle-class parents of today
clearly do not feel themselves to be in any such position of certainty. The milieu in which the youth of America have grown up
bears striking resemblance to the European 1890s as described
by Max Nordau:

> There is a sound of rending in every tradition and it is as
> though the morrow would not link itself with today. Things
> as they are totter and plunge, and they are suffered to reel
> and fall because man is weary, and there is no faith that it
> is worth an effort to uphold them. Views that have hitherto
> governed minds are dead or driven hence, meanwhile
> interregnum in all its terrors prevails and there is confusion
> among the powers that be . . . what shall inspire us? So rings
> the question from the thousand voices of the people, and
> where a market-vendor sets up his booth and claims to give
> an answer, where a fool or a knave begins suddenly to
> prophesy in verse or prose, in sound or color, or professes
> to practice his art otherwise than his predecessors and com-
> petitors, there gathers a great concourse around him to
> seek in what he has wrought, as in Oracles of the Pythia,
> some meaning to be divined and interpreted. . . . It is only a
> very small minority who honestly find pleasure in the new
> tendencies, and announce them with genuine conviction
> as that which is sound, a sure guide for the future, a pledge
> of pleasure and of moral benefit. But this minority has the

gift of covering the whole visible surface of society, as a little oil extends over a large area of the surface of the sea. It consists chiefly of rich educated people, or of fanatics. The former give the *ton* to all the snobs, the fools, and the block-heads; the latter make an impression upon the weak and dependent, and it intimidates the nervous. . . .

Nordau's *Degeneration* is an exaggerated, polemical tract, but much of what he wrote about the malady of his age was pertinent; he realized correctly that ideas, books, and works of art exercise a powerful, suggestive influence far beyond the small circle of the avant-garde:

> It is from these productions that an age derives its ideals of morality and beauty. If they are absurd and antisocial they exert a disturbing and corrupting influence on the views of a whole generation.

The moral and aesthetic ideals of today's avant-garde theater and cinema have certainly had their effect—as have the works of Jean Genet and Frantz Fanon. The deliberate gibberish of recent movies and novels finds its reflection in the involuntary gibberish of certain strands of youth politics; the message of John Cage's "Silent Sonata 4:33" (in which a performer sits in front of a piano for precisely that amount of time, poised to play but never playing) has its parallel in certain aspects of the wider cultural revolution; the theater of the absurd is not unconnected with the politics of the absurd. Indeed, the crisis of rationality has had a powerful impact: affirmation replaces analysis and argumentation; *fin de siècle* revolutionaries arrange happenings and call it a revolution, or discuss *salon* Maoism before enthusiastic audiences and call it radical commitment. Afraid to appear unfashionable or out of step with the avant-garde, those who ought to know better seem willing to take every idiocy seriously, trying to "understand" if not to accept.

Corruptio optimi pessima. The American youth movement, with its immense idealistic potential, has gone badly, perhaps irrevocably, off the rails. For this, a great responsibility falls on the shoulders of the gurus who have provided the ideological justification for the movement in its present phase—those intellectuals, their own bright dream having faded, who now strain to recapture their ideological virginity. There is perhaps some tragedy to be glimpsed in this endeavor of the old to keep pace with the young, but at the moment one cannot permit himself the luxury of a tragic sense.

The doctors of the American youth movement are in fact part of its disease. They have helped to generate a great deal of passion, but aside from the most banal populism they have failed to produce a single new idea. Most of them stress their attachment to Marx. But one need only read *The Eighteenth Brumaire* to find Marx's opinion on the value of bohemianism in the revolutionary struggle; and his polemics against Bakunin leave little doubt as to his feelings with regard to the idea, first propagated one hundred years ago, of a coalition between *lumpenproletariat* and *lumpenintelligentsia.*

Students should not be criticized for ignoring the lessons of the past and the dangers of chiliastic movements. They always do; the historical memory of a generation does not usually extend back very far, and the lessons of historical experience cannot be bequeathed by will or testament. But their mentors do remember, and their betrayal of memory cannot be forgiven.

The American youth revolt was sparked off by Vietnam, by race conflict, and later on by the crisis of the university. At any point along the line rational alternatives could have been formulated and presented. Instead, the movement preferred a total, unthinking rejection, and so became politically irrelevant. Yet a revolution is in fact overdue in the universities. There is nothing more appalling than the sight of enormous aggregations of students religiously writing down pearls of wisdom that can be found more succinctly and profoundly put in dozens of books. There is nothing more pathetic than to behold the proliferation of social-science nonsubjects in which the body of solid knowledge proffered stands usually in inverse ratio to the scientific pretensions upheld. Whole sections of the universities could be closed down for a year or two, and the result, far from being the disaster to civilization which some appear to anticipate, would probably be beneficial.

Unfortunately, this is about the last thing that is likely to happen, for it is precisely the nonsubjects, the fads, and the bogus sciences to which the radicals in their quest for social relevance are attracted as if by magnetic force. As for the consequences of all this, one thing can be predicted with certainty: those to be most directly affected by the new dispensation in the universities will emerge from the experience more confused and disappointed than ever, and more desperately in need of certain truths, firm beliefs.

An American youth movement was bound to occur sooner or later; youth revolt is a natural phenomenon, part of the human condition. But the particular direction the American movement would take was not at all foreordained, and it is therefore doubly sad that in its extreme form it has taken a destructive course, self-defeating in terms of its own aims. It seems fairly certain at this point that the American movement will result in a giant hangover, for the more utopian a movement's aims, the greater the disappointment which must inevitably ensue. The cultural and political idiocies perpetrated with impunity in this permissive age have clearly gone beyond the borders of what is acceptable for any society, however liberally it may be structured.

No one knows whether the right-wing backlash, so long predicted, will in fact make its dreadful appearance; perhaps we shall be spared this reaction. It is more likely that there will be a backlash from within the extremist movement itself, as ideas and ideologies undergo change and come into conflict with underlying attitudes. Insofar as those attitudes are intolerant and irrational, they will not quickly mellow, and for that reason America is likely to experience a great deal more trouble with its *enragés.*

The American youth movement of the sixties, infected by the decadence of the age, missed the opportunity to become a powerful agent of regeneration and genuine social and political change. But decadence, contrary to popular belief, is not necessarily a fatal disease. It is a phase through which many generations pass at various stages of their development. The boredom that gives rise to decadence contains the seeds of its own destruction, for who, after a time, would not become bored with boredom?

In 1890, the prevailing mood in France was expressed in the term *fin de siècle;* the most popular sport was national self-degradation; and everyone was convinced that the decay of the country had reached its ultimate stage. Charles Gide, the economist, compared France with a sugarloaf drowning in the sea. Fifteen years later the crisis was suddenly over. Almost overnight, pessimism was transformed into optimism, defeatism into aggressive nationalism, a preoccupation with eroticism into a new enthusiasm for athletics. No one knew exactly why this happened; French society and politics remained essentially the same, the demographic problem was still in full force, moral and religious uncertainties were as rampant as before.

I do not mean to suggest that recovery is always so certain; indeed, the form the cure takes is sometimes almost as bad as the disease. But generations seldom commit collective suicide. As they rush toward the abyss, a guardian angel seems to watch over them, gently deflecting them at the very last moment. Nevertheless, even the patience of angels must not be tried too severely.

5 From the ashes of the new left: toward a new student movement

TOM KAHN

We turn now from discussion of student movements generally, and of their rationale and historic framework, to a more detailed analysis of the American New Left, particularly the SDS. Tom Kahn finds that although there is a growing disenchantment with the New Left as a movement, essential elements of New Left ideology have gained wide acceptance on the campuses. SDS was proudly nonideological when it first appeared on the scene, but later it developed an antagonism towards the labor movement and an attraction to varieties of communism—both of which developments have contributed to the recent fragmentation of the movement.

Despite its present chaotic state, Kahn sees a possibility for the emergence of a vital and democratic student movement. What is still lacking are those willing to do the necessary rebuilding.

Four years ago I wrote an article for *Commentary* entitled "The Problem of the New Left." It was an attempt to draw attention to some of the elitist and undemocratic tendencies that were then developing within the world of SDS. The article appeared eight months after SDS and the League for Industrial Democracy had broken off relations, a time when many liberals were still hopeful that something good and lasting would emerge from the New Left. Although the article was sharply critical of the New Left, I find upon rereading it that it left the door open for a healthy evolution. The last paragraph said:

TOM KAHN *is executive director of the League for Industrial Democracy.*

There are those who refuse to criticize the New Left because, while they sentimentalize it, they do not take it seriously; they are satisfied that it be *alive* and youthful. There are those who criticize it because they want to destroy it—some because they are reactionaries, others because they have become excessively comfortable in their liberalism. But there are also those, among whom I include myself, who criticize out of a hope growing nearly desperate that this outburst of radical discontent will stick, that it will sink deep roots, that it will energize a new political movement and transform national institutions—in short, that its legacy to the next generation will be a new beginning, not that tiresome mixture of cynicism and nostalgia that grows out of defeat and hangs over us still.

Whether hope is a contrivance of ambivalence or ambivalence of hope, there is no longer any basis for either. There is no point in leaving the door open or keeping a light in the window. The New Left, as an organized movement, is collapsing. Its supporters and apologists are not only betting on an unworthy horse; they are backing a loser. Illusions on this score will from here on be costly.

These conclusions are based in part on a survey of student leaders conducted by the League for Industrial Democracy in the spring of 1970. The survey was carried out by young people on the staff of the LID's Youth Project on Democratic Change. They visited some 50 campuses and interviewed hundreds of student body presidents, campus newspaper editors, and leaders of student organizations. Their findings have been published in a report entitled *The State of the Student Movement—1970,* available from the LID.

Looking at the New Left, the report found that "what once was a more or less unified movement, following a widely accepted leadership, with uniform goals, is now a melange of grouplets, projects, and styles with no shared sense of direction, and very often with profound and even bitter internal differences." The report also found that "there is a growing disenchantment with the New Left as a movement" among students generally and that opposition to the New Left is most intense on those campuses where New Left activity has been most predominant. In other words, where students have had an opportunity to see the New Left *in action*, their attitudes toward it are more unfavorable than on those campuses where New Leftism is represented only by the rhetoric of "participatory democracy," "power to the people," and "there's a change gonna come."

At the same time, the report disclosed a disturbing fact: despite the growing disenchantment with the New Left as a *movement*, essential elements of New Left *ideology* have gained wide acceptance on the campuses. For example, students were asked to respond to the following statement:

> Material affluence and the facade of democracy have made the majority of Americans incapable of understanding or working for meaningful social changes. Precisely because of the charade of freedom, we live under the most oppressive kind of social system—subtle though it may be.

The students were not told that this was a paraphrase from the writings of the philosopher-guru of the New Left, Herbert Marcuse; they were simply asked whether they agreed with it. Although less than 9 percent of the students interviewed could be classified as New Leftists, a majority—some 54 percent—said they agreed.

How explain this apparent contradiction? The answer, the report suggests, lies in the compatibility of certain New Left views with traditional conservatism. A snobbish condescension toward the political capacity of ordinary people and an elitist disdain for their "vulgar materialism" characterize William F. Buckley, Jr., as well as Herbert Marcuse. These attitudes have also characterized endless generations of students, who enjoy, after all, a privileged status.

Elitism, of course, can coexist remarkably well with idealism, and this is especially true of students, who have not yet
taken their places in the economic order. Their conservatism
is mostly rooted in a sense of intellectual and moral superiority,
rather than in a self-interested need to rationalize corporate
wealth or social inequality. Presumably, in the long run the
conservative-elitist bias of college students will be undermined
as higher education expands and the educational level of the
general population rises. At present, however, the bias is strong
and may even have grown stronger in the last decade, especially
among upper middle- and upper-class students. They feel
threatened, I suspect, by the campus population explosion,
which menaces their elite status. In any case, my point is that
student elitism can manifest itself either in traditional political
conservatism or in demands for radical social change. But in
either case there is a tendency toward impatience with the democratic process, a low regard for majorities, a lack of empathy with
the daily problems of working people, and the nagging urge
to short-circuit mass institutions that are slow to accept proffered revelations.

This tendency—and I would stress that it is a tendency,
not an immutable, insurmountable condition of student politics—helps explain why key elements in the New Left ideology
had a resonance on the campus, echoing through institutions
which only a decade earlier had succumbed to political and
intellectual conservatism. The New Left, despite its newness,
did not represent a complete break with the past. Between the
campus conservatism of the fifties and the campus radicalism
of the sixties there are continuities, and these, we can see in
retrospect, profoundly influenced the character of the New
Left. It may be profitable to examine some of the ways in which
the New Left derives from the fifties before we proceed to consider its present collapse and the prospects for a new student
movement.

I

During my undergraduate days in the mid-1950s, my main impression of college was of its encased self-centeredness. It was an ivory tower, not only in that it was a sanctuary, but in that it was a place in which the highest human activity was going on; it was not only away from it all but above it all. Graduates would go forth to lead society, but the intrusion of political activity onto the campus was frowned upon. It seemed to me that the temple of learning, so divorced from social reality, was a provincial place whose inhabitants wanted primarily to be left alone to pursue their careers.

In the 1960s this schizoid conception of the university—as both a wise man with a special right to lead and a virgin whose inviolability must be preserved—appears ironically in the New Left. In its famous Port Huron Statement of June 1962, SDS asked what social force could lead the way in the transformation of society and decided that

> . . . the civil rights, peace, and student movements are too poor and socially slighted, and the labor movement too acquiescent, to be counted with enthusiasm. From where else can power and vision be summoned? We believe that the universities are an overlooked seat of influence.

Indeed, as it turns out, the universities have had an unexpected impact on the American political scene, as centers of opposition to the Vietnam war and as stages for riotous upheavals that have moved public opinion to the right. Faculty senates have committed their universities to official positions on the war. This fall a number of schools will give their students two weeks off to work in the elections. There is now widespread acceptance of the notion that the university is an appropriate assembling area or launching pad for political action in the larger society.

On the other hand, although the university may presumably intervene with "power and vision" in the political life of society, the ivy walls are not to be penetrated by outsiders. The wise men guide the destiny of the tribe, but their own domains are sealed off. Recruiters from Dow Chemical must be barred from the campus, and so must the police, even when they would pursue students guilty of unlawful acts for which other citizens would be apprehended and punished. Teachers and administrators are expected to keep their students beyond the reach of the draft. Protests are directed against the appearance of certain political personalities, or, if they do appear, their speeches are drowned out in hostile clamor. Thus, the university is to be a medieval monastery, wherein protection is afforded from secular authority and heresies are kept to a minimum—and this in the name of a radicalism that would make the university a hotbed of political activism.

My point here is not to condemn the revival of political activism in academia; almost nothing would be worse than a return to the silent generation of the fifties. It is rather to expose the contradiction in insisting on the university's right, politically speaking, to invade society but not to be invaded by it.

Now, the formal educational process per se may need to be sheltered, but political activism cannot be sheltered without becoming warped. Politics is inherently a process of conflict and contention, of opposing forces acting and being acted upon. Shelter it and you break the link between action and consequence. Indeed, this is precisely the issue implicit in the current liberal-radical criticism of the isolation of the presidency.

The link between action and consequence is especially tenuous among the cushioned youth of the affluent middle class (the fountainhead of the New Left), and it is not strengthened by the overall isolation of the university. Academic isolationism did not, of course, originate in the 1950s, but I believe that it was particularly strong then and that it was bound up with the dual idea of the university as a center of moral-intellectual superiority—hence entitled to an almost priestly role—and as a privileged sanctuary, an asylum from public passions.

What has happened in the 1960s is that the ivory tower has been politicized in both of its aspects. Moral-intellectual superiority has largely been translated into political superiority; the priest has turned politician. (Was not Eugene McCarthy the perfect symbol for this development?) And, at the same time, students demand of the university that it protect them from the police, the draft, and the seductions of the military-industrial complex.

The New Left, to the extent that it built upon, or exploited, these notions of the university's role, has not departed from, but has rather revealed its indebtedness to, the academic premises of the fifties. I believe these premises to be conservative and elitist. They are biased and inadequate responses to the uncomfortable fact that the university is two things: a place where formal learning takes place and an institution with an inescapable social and political weight. To find ways of resolving the tension between these two functions is admittedly difficult — and, thankfully, beyond the scope of this paper. Nonetheless, we should recognize that the present conception generates some profoundly undemocratic attitudes, which reinforce the elitist predispositions of affluent youth, and that the influence of the New Left on campus has been achieved not in opposition to these attitudes but precisely in harmony with them. It therefore follows that any effort to replace the New Left with a healthy, democratic student movement must search for new definitions of the university's relation to society.

II

The New Left, of course, does not exist simply within the academic setting; nor has its evolution been determined for the most part by the crisis of higher education. The early demonstrations at Berkeley, one recalls, had nothing to do with free speech or university reform but rather revolved around the issues of race and Vietnam. Although the problems of higher education — mushrooming enrollments, bureaucratization, inadequate student-faculty communication, impersonalization, specialization, and the concentration of many students in one place—although these help account for the resonance of the New Left, they did not predetermine its ideological course. The New Left is a political phenomenon, with off-campus roots and repercussions. Its context is the whole field of American political life, and it must be judged accordingly.

I do not have space here to attempt a full interpretation of the political history of the New Left. Instead I would like to go back to my *Commentary* article of four years ago as a point of departure for several observations. (I do this not in the spirit of self-justification, I ask you to believe, but to suggest that the crisis of the New Left is the logical outcome of early tendencies that were already evident in the mid-sixties.)

When SDS first appeared, it proudly proclaimed its non-ideological character. It wanted to break from the radical dogmas of the thirties. It wanted no part of the sectarian disputations, the scholastic hairsplitting, and the debilitating factionalism of the old left. So, it adopted a vaguely populist stance made up of a romantically appealing rhetoric and an existentially rebellious activism. This stance certainly seemed more compatible with the atmosphere of spontaneity surrounding the blossoming civil rights movement of those days than anything the old left had to offer, and it was applauded by many liberals as a happy combination of radical vision and American pragmatism.

A tiny handful of people on the SDS National Council, including myself, were not so smitten by this nativist rejection of ideology. We thought it was not enough to reject the mistakes of the radical past; lessons had to be drawn from those mistakes and incorporated into a new perspective—a new ideology, if you will—and a corresponding strategy. Naturally, we were denounced as the youth agents of a fossilized sectarianism.

As we look at the SDS today—torn apart by the most incredible ultraleftist factionalism, with each faction trying to outdo the other in Maoist fantasizing, all in a display of infantile leftism far surpassing what Lenin so persuasively condemned—

we must laugh to keep from crying. I, for one, feel reinforced in my innate wariness of political movements that make a principle out of dismissing ideology. Either they are trying to avoid thinking through their ideas in a systematic way or they are already operating on ideological assumptions that they are disinclined to make plain. Whichever was true of SDS, it adopted, in the name of antidogmatism, two postures that have proved disastrous. The first has to do with communism, the second with the labor movement, both of which are subjects of enormous importance to the left.

III

The following excerpt from my article "The Problem of the New Left" indicates how the New Left's attitude toward communism struck at least one observer four years ago:

> Activists of the New Left most frequently describe themselves as acommunist, or as anti-anticommunist. Their writings speak indiscriminately of "*the* ideology of anticommunism," as if the anticommunism of socialists, trade unionists, liberals, McCarthyites, Birchers, and Klansmen were cut from the same cloth. What actually operates here is a kind of reverse McCarthyism which refuses to differentiate between libertarian and rightist opposition to communism. The New Left, precisely by adopting as a cardinal tenet the thesis that the "communist question" is irrelevant, raises the communist question to a standard by which it will judge others. In actual practice, the standard works to the advantage of the procommunist and the indifferentist, neither of whom has reason to raise the question. . . .
>
> The irrelevance of the communist question was at least a discussable proposition so long as the movement confined itself to domestic questions. Anticommunism, after all, is a position deriving in the first place from an analysis of the social system established and ruled by Communist parties, and in the second place from an evaluation of the role of apologists of this system in countries throughout the world. Thus, the New Left could argue the irrelevance

of anticommunism on the ground that there are no significant numbers of communist apologists in this country; as
for other social systems, "We live here, not in Russia." Once
the movement turned toward the war in Vietnam, however,
what began as an admissible (if morally and politically
dubious) disinclination to develop an attitude toward communism, became an indefensible double standard. One need
not support administration policies in Vietnam to recognize that the United States may not be playing the *only*
reactionary or oppressive role in that tragic land. Yet this
is the assumption underlying the SNCC [Student Nonviolent Coordinating Committee] statement on the war of
last January 6.

The SNCC statement had said:

Our work, particularly in the South, has taught us that the
United States government has never guaranteed the freedom of oppressed citizens, and is not yet truly determined
to end the rule of terror and oppression within its own
borders. . . . We know that for the most part elections in
this country, in the North as well as the South, are not
free. . . . We maintain that our country's cry of "Preserve
freedom in the world" is a hypocritical mask behind which
it squashes liberation movements which are not bound, and
refuse to be bound, by the expediencies of United States
Cold War policies.

My article continued:

The SNCC statement is the most extreme example of a
fairly pervasive mode of thought on the New Left. The
danger is not that it paves the way for a resurgence of the
communist movement; it is rather that it encourages a
stance and a species of reasoning that muddies the democratic vision of the left. People who would fight for the
right to vote in Mississippi, and yet support forces which
rationalize the denial of that right, sow great confusion
as to the depth of the American left's commitment to democracy. It is the resurgence of that confusion, which once
before took an enormous toll of radicalism, that we have
to fear.

Although this critique was predictably attacked as, for instance, "red-baiting" and "raising false issues," it now seems clear that, if anything, it understated the case. Who can now insist that the communist question is irrelevant to the New Left? To be sure, the New Left has not caused any significant gains for the Communist party of the United States. Pro-Russian communism is not attractive to most New Leftists; they consider it too bureaucratic and materialistic, that is, too much like the United States. But a resurgence of the Communist party as an organized movement was beside the point some of us were making.

The point was that the defense of communist regimes, as against democratic capitalism, leads to a degeneration of democratic values that will manifest itself in almost every aspect of activity. The New Left's criticisms of the Soviet Union, far from disclosing a residual devotion to democratic values, precisely underscore its utter refusal to make the fundamental distinction between totalitarianism and democracy: the right to organize political opposition to the ruling party or class. The New Left merely prefers the totalitarianism of backward countries, whose bureaucracies are less fully developed and speak a more primitive revolutionary rhetoric, to the totalitarianism of modern industrialized states.

Almost all of the SDS factions now identify themselves as communist, albeit of the Maoist rather than the Kosygin variety. Political democracy is denounced as a bourgeois hoax, totalitarian ideologues are worshipped, and guerrilla warfare and terrorism are openly advocated—and practiced. And as the American people move to the right, in predictable recoil from this grotesque degeneration, the entire left, broadly defined, is the victim. Thus the issue which was not supposed to arise again—the relationship of the left to democracy—did in fact arise again to haunt us. And instead of a new beginning from the movement that called itself the *New* Left, and which the American people considered *the* left, we got only a sickening replay of—to quote Marx in another context—"the old crap."

The best protection against authoritarian ideology is democratic ideology, not no ideology. Granting the sterility of right-wing anticommunism, it was not the only alternative. The anticommunism of democratic radicals had been the product of painful experience, of rethinking old positions, of political, intellectual, and moral soul-searching. This process yielded valuable insights into the character of left totalitarianism, adding new dimensions to radical thought without surrendering to the status quo. In rejecting this experience, the New Left did not escape the mistakes of the old left; it repeated them, blindly, arrogantly, and catastrophically.

It seems to me that the resurgence of "confusion as to the depth of the American left's commitment to democracy" is indeed the bitter legacy of the New Left. But not the New Left alone. The sad fact is that the New Left has been cushioned by a brand of liberalism which seems to exclude the possibility of a majoritarian movement for social change. Liberals of this stripe are of course too genteel to throw bombs or seize buildings, but they *do* contribute to the political atmosphere in which these things occur. They exude contempt for the silent majority, sneer at the hardhats, and flippantly dismiss mainstream institutions as irrelevant; at the same time they rationalize student violence, extol the social inventiveness of the college-educated, and seek salvation in coalitions of militant minorities. Their self-righteous moralizing blinds them to public opinion; indeed, it renders them incapable of feeling the frustrations and resentments that millions of ordinary people are experiencing. And their voguish anti-Americanism makes them vulnerable to the skillful attacks of a Spiro Agnew, whose sharp political eye spots them as the soft underbelly of the liberal movement. Indeed, the insouciance with which these liberals shrug off Agnew's attacks is itself a sign of alienation from the deeper political currents in the country.

Can one be committed to this politics of alienation and still be a democrat? Obviously, one can be alienated from a political system or from institutions out of the conviction that they do not measure up to democratic standards. (On the other hand, it does not follow that one who gives unquestioning loyalty to his society's institutions has strong democratic values.) Yet, in actual practice, it seems to me, a politics that prescribes alienation from existing mainstream institutions—institutions which, rightly or wrongly, command the allegiance of masses of people—tends to run against the democratic grain.

Some liberals and radicals, convinced that the mass institutions are wrong in their policies or structures, automatically conclude that these institutions are therefore unrepresentative of the people or that the people are fools. This, of course, is the easy way out. It demands no attempt to reach people where they are, no effort to understand the ties that bind them to their institutions, and, in short, no need to grapple with the difficult complexities and contradictions of American political life. It offers another convenience: there is no pressure to continually reexamine one's political premises.

Examples of this approach are not hard to find. How many times have we heard certain white liberals cavalierly dismiss the NAACP as being "out of touch with the black community"? Yet the NAACP maintains a membership of roughly half a million, the great bulk of whom are black and not well-to-do. Moreover, it raises from the black community a larger portion of its funds than any other civil rights organization. What these liberals really mean, of course, is that the NAACP is out of touch with those people whom the liberals have appointed as spokesmen for the black community—Black Panthers and other assorted nationalists, separatists, and self-styled revolutionaries. The continuing institutional strength of the NAACP in the Negro community—and the demonstrated inability of liberal-appointed spokesmen to establish a comparable mass base—should have prompted these liberals to reexamine their judgments concerning the mood of the Negro community, the representativeness of the NAACP, and so on. But they have not.

For some liberals and radicals, it would seem, democracy is an abstraction, a blueprint for a future society—perhaps an unexceptionably libertarian and passionately conceived blueprint, but nonetheless only a blueprint. It is not seen as a *process* of social change, as a *mode* of political action, as a *method* of making and applying judgments. Democracy is weakened by this one-dimensional view of its meaning, for, as in the NAACP example, such a view is prone to gross political miscalculation and to elitism.

Thus emasculated, the democratic idea is diminished in its ability to resist authoritarian and totalitarian ideology. What we have described as a tendency among some liberals has reached its logical extreme in the New Left, whose identification with procommunist forces is very much an outgrowth of its alienation from the mass democratic forces for social change in the United States, an alienation foreseeable in the early days of SDS.

IV

Alienation from mass institutions was not invented by the New Left; American radicalism in general has been peculiarly susceptible to this affliction. Yet there is a mass force with which previous generations of radicals identified, even when they did not play a direct role in it, and which the New Left rejected almost from the beginning—the labor movement. This brings me to the second aspect of the New Left's dismissal of the radical experience.

Again, I quote from "The Problem of the New Left":

Whatever their differences, every group, without exception, which has called itself left or radical, has believed that the organized working class, the labor movement, has a unique historical role to play in the creation of the new society. Disagreements as to the precise nature of that role, and as to the political strategy the unions should pursue . . . have rested on a common assumption regarding the socially progressive character of the organized working class. The single new ideological feature of the New Left . . . is the rejection, implicit or explicit, of this fundamental assumption. The reasoning behind this rejection is not that the labor leadership or bureaucracy represses the workers' instinctive radicalism (the Trotskyist formula) or that the workers have been atomized or culturally degraded by mass society (the ex-radical's formula), but that the organized working class has achieved its goals and has itself consequently become part of the power structure.

The article went on to suggest, however, that this criticism of the labor movement was not entirely radical:

The disaffection of intellectuals from the labor movement reached a peak in the fifties, and few students of a liberal or radical persuasion during that time held the labor movement in esteem. It was therefore predictable that when the next wave of radicalism emerged, it would view labor as simply another big institution—and the New Left is very much a revolt against bigness. But it is important to remember that the indifference or hostility to labor grew out of a conservative period, when middle-class prosperity was reshaping the ethos of the university, and the McClelland hearings were convincing millions of Americans that Dave Beck of the Teamsters was the prototype of the labor leader. Thus, while much student criticism of labor comes from the left, it also contains strands of middle-class prejudice—a lack of appreciation for, or identification with, the historic and *continuing* role of the unions in the day-to-day lives of literally millions of working people.

Frankly, these observations seem to me even more pertinent now than when they were written four years ago. Indeed, at that time it was considered hopelessly old-fashioned, atavistically Marxist, to pay much attention to the labor movement, except perhaps as a possible source of funds. Now, however, the role of the unions is once again heatedly debated, and with good reason. In 1962 the Port Huron Statement complained that the

labor movement was "too acquiescent to be counted with enthusiasm"; in 1970 the hardhats no doubt made the New Left
wish that the labor movement, or at least a section of it, were
more acquiescent—and quiescent.

If we look at the actual developments in the labor movement
since 1962, we are struck by how utterly uninformed and lacking
in insight the SDS pronouncement was. For during the decade
of the sixties, the unions made giant strides in organizing "un-
organizable" white-collar professional employees. They laid
the groundwork for the recent historic victories of Cesar Chavez's farm workers. They mounted dramatic and successful
campaigns to unionize hospital workers, sanitation men, and
other low-paid workers. The labor movement also underwent
internal changes. In one large union after another, established
leaders were voted out. In the second half of the decade, the
rank and file increasingly rejected contract settlements negotiated by their leaders, and the number of strikes rose as
workers struggled to catch up with inflation and the profit
boom. The General Electric strike was especially significant
for the unprecedentedly unified support it received from the
entire labor movement—both during the strike itself and earlier
in the development of the coordinated collective bargaining
approach—and for the public's support of the boycott campaign.

Strikes, picket lines, boycotts—these are more exciting
to the New Left, and to young people generally, than the routine
union tasks of settling grievances and servicing members, and
so New Left interest in the labor movement quickened toward
the end of the sixties. But this new concern, it must be emphasized, is based not on an understanding of the essential nature
and role of the labor movement but on its dramatic moments.

Anyone who is familiar with Capitol Hill knows that the
AFL-CIO has been the single most powerful force behind the
social legislation of the last quarter century, and that its vigorous
support has been the decisive factor in the enactment of the civil
rights legislation of the sixties, particularly in the area of fair

employment practices. Labor has not been motivated only by narrow self-interest. The battle for higher minimum wages does not directly benefit the union member (union wages are above the minimum). And the fight against the Carswell nomination had to do with his civil rights record, not his labor stand.

The legislative work of the labor movement is only one aspect of its role. It has an impact on the national economy as a pressure for income redistribution, greater consumer purchasing power, and increased public spending. It also exercises a much overlooked egalitarian influence on our social values. But none of this is grasped by the New Left, partly because of its studied ignorance (facts would conflict with the stereotypes inherited from the fifties) and partly because of its contempt for the social reforms pioneered by labor—reforms which New Left spokesman Tom Hayden has described as "illusory or token, serving chiefly to sharpen the capacity of the system for manipulation and oppression."

The idea that the labor movement (and other liberal institutions) is part of a power structure that has contrived social reforms for the purpose of expanding the capacity of "the system" to manipulate and oppress—this idea lies at the heart of the New Left's elitism and its alienation from liberalism. To be sure, the American welfare state is woefully inadequate, it heaps bureaucratic indignities upon its supposed beneficiaries, and it has doubtless been viewed by some sophisticates in the ruling class as a means of structuring preexisting inequalities. But what this analysis leaves out is the historical reality that the welfare state is the product of struggle by millions of people, in unions and other movements, for economic security and social justice. Their achievements may have fallen short of their goals, but their achievements should not on that account be thought of as the demonic creations of an ingenious ruling class. Was the civil rights legislation of the past decade a trick from above, or was it the fruit of costly and determined struggle from below, in which brave men and women gave their lives?

For all its populist incantations, the New Left has little appreciation of the role of popular movements, at least in the United States. On the world scale, the New Left claims kinship with vast popular revolutionary forces (more accurately, it supports procommunist political movements), but in the United States it sees whatever social advances are made as the work of a tricky Establishment. The people count for nothing. After all, are not "the majority of Americans incapable of understanding or working for meaningful social changes"? Are they not the contemptible silent majority—the money-grubbing, boob-tubing, beer-guzzling, flag-waving, hippie-hating suburban ciphers? And aren't these people the bulk of the labor movement?

This snobbish antagonism toward the labor movement persists as an underlying current in the New Left, but it has lately been obscured by a new fad we are now witnessing: the rediscovery of the working class. There are probably several reasons for this rediscovery. For one thing, the spectacle of silent-majority types walking out of their factories and offices to go on strike, man picket lines, shout slogans, make demands, and, in short, to protest, no doubt prompted some New Leftists to take a second look at the workers. In addition, the more thoughtful New Leftists (and New Politics people), reflecting on the 1968 elections, must have been impressed by the performance of our allegedly moribund labor movement, which almost succeeded in single-handedly electing Hubert Humphrey president of the United States and, in the process, effectively countered Wallace's appeal among workers. Finally, I suspect that the construction workers' demonstrations on Vietnam, while confirming the New Left in its opinion of the unions as reactionary on foreign policy, may also have had a sobering effect on some radicals. After all, there was nothing silent about the hardhats; here was a force that had to be dealt with, one way or another.

Whatever stimulated this rediscovery, it is not confined to the New Left; liberal intellectuals and even the White House are excitedly exploring the mind of the blue-collar worker.

But, interestingly, none of this concern has been translated into significant new support for the labor movement. It is obvious that when factions of the New Left call for a worker-student alliance, they do not mean an alliance with the worker's union. They want a direct relationship between students and workers that bypasses the unions.

Someone has aptly remarked that General Electric wanted a similar relationship with its employees; it got a strike instead. New Left kids who wished to communicate directly with workers on the picket lines have got worse. Some of these kids have discovered to their dismay that, although workers may beef about their unions, they don't want to hear their unions criticized by outsiders, least of all by hairy kids and least of all on the subjects of Vietnam and race. This is no generation gap. It is a kind of class warfare, aggravated by the distinctive politics of the New Left.

Between middle-class radicalism and the labor movement some tension is inevitable. The radicals will almost always be advocating advanced ideas that rub workers the wrong way, that fly in the face of the social or moral codes of working-class life. Yet I would insist, and history provides examples, that a radical movement which had a healthy respect for workers and their problems, which had a historically conditioned identification with their institutions, and which saw its own future as intertwined with theirs—such a radical movement would have been able to reduce the tension to a minimum. Instead, we have had, in the New Left, a movement that has sought to relate to workers and their unions either not at all or on its own terms.

V

The reader may feel that I have dwelt too long and too discursively on the New Left's attitude toward the labor movement. After all, as regrettable or reprehensible as this attitude may be, it surely did not lead to the collapse of the New Left. Granted that a movement which identifies with communism is doomed in the United States, where almost everybody is anticommunist, a movement which is hostile to labor, even though it is radical, will surely find plenty of company.

Perhaps. What I have been trying to suggest, however, is that ideas, at least political ideas, do not exist independently of one another in a vacuum. They are concatenated, linked by threads. The adoption of one idea or value predisposes me to adopt another one similar to it or extended from it.

In this sense, there is a thread connecting the New Left's rejection of the labor movement and its attraction to varieties of communism. These traits, in turn, are interconnected with: the conservative heritage of the 1950s; the isolation and elitism of the universities; the absence of a strong democratic ideology; alienation from mass democratic institutions; and the rise of liberal elitism. I do not list these factors in any necessary sequence, nor do I propose to spell out their precise cause-and-effect relationship to each other. I do contend that a common thread—the degeneration of democratic values—runs through all of them.

Terrorism, violence, manipulation, social pathology, and the trampling of civil liberties are the ugly fruits of the degeneration. The people cannot or will not act? We shall act *for* them, even if in despite of them! History will not move? We shall substitute ourselves for it! Society is logjammed? We shall get dynamite!

Most students did not see all of this in the ideology of the New Left, but when the nightmare materialized on the campus, the most decent among them recoiled. The New Left's base began to shrink, and a movement started falling apart.

VI

With the fragmentation of the New Left, what will happen to the student movement? The LID report *The State of the Student Movement—1970* saw three possibilities:

It is entirely possible that some unforeseen crisis might give new life to those who advocate world revolution and practice petty arson. Nor is it altogether unlikely that disorientation and defeat could exhaust the student left entirely, opening the way for a return to an era of conservatism reminiscent of the 1950s. Yet there is also a third possibility . . . that the student movement will be revived around a new program and a new philosophy which is solidly based on democratic values.

The report went on to describe the obstacles in the way of such a new movement and to suggest ways of overcoming them. I would conclude by quoting at length from the final section of the report entitled "Beyond the New Left":

We would like to suggest that the major obstacle to the creation of a democratic student movement is the attitude of superiority and contempt with which many students and intellectuals view America's lower middle class, its working class, and even many of its poor. . . . In view of this, we propose that projects be initiated which will bring college students, some of whom have led the most ghettoized lives of any Americans, into greater contact with middle Americans, blue-collar workers, white ethnics, and similar population groups. Most important, students should be brought into greater contact with those groups which have good credentials in the struggle for social progress — the trade union movement and the integrationist Negro movement.

Aloofness from the American people is one profoundly conservative sentiment which often appears in the guise of radicalism. Another is the current fashion for racial separatism. Our findings show that separatism has its greatest vogue on the more conservative campuses. Campuses where genuinely progressive attitudes predominate may have greater racial tension, but our respondents from these campuses also feel that race relations are "improved." This is no contradiction. A minority's struggle for equality will indeed create tension, but this tension may be a natural side effect of an essential improvement in race relations. Roy Wilkins and others have criticized black separatism as a misleading "shortcut" to racial equality. This is as true on the campus as in the general community. Those types of colleges which, for example, have been most eager to contrive "black studies" programs are also those which show least improvement in race relations. Those schools which have not established such programs (which are often academically unsound and racially exclusive) have shown greatest improvement.

This finding, along with our interpretation of the history of the student movement, convinces us that strong new efforts should be made to encourage racial integration and integrated student activity for social change. We believe that, just as integrated struggle for change inspired the revival of the student movement in the early 1960s, the collapse of interracialism was among the most important factors in the corruption and disintegration of the movement at the close of the decade. The race question has a symbolic importance in American political life. If it can be solved, then everything is possible. If we accept defeat in this, then a film of pessimism appears over everything else.

The relationship to the black population which students developed during the struggle for integration also provided them with some anchor in political reality. The self-indulgent tactics and language of the latter-day SDS were never accepted by most black people; only when white youth had lost direct contact with the average black and were able to relate to blacks only through those on the political fringes of the black community—the remnants of SNCC or the Panthers—could middle-class obnoxiousness become so important in the style of the student left.

We believe that black and white youth must again work closely together. Perhaps black youth should have their own exclusively black organizations; certainly blacks should take leadership in largely black organizations. *But integration must again become both an ultimate goal and a widely practiced reality in the student movement.* It should be possible for integrationist groups to compete effectively with New Left and separatist forces on the campuses. The apparent failure of separatism in improving race relations has, we believe, created a potential constituency on the campus for an integrationist point of view. This constituency can best be rallied through a direct attack on the segregationists of both the right and the left.

A similar challenge could be put forward to those who are fostering a do-nothing mood in world affairs. Again, this is a case of conservatism dressed up as radicalism. The economic, political, and military problems of the world, especially the developing nations, can only widen if the United States piously retreats behind its wall of nuclear missiles. Those who believe that U.S. policies over the past decade have failed must not yield to the temptations of neoisolationism held out both by some old-fashioned conservatives and by the supporters of the totalitarian left. The evidence that many campus leaders are unwilling to support Israel in a conflict in which Israel is clearly in the right and entirely reliant on American aid is most troubling.[1] A generation that gave life to the Peace Corps and proclaimed the heroic ambition of ending poverty, oppression, and war throughout the world is now turning its back on a small, democratic society—an example of how education and community development can give life to a barren land—which is about to be crushed by a coalition of Arab strongmen and the Soviet military apparatus.

We believe that responsible groups on both sides of the Vietnam debate must join to counteract the isolationist trend on the campus. A national debate on the Middle East, like the debate that took place over Vietnam, should be encouraged. Many young Americans also feel strong ties to Latin America, and student activity in regard to Latin America should be undertaken and supported.

But the greatest need on the campus is for a principled philosophic opposition to both the vehement authoritarian left and to the muted appeals of conservative disengagement. American liberalism has always had a nervous disdain for anything which has the odor of ideology. Those who regret the corruption of student radicalism have usually avoided a confrontation of ideas, hoping instead that some new activity "within the democratic process" could cure

---

1. Fifty-four percent of the students interviewed in the survey felt Israel and the Arabs were equally responsible for the Middle East conflict. Fifty-eight percent did not want the United States to get involved in support of either side.

this condition. But so far such projects have not worked. The Kennedy and McCarthy campaigns, the Vietnam Moratorium, the ecology movement—all these have had their moments of success. But, because they have indeed sought to co-opt or neutralize the extremists in the student left and have avoided principled debate, no lasting alternative to radical elitism has been established.

Young people seeking convictions in a confused world are not likely to be won by those who retreat from the clash of ideas and instead try to mollify and outmaneuver the dissenters. The cleaver tactics usually adopted by "the moderates" on most issues not only fail to inspire the uncommitted, they encourage the most militant disrupters. As sociologist Edward Shils puts it, "The feebleness of those whom they expect to be strong encourages [the protestors'] hostility. The absence of effective positive models and the faintheartedness of those who oppose them open a free field for their aggressive disposition."

Those who want to rebuild a vital and democratic student movement must be willing to fight for their ideals.

In particular

6 "The socialism of fools": the left, the Jews, and Israel

SEYMOUR MARTIN LIPSET

The New Left and its impact on our society are of general concern to all Americans, and the first group of essays in this volume is devoted to consideration of the movement as a whole. In the essays that follow we turn to the specifically Jewish dimensions of the youth revolt: the role of Jewish youth among the activists and the reasons for their participation; the effect of that participation on the American Jewish community; and New Left attitudes towards the Jewish community, Jewish values, and the State of Israel.

From the point of view of Jewish interests, there is no discernable difference between the New Left and the old. As Maurice Samuel commented at Arden House, "The New Left, so called, is an old left in disguise with certain little gimmicks . . . ota hagveret b'shinuy aderet [the same old hag in a new rag—Editor]. . . . fundamentally or predominantly, the left was opposed to the existence of the Jewish people as a people, because it stood in the way [of leftist programs]." As its champions insist, there is no uniformity in the New Left, but, then, neither was there uniformity in the old. But the attitude of the left towards Jewish peoplehood has remained constant and must not be seen as a purely contemporary phenomenon. "We have lived through this assault on the part of the left," declared Samuel, "we lived through it one hundred and fifty years ago, a hundred years ago, seventy-five years ago, fifty years ago, twenty years ago, and we'll live through this one, too."

In the following article, Seymour Martin Lipset analyzes the affiliation of the Jew with radical and

SEYMOUR MARTIN LIPSET *is Professor of Government and Social Relations at Harvard University.*

> *revolutionary movements, old and new. He traces the*
> *alliance through European history and through certain*
> *periods of United States history, and points to the*
> *left-wing anti-West fixation as an important element*
> *in the rejection of Israel by the Third World, since*
> *early Zionist ideology is seen as having developed in*
> *the West, and the only country supporting Israel today*
> *is a Western country—the United States.*

Shortly before he was assassinated, Martin Luther King, Jr., was in Boston on a fund-raising mission, and I had the good fortune to attend a dinner which was given for him in Cambridge. This was an experience which was at once fascinating and moving: one witnessed Dr. King in action in a way one never got to see him in public. He wanted to find what the Negro students at Harvard and other parts of the Boston area were thinking about various issues, and he very subtly cross-examined them for well over an hour and a half. He asked questions and said very little himself. One of the young men present happened to make some remark against the Zionists. Dr. King snapped at him and said, "Don't talk like that! When people criticize Zionists, they mean Jews. You're talking anti-Semitism!"

In discussing the reactions to Israel of liberals, leftists, New Leftists, old leftists, academics, and the like, one is talking about secular versions, in some ways, of various theological doctrines. The history of the relationship between the left and the Jews indicates that the Jews have been intimately associated with the liberal-left side of the political spectrum. The Jews were an issue in the French Revolution, and have continued to concern political men ever since. For a century and a half, the left supported Jewish political and social rights against the existing establishments which tried to deny them. In Catholic feudal Europe, Jews had had few rights, and the universalistic egalitarian ideology stemming from the French Revolution served to break down particularistic restrictions on all groups, and helped thereby to secure the emancipation of the Jews also.

But leftist support for the liberation of the Jews, which helped gain them the right to take their part as citizens, was not an unmixed blessing. Historically the left has assumed (sometimes explicitly, more often implicitly) that one of the payments the Jews would make to the left for having liberated them would be to disappear. Liberal-left ideology of all varieties has assumed that within a free nation (and nationalism was historically a leftist revolutionary ideology in the nineteenth century), Jewish identity—like all other forms of parochial tribal loyalties—would be assimilated into the free, universalistic community. Jews would become members of the nation no different from anyone else: which meant that they would cease being Jews. The maintenance of Jewish particularistic customs—religious, ethnic, and otherwise—was not welcomed by the left. The feeling that Jewish particularism is somehow reactionary, tribal, traditional, and unmodern has continued down to the present.

There is another element in the ambivalent relationship between contemporary left ideologies and movements and the Jews. The socialist and communist movements have opposed anti-Semitism and various restrictions on Jews participating as free citizens, because they shared with other parts of the left the assumption that Judaism (i.e. the Jews) would disappear in the forthcoming universalistic (socialistic) utopia. Unlike liberalism, however, the socialist left has had another special problem, namely, the association of Jews with capitalism encouraged by the disproportionate number of businessmen, bankers, traders, and merchants among Jews.[1]

Anti-Semitism, as August Bebel once pointed out, was "the socialism of fools." In fact, it was perceived as a form of socialism by many in the nineteenth century. Anti-Semitism (some social-

---

1. For an excellent historical discussion of anti-Semitism among socialists and the left, with a useful bibliography, see George Lichtheim, "Socialism and the Jews," *Dissent* (July–August 1968), pp. 314-342.

ists thought or hoped) was a naive, stupid beginning of the recognition that capitalism was evil. Therefore, anti-Semitism in itself was not morally bad, it was simply ignorant and incomplete. Some socialists, including Marx himself, used the symbol of Jewish capitalism—of the Jews as merchants and Shylocks—in their propaganda. Without going into the whole question of Marx's curious relationship with Judaism—it is certainly not a simple one—there can be little doubt that Marx's belief system included some components which must be described as anti-Semitism.[2]

But the major aspect of Marxist nineteenth-century thinking on the subject—and this becomes relevant to some current developments in the American Negro community and to the reactions of leftist intellectuals toward those developments—was to see lower-class anti-Semitism as a form of embryonic class consciousness among workers. To talk about "oppressive Jewish businessmen" and "Jewish bankers" was considered a step in the right direction; it was part of the masses' learning that all bankers and businessmen—all capitalists—were bad. In czarist Russia, some young Jewish revolutionaries hailed the emergence of the anti-Semitic anticzarist *Narodnaya Volya* as evidence that the revolution was really under way. According to J. L. Talmon in his article "Jews and Revolution," published in the *Maariv* of September 21, 1969, three of the 28 members of the executive committee of this organization, which called in 1881 for a pogrom directed against the czar, the nobility, and the Jews, were themselves Jewish (as were many rank-and-file members).

This confused attitude toward anti-Semitism almost prevented the French Socialist party from taking a stand in the major Jewish *cause célèbre* of the Third Republic, the Dreyfus Case. While French radicals (liberals) like Zola and Clemenceau jumped to Dreyfus' defense, recognizing that a major principle

---

2. See Solomon Bloom, "Karl Marx and the Jews," *Jewish Social Studies* (January 1942), pp. 3-16; Edmund Silberner, "Was Marx an Anti-Semite?" *Historia Judaica* (April 1949), pp. 1-52.

was at stake in the persecution of a Jew, no matter who he was, a debate emerged among the socialists. A number of them, particularly those on the revolutionary left, argued that socialists should not be concerned about Dreyfus since he was a professional soldier, a captain in the Army, and that whether Gentile militarists or capitalists persecuted Jewish militarists or capitalists was of no concern to revolutionary socialists.

Jean Jaurès, the famous French revisionist socialist leader, saved the glory of the socialist movement by insisting that whenever injustice was done, socialists and radicals had to be in the forefront of the battle, that it made no difference whether injustice was done to a capitalist, a general, a Jew, or anybody else. He argued the case for socialist involvement in the defense of Dreyfus on a broad idealistic basis that had nothing to do with historical materialism or class struggle. Jaurès laid down the principle that the left must always oppose religious and racial discrimination regardless of the social or economic status of the victim.[3]

In general, between the French Revolution and the end of World War II, the political history of continental Europe has suggested that most of the tendencies classified on the right have been somewhat anti-Semitic, whereas those on the left have been more defensive of Jewish rights. The traditional religious-linked right groups regarded the Jews as outside of Christendom and hence not properly qualified to be full citizens. Some more populist-oriented rightist movements used anti-Semitism as an antielitist tactic to win mass support against the blandishments of the socialists. There were, of course, some major exceptions to these generalizations, particularly among monarchical and aristocratic elements concerned with protecting *their* Jews against the vulgar prejudices of the masses or the materialistic middle classes. The socialists also tolerated some overt anti-Semites in their ranks, particularly in central Europe.

3. Edmund Silberner, "French Socialism and the Jewish Question, 1865–1914," *Historia Judaica* (April 1957), pp. 13–14.

This historic link between position on matters of Jewish rights and the broader political spectrum helps to explain the presence of large numbers of Jews in the various leftist movements, particularly many wealthy Jews, who have supported radical left causes. For much of European history, Jews had no alternative but to support a variety of left tendencies. This was especially true within the Czarist Empire before World War I. This limitation on political alternatives was paralleled socially. The German political sociologist, Robert Michels, accounted for the left propensities of many affluent Jews as a reaction to this phenomenon in his justly famed study of the structure of socialist parties, *Political Parties*:

> The origin of this predominant position [of the Jews in the European socialist movement] is to be found, as far at least as concerns Germany and the countries of Eastern Europe, in the peculiar position which the Jews have occupied and in many respects still occupy. The legal emancipation of the Jews has not been followed by their social and moral emancipation. In large sections of the German people a hatred of the Jews and the spirit of the Jew-baiter still prevail, and contempt for the Jew is a permanent thing. The Jew's chances in public life are adversely affected; he is practically excluded from the judicial profession, from a military career, and from official employment. . . .
>
> Even when they are rich, the Jews constitute, at least in eastern Europe, a category of persons who are excluded from the social advantages which the prevailing political, economic, and intellectual system ensures for the corresponding portion of the Gentile population: Society in the narrower sense of the term is distrustful of them, and public opinion is unfavorable to them.[4]

The links of Jews to the left in Europe affected the political behavior of those who emigrated to America. Although the issue of Jewish emancipation, civil and social rights, did not concern American politics (and in any case, in the second half of the nineteenth century it was difficult to assign left-right labels to

4. Robert Michels, *Political Parties* (n.p., 1915), pp. 260–261.

the two major U.S. parties which corresponded to the European divisions), the general ideological commitment of many Jews led them to support efforts to form leftist socialist and anarchist movements.

The small socialist-anarchist groups apart, Jews found it extremely difficult to respond in group self-interest or value terms to the American party system. Those attracted to the abolitionist and civil rights causes were faced with the fact that the Republican party, both before and after the Civil War, had strong ties to antiimmigrant nativism, that most Know-Nothings of the 1850s had become Republicans, including many top leaders of the party. The appeal to Jews by various agrarian elements and social reformers who sought to create anti-System left-wing third parties was limited, since many of these (from the independent parties of the 1870s to the Populists of the 1890s) included among their spokesmen leaders and writers who emphasized the exploitative role of the Rothschilds and other international Jewish bankers. Although some serious students of Populism report little or no anti-Semitism in the local publications of the movement in the Midwest, there can be no doubt that the party welcomed into its ranks many who focused on the Jews and who produced an American version of "the socialism of fools."

The nomination of William Jennings Bryan for president in 1896 by both the Democratic and Populist parties in opposition to William McKinley, the proindustry candidate of the Republicans, seemingly gave a left-right dimension to the two-party system, one which might have affected the political orientation of left-disposed recent Jewish immigrants. Yet Edward Flower, who has studied that election, reports strong streaks of anti-Semitism in the Populist and Free Silver elements who made up a considerable part of Bryan's campaign organization. An Associated Press dispatch from St. Louis at a time when both the Populist and Free Silver conventions were meeting is particularly noteworthy on this point:

One of the striking things about the Populist Convention, or rather the two conventions here and those attending them, is the extraordinary hatred of the Jewish race. It is not possible to go into any hotel in the city without hearing the most bitter denunciation of the Jews as a class and of the particular Jews who happen to have prospered in the world.[5]

Flower's examination of American Jewish publications of the day indicates considerable concern about the presence of anti-Semitism in the Bryan 1896 campaign generally and among the Populists in particular. There were a number of references in these papers to anti-Semitic speeches by Populist and Democratic leaders. Mrs. Mary Lease, a prominent spokesman of Kansas Populism, toured the country speaking for Bryan in a manifestly anti-Semitic vein. After the election, Jewish Democratic politicians complained that Bryan had lost many Jewish votes because of the gibes of Populist orators.

The peculiar appeal of anti-Semitic beliefs which emphasized the negative role of Jewish wealth and banking among left-wing agrarians continued through the 1920s. Thus Tom Watson, the most prominent leader of Southern Populism, who had opposed the coalition with the Democrats in 1896, and who tried to revive the party by running for president in 1904 and 1908, had become a flaming bigot by the second decade of the century. *Watson's Magazine* strongly attacked Negroes, Catholics, Jews, and Wall Street, and supported revolutionary left-wing movements abroad. Watson practically organized the lynching of Leo Frank, a wealthy Atlanta Jew, who had been accused of murdering "a working-class Gentile" girl; and he supported the czarist government's charges that Mendel Beiliss had engaged in a ritual murder of a small Christian boy. The revived Ku Klux Klan was formed in 1915 by members of the

5. Edward Flower, "Anti-Semitism in the Free Silver and Populist Movements and the Election of 1896" (Master's thesis, Columbia University History Department, 1952), p. 27. The original quotation is from the *New York Sun* (23 July 1896), p. 2.

Knights of Mary Phagen, an organization formed under Tom Watson's sponsorship to make sure that Leo Frank died for Mary Phagen's murder.

Yet Watson opposed America's participation in World War I as subservience to "our Blood-gorged Capitalists." He strongly defended Eugene V. Debs, the socialist leader, for his opposition to the war. Elected to the Senate in 1920, he attacked the oil companies and the U.S. Steel Corporation, praised the Soviet Union, and demanded that the United States recognize it. Professor C. Vann Woodward's description of reactions to his death in 1922 illustrates the confusion that attends any effort to line up a consistent appeal of a rational democratic left:

> Eugene Debs, recently released from the penitentiary, wrote in a letter to Mrs. Watson: "He was a great man, a heroic soul who fought the power of evil his whole life long in the interest of the common people, and they loved and honored him. . . ."
>
> Most conspicuous among the floral tributes [at his funeral] was a cross of roses eight feet high, sent by the Ku Klux Klan.[6]

During the 1920s the most prominent advocate of anti-Semitic sentiments in America was Henry Ford. His weekly newspaper, the *Dearborn Independent,* distributed by the hundreds of thousands, denounced the Jews for everything evil under the sun, from communism to short skirts, from bootlegging liquor to fomenting strikes, from control of Wall Street to control of the labor movement, from corruption in baseball to deliberate murder. But Ford and his paper also attacked non-Jewish international bankers, Wall Street, and the monopolies. And when dissatisfaction with conservative control of both major parties resulted in a movement in the early twenties to create a third Progressive party, Henry Ford

6. C. Vann Woodward, *Tom Watson: Agrarian Rebel* (Gloucester, Mass.: Peter Smith, 1963), p. 486.

was boomed for the nomination. A poll conducted by *Collier's Magazine,* in 1923, reported that over a third of those queried were for Ford. Senator Robert La Follette, who was himself to be the presidential nominee of the Progressive and Socialist parties in the 1924 election, declared in the summer of 1923 that "Ford had great strength among the Progressives." A student of the Progressive campaign, Gordon Davidson, reports that

> a group of Progressives, Farmer-Laborites, Independents, and Liberals from fifteen states met in Omaha on November 21 [1923] at the request of Roy M. Harrop, national temporary chairman of the Progressive party. They passed a resolution endorsing Ford for president on a ticket to be known as the People's Progressive party. . . .[7]

Ford, fortunately, was unwilling to run. The willingness of many of the leaders of what was then the largest left tendency in the United States to support Ford in spite of his vitriolic anti-Semitism illustrates again the extent to which segments of the left have been willing to accept anti-Semitism as a foolish but potentially progressive version of antielitism or anticapitalism.

It is hard to generalize about the predominant political location of the mass of American Jews before 1928, although it appears true that East European Jews contributed heavily to the membership and support of the small Socialist and Communist parties. The identification of Jews with progressive and underdog causes as well as their opposition to Prohibition probably led the vast majority of them to back Al Smith for president in 1928. And from the 1930s on, American Jews not only were linked disproportionately to the radical left, they also in the main increasingly identified with Franklin Roosevelt and his New Deal.

The events of the years 1930–1945 clearly served to intensify

7. Gordon W. Davidson, "Henry Ford: The Formation and Course of a Public Figure" (Ph.D. thesis, Columbia University History Department, 1966), p. 286.

the ties in many countries between Jews and the parties of the left, both moderate like the Democrats or Social Democrats, and extreme like the Communists. For portions of this period (especially 1936–1939 and 1941–1945), the Communists and the Soviet Union had a special appeal as seeningly the boldest and most prominent organizers of the anti-Nazi struggle.

This success of the Communists among American Jews occurred in spite of the fact that the most flagrant examples of leftist willingness to collaborate with anti-Semites who also espoused a version of socialism were the relations between Communists and Nazis in 1931–1932 and again in 1939–1941. During the first period, the German Communist party joined on occasion with the German National Socialist Workers party (NSDAP) in sponsoring strikes and a referendum which brought down the Social Democratic government in Prussia. This latter event ended the police action against the street terrorism of both extremist parties. During the second period, Molotov actually sent official fraternal greetings from the Soviet Communist party to the German Nazis saluting their mutual interests. The French Communist party applied to the Nazi occupation authorities for permission to publish the party organ *L'Humanite* (and to function in the occupied zone) on the grounds that the party's main concern was the defeat of the Allied imperialist forces. Although many quit the party in Western countries, these events (including cooperation of Stalin's Russia with Hitler's Germany in invading Poland in 1939) did not destroy the hard core of the party, nor did it prevent many Jews from remaining members or fellow travelers in the United States, Britain, Canada, and elsewhere.

Cooperation with the worst anti-Semites in history did not prove sufficient to alienate revolutionary leftists—Jews and Gentiles—from the communist movement.

The heavy dependence of many liberal and leftist parties on Jews as leaders and financial backers and as a mass base has concomitantly pressed such groups to react to Zionism more strongly than might have been anticipated given its limited size and scope. The moderate liberal left in America and Europe—the Democrats, Liberals, and Social Democrats—have tended to be strong supporters of Zionism, accepting it as an appropriate response to the plight of Jews in other countries who suffered from persecution. Jewish moderates who adhered to such parties have tended on the whole to be less alienated from a Jewish identification than those supporting the extreme left, and, therefore, more likely to be willing to identify openly with Jewish causes.

The Marxist left also reacted to Zionism more stongly than its status as a movement would appear to have warranted. Its reaction tended to be one of total opposition. From its general ideological position, the Marxist left considered Zionism a bourgeois philosophy, an outmoded expression of nationalism which had to be opposed by socialist internationalists. The East European left had opposed Zionism in part because in the Czarist Empire (in Poland, the Ukraine, Russia, and Rumania, where there were very large, impoverished Jewish populations who were denied legal, political, and social rights), Jews were an important source of mass support for the various left-wing oppositionist movements. For the East European left, therefore, Zionism became a major rival political tendency competing for the support of the Jewish masses. The Jewish radicals, Socialists, Anarchists, and Bolsheviks, saw Zionism, quite naturally, as a political opponent and strongly opposed it. Much of the opposition of the Soviet Communist party to Zionism, after 1917, flowed from the earlier antagonism of the Jewish-Socialist *Bund* and other Jewish radical leftists to Zionism. Another source of the Jewish radicals' bitterness to Zionism derived from the fact that participation in the socialist and communist world meant, for many Jews, a way of escaping their Judaism, a way of *assimilating* into a universalistic non-Jewish world.

The extent to which Jewish radicals—left-wing socialists and communists—turn out to be much more anti-Zionist than the non-Jewish radicals has been striking, and it is worthy of special comment. The non-Jewish radicals could look upon Zionism as simply another movement, another opposition tendency, but only one among the many movements to which they were opposed. The Jewish radicals, both European and American, had to resist Zionism much more strongly since many of them not only felt tied to it in some ways but also experienced the need to disassociate themselves from anything which smacked of their hated inferiority status as Jews. They argued in classic left terms that the solution to anti-Semitism lay in Jewish assimilation in a socialist society, where presumably all forms of nationalistic particularism would disappear.

THE STATE OF ISRAEL

Whatever divisions existed about alternatives to European anti-Semitism faded during World War II, under the impact of the holocaust. Six million Jews were murdered. By 1948 and the creation of the State of Israel, there was, for a very short, very unique period, almost complete unanimity about the value of creating a Jewish state. The justifications which produced this unanimity varied greatly, but clearly the holocaust settled the argument advanced by many socialists, that Jews should not emigrate to Palestine, that they should "remain and fight to create socialism at home." No one could really argue any longer that Jews should stay on in lands in which almost all of their brethren had been decimated.

The Soviet Union found it in its interest to support the creation of the State of Israel, which meant that the international communist movement also gave enthusiastic support to the emergence of the state. This period, of course, lasted for only a moment as far as world history is concerned; shortly thereafter, Stalin's paranoia, focusing on the Jews as "foreign agents," gave birth to a new wave of Soviet anti-Semitism: in the Doctor's Plot in the U.S.S.R., in the various treason trials in Rumania and Czechoslovakia, and in the trials of economic speculators, as well as in the repression of various Jewish rights in the Soviet Union.

It has been suggested that the creation of Israel itself contributed to the revival of anti-Semitism in the Soviet Union— because of the clear evidence that the Jews of the Soviet Union (and other Eastern European countries) were as positively and enthusiastically impressed and gratified by the creation of the State of Israel as Jews in the West or anywhere else. Russian Jews exhibited their strong support for Israel publicly in many ways. When Golda Meir went to Moscow as the first Israeli ambassador, she was greeted by tens of thousands of Moscow Jews. There were scores of comparable incidents which showed the passion of Russian Jews for Israel. Such behavior was viewed as evidence of disloyalty by Stalin, for it suggested that the Jews did not have a total commitment to the Soviet Union. Some Russian experts have pointed to Stalin's long-time personal history of anti-Semitic sentiments and behavior. But whatever the source of Stalin's revival of anti-Semitism, the fact is that the Soviet Union quickly turned from a supporter to an enemy of Israel, a role which it has maintained under all of Stalin's successors. Governmental support for anti-Semitism within the Soviet Union and the rest of Eastern Europe has had its ups and downs, its ebbs and flows, but it has never been totally repudiated and has continued to exist.[8]

The persistent Russian opposition to Israel, of course, has affected a part of the left, that still considerable section which sympathizes with the Soviet Union. China and its followers in the communist world have been even more vitriolically anti-

8. See William Korey, "The Legal Position of the Jewish Community of the Soviet Union," in Erich Goldhagen, ed., *Ethnic Minorities in the Soviet Union* (New York: Praeger, 1968), pp. 316–350; Moshe Decter, "Soviet Jewry: A Current Survey," *Congress* (5 December 1966), pp. 6–40; Zygmunt Bauman, "The End of Polish Jewry — A Sociological Review," *Bulletin on Soviet and East European Jewish Affairs* (January 1969), pp. 3–8.

Israeli, although Israel was one of the first countries to recognize Communist China. Technically Israel still recognizes it, although Communist China has never recognized Israel. (In the United States, those organizations which by their own description are pro-Maoist communists include both wings of SDS, the right-wing Revolutionary Youth Movement and the left-wing Worker-Student Alliance, the Progressive Labor party, and the Black Panther party. Most recently, however, the latter has shifted somewhat, forming an alliance with the original pro-Russian Communist party.) The emergence of the antiimperialist Third World bloc, a nonaligned group of countries mainly in Asia and Africa, also has affected the relations of the left to Israel, since much of the Arab world joined with various other new nations to form this nonaligned group.

The Arabs successfully demanded that Israel be excluded from this camp, even though Israel made some initial gestures to establish its role as an Asian state that was part of the Afro-Asian world. The Arabs, however, had a lot more votes in the United Nations and more political power, and that part of the Afro-Asian world which, though not directly a part of the communist world, had strong ideological links to it (e.g., Indonesia, Guinee, Mali, and Tanzania) pressed for the rejection of Israel. Israel has never been able to become part of the Afro-Asian world, although it has succeeded in establishing strong links with many countries in black Africa. The leaders of the Afro-Asian group of nonaligned countries have defined themselves as strongly in opposition to the Western imperialist countries, among whom they place Israel. The Arabs have continued, with greater or lesser success (depending on the part of the world they address), to argue that their conflict with Israel is essentially a continuation of the anticolonial struggle with imperialist powers, that Israel is essentially a satellite of the United States—of the European-American world—thrust into the Afro-Asian border areas, and, therefore, that it has to be eliminated.

This image of Israel inevitably has had a great deal of in-

fluence. Its acceptance is, of course, not just a propaganda success, but also reflects a degree of validity. Clearly, in the context
of having been rejected by the Soviet Union and China, of not
being welcomed by the Afro-Asian alliance countries, and of
being strongly dependent on financial support from American
Jewry and political support from Washington, Israel has had no
alternative but to maintain strong links with the United States
and Western Europe. Realistically, whatever the sources of its
original international position, Israel had to become part of the
American alliance—the grouping of states which emerged
around the United States.

In spite of the opposition of China, the Soviet Union, and
many Afro-Asian states to Israel, much of the left retained a
strong sense of identification with Israel until the Six-Day War.
The existence of a large viable cooperative movement and economy in the form of the Histadrut and the kibbutzim; the fact
that all Israeli governments have been dominated by socialist
parties; the strong enthusiasms for Israel and its institutions
voiced by the highly influential group of left-oriented Jewish
intellectuals; and the strong sense of guilt felt by many for their
ineffective response to the Nazi holocaust—all these factors
served to maintain Israel's credit within the liberal-left movement (including almost all socialist parties in developed countries and in many communist ones as well).

The Six-Day War, however, had a decisive effect in
changing the reaction of the left to Israel because (and I think
this is also true with respect to much of the Christian world)
Israel by its quick victory ceased being an underdog nation.
Leftist values, as well as religious sentiments (particularly Christian ones), tend to make common cause with underdogs against
the more powerful. Many seem to believe that anybody who
looks underprivileged and poor must be right and should receive moral support. Jews and Israel were long regarded as the
underdog, as victims—an image reinforced by their treatment
by the Germans in the last war, by the communist world's mas-

sive opposition to Israel and by Israel's being surrounded by a hundred million Arabs. But from this perspective, the Israeli victory in June of 1967 was much too good, much too quick to maintain sympathies and solidarities. The Arabs became the underdog for many on the left as well as throughout Christendom. Israel is now held to be a strong and rich nation, whereas the Arabs are weak, underdeveloped, poor. Anybody defined as an underdog is good, anybody thought to be powerful is bad. This sentiment has affected and continues to affect the images of Israel and the Arab world. The only way Israel can change it is to lose.

THE NEW LEFT

The most important political event affecting Israel in Western politics in recent years has been the rise of the New Left. Without going into the reasons for its emergence, there is no question that the New Left movement has been significant. Though it arose mainly as a campus phenomenon, it has also affected the older world of left intellectuals. New Left ideology originally was new or different from that of the old left in that it opposed all powers by announcing its hostility to *all Establishments,* including some in the communist world—in Russia in particular and to some extent (it varies from country to country) in China as well. Unlike earlier Western student groups, the movement was unaffiliated with the major adult left-wing parties. Basically it lacked a clear-cut, positive program about what it wanted— how it was to achieve power and how it was to change society fundamentally. Increasingly, however, its need to find a defensible ideological position led it into an association with dissident forms of communism, mainly Maoist.

At the 1969 convention of SDS, the most important New Left group in the United States, all major factional tendencies proclaimed themselves as Marxist-Leninist pro-Maoist communists. They even used quotes from Stalin (who is still viewed positively by the Maoists) against each other in debate. The weekly New Left newspaper, the *Guardian,* concluded in its editorial on the convention: "The new left as it has been known during this decade disappeared during the Chicago SDS convention. It is being replaced by Marxism-Leninism"[9].

The New Left, particularly since June 1967, has identified Israel with the American Establishment. This view has been affected by the relationship of Jews and Negroes in the United States, the growth of black nationalism, and the links of certain radical Negro groups with the Arab world. This Negro view of the Arab-Israeli conflict is related to the growing tension between a section of the black militant leadership and some Jews. The conflict is largely a result of American events, and there is not very much Israel can do about it. Even though various black leaders in this country (viz., Stokely Carmichael and others) have become overtly pro-Arab, I do not think this derives from a serious view of the Arabs as oppressed peoples, or even a conception of black (Arabs) versus white (Jews), which sometimes seems to be implied in black nationalist literature.

The split between the Jews and the Negroes, which has affected attitudes towards Israel, stems much more from the American situation than the Middle East conflict. Ironically enough, part of the tension stems from the fact that Jews have been so involved in civil rights. The integrationist movement was largely an alliance between Negroes and Jews, who, to a considerable extent, actually dominated it. Many of the inter-racial civil rights organizations have been led and financed by whites, and the majority of their white members have been Jews. Insofar as a Negro effort emerged to break loose from involvement with whites, from domination of the civil rights struggle by white liberals, this meant concretely a break with Jews, for they were the whites who were active in these movements. The black nationalist leadership had to push whites (Jews) "out of

9. The *Guardian* (15 July 1969), p. 12.

the way" and to stop white (Jewish) "interference" in order to get whites (Jews) "off their backs."

Perhaps more important than the struggle within the civil rights movement has been the conflict inherent in the historical fact that most Negro ghettoes in the North were formerly Jewish ghettoes. Negroes moved into Jewish areas such as Harlem, Bedford-Stuyvesant, Roxbury, and Watts, as well as Jewish districts in Washington, Chicago, Philadelphia, and many other cities. The reasons for this pattern of ethnic succession attest to positive aspects in Jewish racial attitudes—they were less resistant to Negroes moving into their neighborhoods, they reacted much less violently, than other white communities. This process meant, however, that though Jews eventually moved out as residents, some of them remained as landlords and storeowners. Hence many Negroes came to see Jews not as neighbors, but in the role of economic oppressors.

Reinforcing these consequences of ecological succession have been the effects of the fact that during the 1930s large numbers of able Jews found that the only place they could secure employment was in government service, as teachers, social workers, or other professionals. Thirty years later, many of these same Jews (now in their fifties and sixties) are at the summits of the civil service hierarchy as, for instance, school principals, and division heads. And as Negroes follow the Jews into the civil service, they find that the directors of units operating in Negro areas are often Jews. The request that blacks be given top jobs in such organizations often has become a demand that Jews be removed from positions which they obtained through merit and seniority.

These economic relationships, which have helped produce the tension between Negroes and Jews, have had their obvious effect on the white New Left (which is itself disproportionately Jewish). It is clearly expressed by the black nationalists: "We don't want whites, but we particularly don't want Jews, and we are expressing antagonism to Jews in the form of opposition to

Israel." They attack Israel and Zionism as an expedient way of voicing their anti-Semitism. In essence, therefore, the attack on Israel on the part of some sections of the Negro community reflects tensions in the local American scene, not in the Middle East.[10]

I should stress, however, that the large majority of the Negro community, even the majority of those active in various black militant organizations, are *not* anti-Semitic or anti-Israel. The data available from various public opinion polls show that the level of anti-Semitic feeling in the Negro community is no greater than it is in the white community, that it remains relatively low in both. The existence of black anti-Semitism is being highlighted because of the expression of anti-Semitic sentiments by the most militant and radical leaders and organizations; and it is they who get the most publicity from the white-controlled mass media. These sentiments should not be ignored, however, since they are growing among younger black spokesmen, who are unaware of the close ties between Jews and Negroes in the past.

These sentiments also have an impact far exceeding their importance within Negro public opinion among those sections of the white population whose guilt feelings about being white or whose desire to use the Negro to build a mass radical movement lead them to follow the political path of the most militant black leaders. As one SDS leader has described the process:

10. It is particularly ironic that much of black Africa has a strong antipathy to the Arab world. The Arabs are the historic slavers of Africa; a small African slave trade which arranges the shipment of blacks to portions of Arabia to serve white masters *still* exists. In addition, there are two hot wars between Arabs and African blacks in the Sudan and the Chad. In the Sudan, the dominant Arabs in the north are fighting black Christian and animist rebels who seek equal political rights. In the Chad, the formerly dominant and more advantaged Arabs of the north are the rebels seeking to overthrow the government of the animist and Christian Africans, who are the majority of the country. I have seen no evidence that any American black organization has devoted the slightest attention to the civil wars in the Sudan and the Chad.

"S.D.S. has consistently supported the political viewpoints and actions of the most militant segments of the black movement and has consciously shaped its own analysis and program in response to those elements as they have evolved during the sixties from Malcolm X to SNCC to the Black Panther party."[11] Thus, the anti-Semitism, "the socialism of fools," occasionally voiced by groups such as the Black Panthers, SNCC (now the Student National Coordinating Committee), and other black militant organizations has had a considerable impact on their white fellow travelers inside SDS and other sections of the left.[12] The earlier Marxist attacks on anti-Jewish appeals have been forgotten, and the contemporary New Left has been condemned to repeat the foolishness.

The task of analysing the impact of the New Left on Israel's position is further complicated by the fact that Jews play a very great role in the student-based New Left, a role considerably disproportionate to the number of Jewish students on campus. This is not only true of students; it is also characteristic of the older left community as well. Many of these Jewish leftists exhibit familiar forms of Jewish self-hatred, of so-called Jewish anti-Semitism, of the sort which were widespread within the left before the Nazi holocaust and the creation of the State of Israel. Self-hatred is becoming a major problem for the American Jewish community. There is a real need for some serious

11. Michael Kazin, "Some Notes on S.D.S.," *The American Scholar* (Autumn 1969), p. 650.
12. For example, *Black Panther,* the weekly organ of the Black Panther party, published an article by Field Marshall Don Cox, entitled "Zionism (Kosher Nationalism) + Imperialism = Fascism" in its issue of 30 August 1969, in which Zionism is described several times as "Kosher nationalism" and as a variety of "fascism." The article refers to the "fascist Zionist pigs." The *SNCC Newsletter* of June–July 1967 contained a two-page center spread on "The Palestine Problem," which among other statements asked its readers whether they knew "*that* the famous European Jews, the Rothschilds, who have long controlled the wealth of many European nations, were involved in the original conspiracy with the British to create the 'State of Israel' and are still among Israel's chief supporters? *That the Rothschilds also control much of Africa's mineral wealth?*" (emphasis in original).

analysis of the sources of Jewish anti-Semitism. It is not an in-
considerable phenomenon, and one of the forms it takes among
Jewish youth is the denunciation of their parents as hypocrites
(a criticism which attests to the fact that their values are not
terribly different from those of their families; otherwise why
accuse them of hypocrisy?).

Various studies of American student militants indicate that
the left activists tend to come from liberal-left families, disproportionately Jewish. Basically there is continuity in family
ideology, rather than a break. To see the New Leftist students,
in Kenneth Kenniston's phrase, as "Red Diaper Babies" is not
an exaggerated image. Many of them come from families which,
around the breakfast table, day after day, in Scarsdale, Newton,
Great Neck, and Beverly Hills, have discussed what an awful,
corrupt, immoral, undemocratic, racist society the United
States is. Many Jewish parents live in the lily-white suburbs,
go to Miami Beach in the winter, belong to expensive country
clubs, arrange bar mitzvahs costing thousands of dollars—all
the while espousing a left-liberal ideology. This is their hypocrisy, and it is indeed the contradiction which their children
are rebelling against. Many Jewish parents, unlike Gentile
parents of equivalent high economic class background, live a
schizophrenic existence. They sustain a high degree of tension
between their ideology and their life style.

Some years ago, Nathan Glazer, Herbert Hyman, and I did
a study of Jewish behavior and attitudes, through secondary
analyses of various public opinion studies that had been gath-
ered in New York and other places. We isolated large samples
of Jews and discovered, among other things, that at the same
middle-class income level, 40 to 60 percent of the Jews had part-
time servants, as against 0 to 5 percent of the Protestants. People
outside the South who had a full-time servant were preponderantly Jewish.[13] Relatively few Christians had one. We found

---

13. Since these servants are almost invariably Negro, this fact re-
inforces the image in the black community of the Jew as an economic
exploiter.

a pattern, a style of social life, of relative asceticism among middle- and middle upper-class Protestants which did not exist among Jews on an equivalent income level. But, though affluent Jews lived well, spent considerable sums on housing, vacations, servants, and costly cars, they also as a group continued to maintain a relatively liberal-left view of the world. This left-wing outlook and right-wing style has created grievous tension between parents and children.

Young Jews take seriously the leftist ideologies they imbibed at home, particularly when they move to the liberal campus environment. They see American Jewish life as essentially immoral and hypocritical, and not a few of them extend this view to Israel's relations with Arabs. Israel, in effect, seems to be behaving like their parents. Israel itself does not really interest them. They are essentially reacting to American Jewish conditions and to the American way of life. But the very significance and the quantitative importance of the Jews within the American left—and even within parts of the European left—mean that Jews are beginning to take the lead in an attack on Israel and on Jewish customs. This fact serves to alleviate any senses of guilt or tension about anti-Semitism which non-Jewish leftists might have.

THE BREAKING POINT

What is being done about this? One thing which presumably might have some positive effect on the left's attitude toward Israel is a revival of the image of Israel as a center of social experimentation. The kibbutz still remains the only viable example of a decentralized, anarchist-socialist society. Those who want to see participatory democracy in action—the workers actually running their institutions—can point to nothing as successful as the kibbutz. Here it must be acknowledged that Israel and its public relations may be more at fault than the New Left youth for their ignorance on these matters. In the past decade, Israel has done little to establish itself as an example of social reform, of institutional experimentation. In its efforts to secure investments and contributions from wealthy Americans, it has placed more emphasis on creating an image of Israel as a successful, free-enterprise "boot-strap" operation, a sort of small-scale Japan. But in selling itself thus to the business community, it may well have contributed to weakening a major portion of its political base.

Yet in this connection it may be useful to examine the contents of a recent book, *Obsolete Communism: The Left-Wing Alternative,* by Daniel and Gabriel Cohn-Bendit. "Danny the Red" was one of the major leaders of the French student revolt of May 1968, and the Cohn-Bendit brothers emerge in this book as anarchists. As a positive example of anarchism in action, they point to the Makhno movement in Russia of 1918 and 1921, which dominated a large area of the Ukraine. Yet, though they discuss politics in many countries they do not say a word about Israel or the kibbutzim. Evidently they are not "revelant" to the proposals for new anarchist forms of society. This, surely, is not a result of ignorance, since some years ago Danny Cohn-Bendit spent several months in Israel, mainly on a kibbutz, and even considered settling there. He tries to make a case for anarchist institutions, but does not even mention the one country where concrete examples of such institutions exist. He also fails to mention the fact that there were Al Fatah Arab terrorist booths in the Sorbonne during the 1968 student sit-ins, and that the New Left anarchist as well as the Marxist-Leninist groups supported them. Danny Cohn-Bendit, who admires the anarchist Makhno but does not know the Israeli kibbutzim, is not an atypical Jewish boy. We will be seeing many more like him.

Older left-wing critics of Israel such as I. F. Stone and Professor Noam Chomsky also cannot be accused of ignorance concerning the Israeli socialist movement or its radical institutions. Both men, who now write harshly about Israel, have visited the country on a number of occasions and are personally well acquainted with the Israeli left, the Histadrut, and the kibbutzim. Like Daniel Cohn-Bendit, Chomsky considered settling in Israel and also appears to have strong anticommunist anarchist sympathies. But Stone, Chomsky, and Cohn-Bendit are today committed supporters of the international revolutionary left. And that left currently defines the Al Fatah terrorists as "left-wing guerrillas" and Israel as "a collaborator with imperialism," if not worse. One doubts whether even the most sophisticated presentation of Israel's case could ever regain their support.

The moderate left, of course, can still find a basis for strongly supporting Israel, since it is concerned with the preservation and extension of political democracy. The case for Israel in these terms has been strongly put by a new group, the Youth Committee for Peace and Democracy in the Middle East, organized by members of the Young People's Socialist League, but including a wide range of youth leaders, such as James Blake, the vice-president for Youth Affairs of the NAACP, Spencer Oliver, president of the Young Democrats, Joe Burke, the Civic Action director of the Catholic Youth Organization, and others. Their statement points out:

> Whatever its shortcomings, Israel is a democratic country. The governments of her Arab opponents, by contrast, are all to one degree or another staunchly authoritarian. Iraq, Syria, and Egypt are one-party states, in which all political rights have been suppressed. The same is true of the Kingdom of Jordan and the anachronistic sultanate of Saudi Arabia. The press in these countries is rigorously controlled. So are the courts. . . .[14]

In fairness, I should note that the various wings of the far left, while all anti-Israel, are not united in their estimate of Al Fatah or the positive worth of Arab terrorism. The Russians and their followers in the communist movement exhibit some opposition to terroristic and guerrilla tactics by Arab groups.

14. See "Student Group Formed on Middle East," and "Youth on Middle East," *New America* (29 September 1969), p. 12.

In the March 1969 issue of *Dokumentation der Zeit*, a magazine published by the East German Institute for Contemporary History, Al Fatah was described as a group whose student founders were inspired by "the reactionary terrorists of the Moslem Brethren," and who now secure most of their funds and supplies from "the Arab oil states of Kuwait and Saudi Arabia." The article argues:

> The slogans and general tendency of Al Fatah represent the most extreme elements of the resistance movement. By strictly prohibiting any political and ideological activity of its members, Al Fatah is preventing the necessary process of ideological clarification among the resistance organizations and trying to pin the movement down to a rigid extremist line, which in the last resort, amounts to nothing but a reinforcement of imperialism through a policy of left adventures.

The considerable support which the intellectual left once gave to Israel is gone, and it is not likely to be revived, certainly not on the same basis.[15] Israel must expect to be criticized by the extreme left for the foreseeable future. Since left intellectuals have been and continue to be important in forming public opinion, this is obviously a major loss to Israel's public position. It is also important to recognize that short of another war, the almost unanimous support that Israel has received from the Jewish community will not continue. The division (partly a matter of age and partly ideological) between younger and older Jews, and between left groups and Jewish-identified groups, will continue to affect attitudes to Israel. The Jewish community in America, particularly, is likely to become much more polarized politically than it has been for a long time. We

---

15. Ironically, the reverse process appears to have occurred in the communist countries of Eastern Europe. There, Israel has become a symbol among protesting students and intellectuals of a free small power which has stood up to powerful bullies (backed by the Soviet Union). To support Israel in Poland, Russia, etc., is a way of voicing opposition to the anti-Semitic policies of their communist governments.

are going to see an upsurge of large numbers of overtly conservative Jews. A kind of backlash is occurring among Jews who remain more identified with Israel and Zionism—or with the synagogue—as a reaction to the attacks on Jews and Israel coming from the left and the black nationalists.

But if Israel has lost support on the left, it has gained among groups not previously known for their sympathy for Jewish causes. Those aspects of Israel's foreign and military policies which alienate left-wing sympathy attract rightist support. Many non-Jewish conservatives see in Israel's successful military resistance to the Arab world and its defiance of United Nations resolutions an example of the way in which a nation which has self-pride—and which is not "corrupted by the virus of internationalism and pacifism"—can defend its national self-interests. Some see in the Israeli defeat of the Arabs the one example of an American ally which has decisively defeated communist allies in battle. Thus, Israel and its supporters find themselves with friends on the right and enemies on the left.

Although many archconservatives (e.g., Barry Goldwater and some of the contributors to William Buckley's magazine, the *National Review*) are now strongly pro-Israel, the extremist right, like the extremist left, remains very hostile, an attitude linked to their continued anti-Semitism. Thus, the *Thunderbolt*, the organ of the racist National States Rights party, stated in April 1969 that it supports "a strong Arab stand against the brutal aggression of Israel." Gerald L. K. Smith's *Cross and the Flag* repeatedly condemns Israel for crimes against the Arabs. The Italian neo-Fascists strongly back Al Fatah and (like the New Left) reprint much of its propaganda. The fascist magazine *La Nation Europeenne* also supports Al Fatah and advertises its publications. The German National Democrats, in their paper *Deutsche National Zeitung,* take a similar pro-Arab terrorist line. I do not think it would be unfair to say that the revolutionary fascist right and the revolutionary communist left have similar positions with respect to Middle East conflict and the role of Al Fatah. But it should be stressed that the opposition of the left extremists is by far more powerful than that of the fascists, who have little influence.

The pattern of increased support for Israel among the democratic conservative or rightist groups has been paralleled on the American homefront with respect to domestic issues. Those Jews who are concerned with the adverse consequences of Negro militancy on areas of Jewish concern (e.g., the preservation of the merit system in civil service employment, standards of admission to universities, and the rights of Jewish business men in the ghetto) find more support from conservatives than from liberals. Conservatives eager to gain Jewish support have made overtures to the Jewish groups. Recent local elections indicate that the vaunted "near unanimous" commitment of Jews to liberal and Negro causes is breaking down.[16]

The separation of the Jewish population into the same constituent parts that divide the American electorate as a whole may be testimony to the end of the almost two-century period

16. In the 1966 referendum on the retention of a civilian police review board in New York City, Jews divided in this way: 40 percent for keeping the board, 55 percent for abolishing it. In the 1965 mayoralty election, the Tammany candidate Beame secured 56 percent of the Jewish vote as compared to 41 percent for the Republican-Liberal Lindsay. In 1969, Sam Yorty, running against a moderate Negro candidate, Tom Bradley, for mayor of Los Angeles, did much better than anticipated in Jewish districts in the final election, securing 35 to 40 percent of the vote. And in the New York City Democratic mayoralty primary in June 1969, the Jewish Democratic vote split into three parts. Slightly less than a third went to the more conservative "law and order" candidate, Mario Proccacino; another third backed the centrist candidate and former mayor, Robert Wagner; and somewhat more than a third divided among the three more liberal candidates, Badillo, Sheuer, and Norman Mailer.

In the November election, according to an NBC computer precinct analysis, John Lindsay, the victorious Liberal party nominee, who defeated the more conservative Democratic and Republican candidates, secured 42 percent of the Jewish vote, exactly the percentage he received among the electorate as a whole. The more affluent, younger, and irreligious Jews tended to vote for Lindsay, whereas the less privileged, older, and religious ones opted for his more conservative rivals.

in which the politics of Jewry has been a subtheme to the politics of revolution. The identification of Jewish causes with those of the left reached an all-time high point between 1930 and 1950, periods dominated internationally by the anti-Nazi struggle and the fight to create the State of Israel. Within the United States, this link was reinforced by the strong involvement of Jews with the civil rights cause which lasted through most of the 1960s.

The rise of the New Left, the shift in the international position of Israel, and the tensions between sections of the Jewish and Negro communities have all contributed to breaking the relations between the left and Jewry. Jews will, of course, continue to contribute in heavily disproportionate numbers to the activist left, particularly to that section which derives its main strength from the university and intellectual worlds. But they will also increasingly sustain moderate liberal and conservative politics. Israel will probably find its greatest supporters among American Jews and non-Jews in the ranks of such center groupings, and this may well make life difficult for those who seek to remain both socialist and Zionist.

7   The new left and Israel

LEONARD J. FEIN

The clamor for national survival—for distinctive identity—has reached massive heights around the world, and at the same time opposition to Jewish national survival has reached unprecedented proportions. Leonard J. Fein emphasizes that Jewish nationalism, as represented in the Zionist movement and by the State of Israel, is, first, an authentic reflection of the Jewish tradition and not, as some would argue, a deviation from that tradition; second, that in the most literal sense Jewish nationalism is revolutionary; and third, that the nature of Jewish nationalism offers useful precedent and helpful insight into how the typically reactionary consequences of particularistic nationalism may be avoided. Because it does offer such insights, he writes, the Jewish dream, as authentically reflected by the State of Israel, is a dream which both challenges our conventional modern wisdom and excites our creative imagination.

Fein identifies the problem of Jews in the New Left vis-a-vis Israel as constituting less of a problem with Israel than with their own Jewishness.

I am neither spokesman for, nor analyst of, the New Left; I know neither who is "new" and who is "old," nor, for that matter, who, any longer, is left and who is nonleft. Why some of those who identify themselves as part of the New Left should have chosen to be hostile to Israel is an issue I can only speculate about, and I find such speculation idle. The substance of the hostility is, on the other hand, a matter of record, and I think it evident that if we discount the growing volume of crude distortion and the appalling ignorance, we are left with a debate that is not new

LEONARD J. FEIN *is Associate Professor of Politics and Social Policy and Director, Hornstein Program in Jewish Communal Service, Brandeis University.*

at all but is, instead, a continuation of the debate between Jewish nationalism and Jewish universalism that has dogged the Zionist movement since its inception.

There are those, of course, who have wearied of these issues. They can hardly be blamed if their response to 1960 restatements of 1890 insights is a yawn. Neither, however, can the young, born, in Koestler's phrase, without an umbilical cord, be blamed for their excitement. If "it should be obvious why it will be the Moynihans we go after first rather than the southern sheriff,"[1] perhaps it is obvious why some young radicals take special pleasure in attacking Israel rather than, say, Saudi Arabia. All the more so since Arab rhetoric has shifted from genocidal-fascist to revolutionary-liberationist. But, surprise or no, and motive aside, we are, it seems to me, called upon once again to restate the case for Zionism, and, if those of us who had supposed that we were done with the debate in 1948 or in 1967 have now a rather *déjà vu* reaction, we might also treat the exercise as opportunity: in restatement, there is, at least, the chance for rediscovery and, perhaps, for new insight as well.

The problem which Jewish intellectuals—and, as I shall argue in a moment, Jewish nonintellectuals as well—have had with Israel is not, in the first instance, a problem with Israel at all but is, instead, quite clearly a problem with their Jewishness itself. Israel merely serves to intensify that problem and, for some, to bring it to a head. Hence I begin with some comments on the problem of Jewishness in general before moving to the special case of Israel.

I

We may take as our entering wedge here the concept of the non-Jewish Jew. To be ever so much clearer, why not simply the non-Jew? Because there were formidable obstacles in the path

1. Julius Lester, *Look Out, Whitey! Black Power's Gon' Get Your Mama!* (New York: Dial, 1968), p. 54.

of this alternative. First, though a Jew might choose to assimilate completely, non-Jewish society might not be especially gracious in its welcome.

Second, and more important than the barriers erected by non-Jewish society, have been the internal obstacles. Through most of European history, to cease to be a Jew meant, necessarily, to become a Christian. There was no third option, no gray area of secular life to which a Jew could easily repair. And to become a Christian meant not only to stop being a Jew but also to join the enemy. It was, therefore, a thoroughly dishonorable thing to do.[2]

Yet there were Jews who, all things considered, were prepared and even eager to give up their Judaism and to join the nonmarginal majority. Conversion was not, given the issue of honor, an option open to most, but there have been moments in Jewish history in which a third option became available, an option which permitted an end to Jewishness without requiring a beginning to Christianity. The most outstanding examples of such third options are the radical movements of the nineteenth and twentieth centuries and the scientific-academic community of the twentieth century.

These two arenas were, and are, manifestly secular in orientation. They held religion to be, at best, an unfortunate atavism, perhaps meriting indulgence but destined in the end to be discarded on the junk pile of history. And ethnic identification, while not necessarily a matter of great moment, was contrary to the universalist ethic which infused both radical ideology and scientific mores. Most important, even if both the radical and the scientific communities were actively hostile towards religion, neither required a formal renunciation of Jewishness

2. See, for example, Rudolph Maurice Loewenstein, *Christians and Jews: A Psychoanalytic Study* (New York: Dell, 1951); and, for a somewhat different interpretation, Philip Roth, *Portnoy's Complaint* (New York: Random House, 1969), pp. 220–228, and especially, p. 225.

in favor of Christianity. Hence movement into these communities could not be regarded as dishonorable per se.

Both radicalism and science offered the Jew a way of not being Jewish. More than this, they offered him a hope of solving the Jewish problem in general. For each promised the advent of a rational utopia in which the Jewish problem would become obsolete. If the workers of the world would unite under socialism's banner, there would be no one left to conduct anti-Jewish pogroms. And if science were to emerge victorious, it would undermine the medievalism which Jews blamed for anti-Semitism. Thus the individual Jew attracted by these revolutionary communities could easily believe that in being so attracted he was remaining faithful to the transcendent needs of his people, even if his family and friends might express distress.

The attraction was described by Isaac Deutscher with special force:

> The Jewish heretic who transcends Judaism belongs to a Jewish tradition. Spinoza, Heine, Marx, Rosa Luxemburg, Trotsky, and Freud . . . all went beyond the boundaries of Jewry. They all found Jewry too narrow, too archaic, and too constricting. . . . They were a priori exceptional in that as Jews they dwelt on the borderlines of various civilizations, religions, and national cultures. They were born and brought up on the borderlines of various epochs. Their minds matured where the most diverse cultural influences crossed and fertilized each other. They lived on the margins or in the nooks and crannies of their respective nations. Each of them was in his society and yet not in it, of it and yet not of it. It was this that enabled them to rise in thought above their societies, above their nations, above their times and generations, and to strike out mentally into wide new horizons and far into the future.[3]

It is true that Deutscher was committed to a universalist utopia: "I hope . . . the Jews will ultimately . . . find their way

3. Isaac Deutscher, ed., *The Non-Jewish Jew: And Other Essays* (New York: Oxford University Press, 1968), pp. 26-27.

back to the moral and political heritage that the genius of the Jews who have gone beyond Jewry has left us—the message of universal human emancipation."[4] But what kept him a Jew, a man who saw himself as a Jew? "This is a [bourgeois] society which at every moment of acute insecurity whips up racialism, nationalism, xenophobia, the hatred and fear of the alien. And who is more alien than the Jew?"[5] This is the sum of Deutscher's answer. He does not like the Jews. He is deeply upset by Israel. Yet he fears a resurgence of anti-Semitism. Does the fear itself provide the motive for remaining a Jew? Deutscher does not imagine that his continued identification as a Jew will reduce the possibility of anti-Semitism. On the contrary, he was clearly wise enough to recognize that insofar as his Jewishness had any bearing at all on the subject, it would increase such a possibility, since he was more alien than most. Yet that is what we are left with, which is, in the end, honor. And what, in Deutscher's view, is the ultimate answer? "As long as the nation-state imposes its supremacy and as long as we have not an international society in existence, as long as the wealth of every nation is in the hands of one national capitalist oligarchy, we shall have chauvinism, racism, and, as its culmination, anti-Semitism."[6] In short, Deutscher remained a Jew, which he did not like doing, because it would have been dishonorable not to do so. But anti-Semitism would remain a problem only so long as capitalism remained in power. Destroy capitalism and you destroy anti-Semitism, and then, of course, Deutscher could stop being a Jew, could go "beyond Jewry."

One may be inclined to argue that the commitment to secular messianism by Jewish radicals was no more than an informed response by peculiarly sensitive people to intolerable social conditions. Such an argument, however, fails to account for the

4. Ibid., p. 41.
5. Ibid., p. 57.
6. Ibid,, p. 58.

significant overrepresentation of Jews in the radical movements of the past century.[7] Further, it fails to give proper weight to the Lasswellian formulation that politics is the displacement of private motives onto public objects.[8] So, Riesman:

> [The] rebel Jews of the nineteenth century found their security, found the end of their seeming marginality, in their clear vision of a future in which no irrational margins of class, or ethnic group, or caste, would be left. . . . They held only to the future, with such tenacity that they could be violently anti-Semitic without self-hatred.[9]

The non-Jewish Jew, in his radical version, is an ideal type. His counterpart in the real world will not necessarily be a self-hater, nor even a denier of his Judaism. But he will be a person to whom Jewish history is fundamentally irrelevant, except as it is imposed from without. His metier is the universal, his utopia is secular, and his religion, as distinguished from his name tag, is enlightenment. His solution to society's Jewish problem is to create a world without superstition, personal or institutional, and his solution to his own Jewish problem is to work for the advent of such a world.

The case of the Jewish scientist-intellectual-academic is rather more delicate. Radicalism manifestly disputes religion, and its temper is explicitly eschatological. The university is more subtle in its demands and more diverse in its commitments. To be sure, in the wake of the events of the 1960s, it is not easy to recall the moral basis of the academic persuasion in earlier and more placid times. Yet it is not too much to say that the

7. See Nathan Glazer, *The Social Basis of American Communism* (New York: Harcourt Brace Jovanovich, 1961); and Kenneth Keniston, *The Young Radicals: Notes on Committed Youth* (New York: Harcourt Brace Jovanovich, 1968), pp. 306-307.
8. The reference is to Harold Lasswell, *Psychopathology and Politics* (New York: Viking, Compass Books, 1960), especially pp. 65-77.
9. David Riesman, *The Lonely Crowd* (New Haven: Yale University Press, 1950), p. 158.

critical rationality which informs academe frequently implies a social and political ambience, if not an ideology.[10] The scientific community is transnational and, in important degree, stands outside history as well as place; its members commonly see themselves as possessed of a higher, and hence more nearly utopian, morality. In large measure, the twentieth-century university is the institutionalization of the Enlightenment; however brutal the world of nations, and however remote the end of days, the university is civilized—civilized because rational, as all men must become.

Milton Gordon, in his very useful *Assimilation in American Life,* develops a conceptual framework that helps us to understand the importance of ethnicity and class in contemporary America.[11] But he finds it necessary to describe the academic community as a separate phenomenon not comprehensible within the general framework of group behavior.[12] And, as to the degree to which men of academe perceive their world as a rational universalist alternative to pre-Enlightenment understandings, we have Gordon's own observations:

> [The academic community] serves the rest of the nation as a symbol of the possibility of interethnic harmony and integration at the meaningful primary group level of communal living. . . . It provides a testing ground for the problems and processes inherent in the achievement of . . . [an integrated] society and stands as a symbol of its potential development in larger scope.[13]

The academy thus is utopia writ small.

It also offers an appealing option to those who seek to resolve their problem of marginality; the academic community

10. The concept of critical rationality is from Talcott Parsons, "Sociological Aspects of Fascist Movements," in Talcott Parsons, ed., *Essays in Sociological Theory,* rev. ed. (New York: Free Press, 1954), especially pp. 131-132.
11. Milton Gordon, *Assimilation in American Life* (New York: Oxford University Press, 1964).
12. Ibid., especially pp. 224-232, 256-267.
13. Ibid., pp. 255-256.

is "the classic sociological enemy of ethnic parochialism."[14] It is true that the academic man is himself marginal, but his marginality is quite different from that of the Jew. The academic man can, if he wishes, isolate himself to a large degree from those whose culture he studies, identifying himself instead with the culture of the observer; he can be cosmopolitan rather than local, sharing community with the other readers of the *New York Times,* rather than with his physical neighbors. In this sense, though inducted into two cultures, he can fairly easily reject one in favor of the other. Society even appears to endorse such a choice by expecting the professor to behave peculiarly. And, with respect to the specific problem of status inconsistency, the status ascribed to *Professor,* however ambiguous society is in its feelings, is surely higher than that ascribed to *Jew.* Like the radical, therefore, the academic labors for a secular utopia in which status will derive from achievement. Unlike the radical, he awaits utopia in comfort, of sorts.

II

There is a curious footnote to these musings. One may well be inclined to argue that the concept of the non-Jewish Jew is not very helpful, since it has such limited currency. There is, as against this, the possibility that this concept is enjoying a new wave of popularity among the young—the radicals begat the professors, and the professors, in turn, begat the radicals, all in their own image begat they them—but I am not at all certain, even so, that we are talking about a position taken by only a small, rather inbred circle of intellectuals. Instead, I suggest that Deutscher, who himself believed that his own involvement as a Jew would be, as he put it, "considered subversive, heretical, and thoroughly un-Jewish to all the congregations of the Synagogues of New York, Paris, and London," was presenting a

14. Ibid., p. 58.

position not far removed from that endorsed by large numbers of nonintellectual Jews, at least in this country. As evidence for such a perception, we have the fascinating answers given to Marshall Sklare's question in the Lakeville study, "What does a person have to do in order to be a good Jew?"

The answers are broken down into what it is essential for a Jew to do, what it is desirable that he do, what is basically irrelevant, and what it is essential he not do. For a summary of these answers, see the table on page 141.

In short: It is essential, in order to be a good Jew, that one engage in secular good deeds; the only specifically Jewish essential is readiness to acknowledge that one is a Jew, the issue, once again, being one of honor. It is desirable, though not essential, that a Jew maintain some identification with the community and have some knowledge of its history. Ritual is a matter of indifference, and acts of extreme parochialism, such as voting for candidates because they are Jewish or promoting the use of Yiddish, are specifically forbidden. They are not, you will note, matters of indifference; a person who does such parochial things is not a good Jew, he is a bad Jew, and he has done something Jews ought to avoid doing.

Deutscher might have thought that he would be condemned by the congregations of New York, but now we know better. The congregation of Lakeville, at least, would see in him a brother, a kindred spirit, whose understanding of Judaism and its obligations—in particular, the obligation to rise above Judaism—they share in large measure themselves. It is not, I believe, too much to suggest that the Jews of Lakeville, no less than the non-Jewish Jew I have been quoting, are Jews out of honor rather than conviction.

III

Yet the overwhelming ambiguity—one might even say contradiction—of the modern era may be stated as follows: pre-

The image of the good Jew: attitudes of respondents in the Lakeville study (in percentage)

Item	Essential	Desirable	Makes No Difference	Essential Not to Do	No Answer
Accept being a Jew and not try to hide it	85	13	2	—	—
Contribute to Jewish philanthropies	39	49	12	—	—
Support Israel	21	47	32	—	—
Support Zionism	7	23	59	9	2
Support all humanitarian causes	67	29	4	—	—
Belong to Jewish organizations	17	49	34	—	—
Belong to a synagogue or temple	31	44	25	—	—
Attend weekly services	4	46	49	1	—
Lead an ethical and moral life	93	6	1	—	—
Attend services on High Holidays	24	46	30	—	—
Observe the dietary laws	1	11	85	3	—
Be well versed in Jewish history and culture	17	73	10	—	—
Know the fundamentals of Judaism	48	48	4	—	—
Have mostly Jewish friends	1	10	81	8	—
Promote the use of Yiddish	1	6	69	24	—
Give preference to Jewish candidates for political office	1	6	39	54	—
Gain respect of Christian neighbors	59	32	9	—	—
Promote civic betterment and improvement in the community	67	29	4	—	—
Work for equality for Negroes	44	39	16	1	—
Help the underprivileged improve their lot	58	37	5	—	—
Be a liberal on political and economic issues	31	32	35	2	—
Marry within the Jewish faith	23	51	26	—	—

cisely at a time when the rhetoric of universalism has reached such an unprecedented peak, and precisely at a time when the myths associated with universalism have become part of the conventional wisdom, the tribal instinct has reasserted itself with extreme vigor. Far from an atavistic anachronism, nationalism now comes to be seen as the wave of the future, and the operational question, which so recently was widely taken to be how the last residues of nationalism might once and for all be extirpated and eschatological visions made real, has now turned to a seemingly less ambitious concern with the management of diversity.

It is not surprising that the enlightenment doctrine should still seem plausible. The diffusion of advanced technology, although a much slower process than had originally been predicted, continues to promise a standardization of consumption around the world. The emergence of a major nonnational community of significant size and still more significant power—to wit, the transnational community of intellectuals—suggests a universal priesthood entirely in keeping with universalist doctrine. Even the advent of national superpowers and regional alliances, however disconcerting in other connections, may be seen as a movement away from the tribe and towards the family of man.

What is suprising is the resistance one now encounters in almost every nation to the passing of place as a meaningful reference point and to the destruction of past as a useful handle on the future.

The question that quite naturally arises is what view enlightened men, as distinguished from men of the Enlightenment, may take of this contradiction. Shall we persist in the conventional view that the tribal instinct is an insidious urge, to be indulged from time to time on tactical ground but still to be opposed as a matter of strategy? Shall we continue to believe that education will, in the end, liberate us from the constricting bonds of nationalism? Shall we now, as we have in the past, set as our goal the emergence of universal brotherhood in fact as well as in theory? Shall we, in short, view the current assertiveness of groups within the family of man merely as an index of how far we have yet to go, of how much work still needs to be done?

Or shall we, instead, cast aside our central convictions regarding the desired shape of the future? Shall we take the mounting evidence that the rhetoric of universalism does not describe the reality of nationalism as further evidence that our theories, and not those who in their deeds reject them, are flawed?

My central thesis is that Jewish nationalism, as represented in the Zionist movement and by the State of Israel, is, first, an authentic reflection of the Jewish tradition and not, as some would argue, a deviation from that tradition; second, that in the most literal sense, Jewish nationalism is revolutionary, specifically in its early and explicit rejection of the assumptions of universalism; and third, that the nature of Jewish nationalism offers useful precedent and helpful insight into how the typically reactionary consequences of particularistic nationalism may be avoided, permitting the development of a theory which satisfies both the modern liberal disposition and the tribal instinct simultaneously.

If I speak of Zionism as an authentic reflection of the Jewish tradition, I do so not on episodic historical grounds. Obviously, the emergence of Zionism as a political movement at a specific time and in a specific place, the struggle of Zionists to establish a nation-state, and the success, eventually, of that struggle constitute a set of specific responses to the historical conditions of the moment. There was a confluence of capability and opportunity, and Israel came to life. But my argument is that the idea of Israel was always present, however embryonically, in the Jewish understanding and that, fundamentally, the State of Israel was logically and hence inevitably implied by that understanding.

I would not presume to suggest either an Old Testament

genesis for Jewish nationalism nor a New Testament refutation of nationalism, although I must confess that my superficial familiarity with the literature leads me to think both suggestions plausible. But it is clear that throughout Jewish history and Jewish literature, both secular and sacred, the urgency of the preservation of the Jews as a distinct group has been central — and it is undoubtedly central even in Lakeville today. The concept of election has supported that perception; the liturgy is replete with references endorsing it, and, most important, the stubborn refusal of most Jews to opt for what must surely have been seen as the easier course of assimilation reflects it. In short, whether the chief cause is seen essentially as theological presupposition, cultural pattern, or historical experience, the centrality of Jewish survival must be taken as the key to the Jewish understanding. I speak, you will note, of Jewish survival, and not merely of the survival of Jews.

How can that instinct for distinctive survival be explained? Conventional explanations do not suffice, for it is clear that the survival of the Jew as Jew was not, in general, regarded as a prerequisite to salvation and that such survival was not coterminous with the survival of any given way of life. Nor is it sufficient, in my judgment, to suggest that Jews were forced to opt for distinctive survival since their hosts around the world were nowhere prepared to view Jews as other than Jews. Indeed, I do not find in any of the literature a persuasive statement of the ideology which presumably leads to the instinct. It is almost as if Jews have become fixated on survival for its own sake, without ever having been very eloquent about why it is that such survival matters. That, in fact, is why I use the term *instinct*.

It is the persistence of Jews in their apartness that has troubled so many people for so many years. The Church has never understood it very well; Lenin was furious about it; and Arab nationalists have failed to accept it. Perhaps the fault lies with the Jews, who could hardly expect others to understand what they themselves did not understand but knew without understanding. In this generation, of course, the understanding is a bit easier, for this is the generation of Auschwitz, and that may be all that is required to understand the urgency of survival, an urgency expressed so clearly during the days before the Six-Day War. But, for better or worse, the memories of Auschwitz will fade and with them, once again, the explanation; the instinct, if history is any guide, will not.

To have insisted on apartness, of course, has meant also to reject the liberal dogma of universalism. The extraordinary tension within the Jewish communities of Europe between those who saw the Enlightenment, with its presumed tolerance and humanity, as the best hope for Jewish survival and those who insisted on clinging to more traditional and more parochial patterns is an argument which has not yet been put to rest for Jews or for others, although the idiom has changed substantially. It is an argument which has not been put to rest because it is not capable of resolution; there is so much impressive evidence on either side of the debate. It is true, of course, that the Enlightenment proved to be far less enlightened than its authors had intended and the tradition more viable than its detractors had predicted. But the central question has remained: is it possible to imagine a pacific world society still moved by ethnocentrism, or does ethnocentrism not inevitably lead to hostility, and ultimately to madness? Can we regard fraternities that are less than the whole as legitimate? Is it not obvious that members of any one fraternity will come to view all nonmembers as enemies? And, on the other hand, can we plausibly expect men to attach themselves to a society so large as the family of man? In a world of universal brotherhood, in a world in which everyone is your brother, what can brotherhood possibly mean?

Israel must be understood as the Jewish effort to answer these questions creatively and in deed rather than word. Israel is, in a fundamental sense, the procreant resolution of the tension between the tradition of the Enlightenment and the tradition of the Tradition. For, most simply put, it was, and is, an effort to produce a society parochial in structure but universal in ideology. And that, it seems to me, is precisely what Jewish history has all been about. The absurd aspect of Jewish history, of course, is that we would normally have expected a people exposed to what the Jews have been exposed to and subjected to what the Jews have been subjected to to have been withdrawn, embittered, certainly disenchanted. Whose innocence has been violated more often or more comprehensively? And who has remained, at the same time, more steadfastly committed to the vision of the end of days and to the behaviors required to translate the vision into reality?

I put it to you as simply as I know how: if, through some blinding alchemy, Israel could suddenly be transformed into an island state, surrounded by neutral and placid waters — if, that is to say, the harsh facts of hostility in the Middle East could be cast aside — Zionism and its product, the State of Israel, would be seen everywhere as a creative effort to confront and to resolve the modern dilemma rather than as a gnawing irritant or a tragic predicament. I do not mean to trivialize the tragedy of the Middle East by suggesting that we can disregard the conflicts there; I mean instead to propose that the Jewish dream, as authentically reflected by the State of Israel, is a dream which both challenges our conventional modern wisdom and excites our creative imagination.

It is not, of course, a dream without problems, both internal and external. The internal problems, which are not here our direct concern, seem to me to be manageable. It is the external problems, of course, which threaten to convert the dream into a nightmare. For Jewish nationalism, however authentic, has not been expressed in a vacuum; it has been expressed in a setting bitterly uncongenial. It is a bone in the throat of liberals, who, if they endorse Israel at all, do so chiefly out of guilt rather than out of ideological persuasion; it is a bone in the throat of the left, which has always viewed the Jews as too committed to bourgeois behavior; and it is worse than a bone in the throat of its neighbors, with whose own resurgent nationalism it conflicts almost directly. Though the State of Israel will surely survive these problems, it is possible that they will, in the end, mean defeat for the idea of Israel. That is to say, they will force Israel towards a destructive parochialism.

Yet I find it interesting and instructive that now, some twenty years after Israel's national rebirth, the clamor for national survival—for distinctive identity—has reached such massive heights around the world. Of course, we may, as so many do, continue to view the assertions of identity as tragic symbols of how far we have to go to find the new freedom, or we may, as I prefer, take them as evidence of how wanting liberal univeralism is as a compelling theory of human organization. We may, that is, conclude that others are now discovering for themselves that responsible universalist ideology permits, and very likely even requires, continued particularism in structure. It is as if everywhere people were saying that universal brotherhood, because it is too big to contemplate, offers too meager rewards and were endorsing instead a kind of universal cousinhood, acknowledging their kinship in the family of man but insisting on their right to be somewhat more selective in their fraternity.

Contemporary sociological wisdom should be open to such a perspective. Have social critics not railed against the destabilizing consequences of mass urbanization and the attendant loss of place and of perspective? Have we not lamented rootlessness, anonymity, and anomy; have we not characterized the modern condition as that of the lonely crowd? Surely insights such as these should lead to a warm embracing of those who seek to convert the lonely crowds into meaningful entities, who seek to rebuild the walls the Enlightenment had torn down, on the grounds that the walls serve to stave off the uprooting flood.

But sociology and the liberal community it serves are informed by universalism and, therefore, have been far more concerned with the conflicts the walls appear to generate than with their stabilizing function. Sociology has systematically avoided confronting the problem of stability and the problem of tolerance simultaneously, preferring instead to divide itself into ideological sects, with the most powerful voices raised against tradition and for the universal ethic.

If I say that Israel represents a genuinely revolutionary phenomenon, I do so because Israel has, at least, made the effort to solve this timeless and apparently intractable dilemma. I say that Israel offers insight to us all today. It is no accident that the early Zionist literature is now studied with care by black militants in America; that Israel has become a chief symbol to Eastern European revolutionaries seeking to reassert their own particular destinies against the Soviet monolith; that, wonder of wonders, the recruitment rhetoric of Al Fatah is so similar in tone and even in wording to the Zionist literature of 1947. It is not that each of these and all the others seek the same kind of answer the Israelis have found. It is, instead, that each confronts precisely the same dilemma, the dilemma of reconciling, somehow, the two contradictory impulses of the modern temper.

IV

Now it may be argued that such reasoning, however valid, has as much to do with the reality of the Middle East today as do the romantic appeals for a coalition between Arab and Jewish workers against their respective exploiting elites—which is to say, very little, if anything. Yet it seems to me that several implications flow rather directly from this set of perceptions. It does not derogate from the pathos, or even justice, of the Arab case to state that an Israel de-Zionized is an Israel sheared from its history, which is, in the end, its only justification. This conclusion clearly follows from the preceding analysis. What others sometimes take to be the artificial character of Israel is, instead, its only genuine claim to authenticity. De-Judaizing it or, for that matter, secularizing it, as some propose, would be the surest way to convert authenticity into artificiality.

The only genuinely interesting question about the real Middle East, the Middle East of blood and bloodshed and not the Middle East of American intellectuals, much less of troubled Jewish American intellectuals, is whether Arab claims are entirely irreconcilable with Jewish claims or whether there is not some way which can yet be found to give expression to the claims of both without denying the purposes each has chosen for itself.

I take very seriously indeed the emergence—some might say resurgence—since 1967 of a Palestinian identity. For that identity, still testing its limits and its capabilities, suggests at last the possibility of a settlement between Israel and those whom its presence most directly affects—that is, the Arabs of what once was Palestine (but became, in 1948, Israel), a piece of Jordan (the West Bank), and a territory controlled by Egypt (the Gaza Strip). Whether other Arab regimes feel fraternally tied to the Arabs of Palestine or whether they seek to exploit the tensions for their own domestic political advantage, surely the Palestinians themselves ought to play the leading role in any negotiations with Israel. Until recently, the Palestinians had no vehicle for self-expression. They were required, instead, to influence, as best they could, the Hussein regime in Jordan and the Nasser regime in Egypt. Now, with the emergence of the guerrilla movement, a Palestinian state becomes a possibility.

We ought not exaggerate the power of the guerrillas, nor romanticize their methods. Killing civilians is mean, and tossing grenades into air terminals is less an act of calculated warfare than an act of cowardly desperation. The guerrilla leaders, who include a number of serious intellectuals, hardly speak for the guerrilla masses, who are, typically, recruited from the most backward elements of refugee society. But the guerrillas, at the very least, are authentic; unlike, say, the Iraqis, they have a genuine causus belli, and the only serious question is whether their developing aspirations are entirely incompatible with Israel's continued existence.

If what the guerrillas seek is Israel's destruction, then there can be little hope for an enduring peace settlement with or without peace treaties, with or without imposition from the outside. For if Israel's destruction is their aim, the guerrillas will simply refuse to accept any settlement arrived at by formal governments, thereby quite probably bringing intolerable pressure to bear on Hussein and certainly forcing the Israelis to respond to their incursions with force. But if, instead, the guerrillas have a positive goal—if their aim is to find political expression for their developing Palestinian identity—their present struggle with Israel might well be diverted into more productive channels not incompatible with Israel's own needs.

Specifically, we might remember that the Palestine for which Britain was awarded a League of Nations mandate in 1920 included both Israel and Jordan. The Hashemite Kingdom of Jordan, in other words, dates back only to 1923, when Britain carved Palestine in half, creating Transjordan. As to the West Bank, it has been part of Jordan only since it was annexed in the course of the 1948 Israel-Arab war, an annexation recognized to this day only by Britain and Pakistan. Hence the country we know as Jordan is, in the sweep of history, almost a contemporary of Israel; a mere twenty-five years separate their birth. If the issue at stake in the Middle East today is the development of an opportunity for political expression of a Palestinian identity, Jordan is as plausible a target as Israel—indeed, more plausible, since a Palestinian Jordan would require no massive displacement of people, no incompatible contest for the same piece of territory, no blood bath. All that it would involve, basically, is a change of regimes in Jordan—an end to the monarchy and its replacement by an indigenous representative government.

In this view, the emergence of the guerrillas as a real force in the Middle East may be regarded as presenting a new basis for settlement of the dispute. It is clearly premature to expect that settlement just around the corner, for the guerrillas still have to develop a more coherent ideology, to say nothing of a more impressive self-discipline, before they will be prepared even to think about redirecting their energies, just as the Israelis still have to learn to stop deprecating the concept of a Palestinian identity. But this particular scenario has one advantage over any other; if it works, it will bring both peace and security, since it will reflect a new sense of reality on all sides and an authentic response to the aspirations of Arabs and Jews.

In summary, if the story of Israel and the emergent story of a dozen other and more recent experiments in national liberation are to have any durability, they can endure only if and as they confront quite squarely the modern dilemma, that is, the problem of creatively combining the tribal instinct and the universal ideology. To argue for an exclusivist solution, a solution in which the national instinct of one group is expressed at the expense of the no less authentic national instinct of another, is to violate that mandate. This is a lesson that Israel will find it hard to learn, given recent history, but it is a lesson to which the Jewish experience is almost uniquely open. It is a lesson that I can only pray the Arabs will learn, not only because what little I know of Islam tells me that it is a congenial lesson, and not only because as a Jew I dread the consequences of continuing exclusivity, but finally because the bold experiment with national expression which now unfolds before us everywhere can as easily become the harbinger of a new brutalism as of a new creativity. It can as easily seek to solve the modern dilemma by retreating from it as by addressing it directly. There are, in short, more challenging conquests to be made than the continuing and fruitless conquests of each other. It is to these creative conquests that we—and even the non-Jewish Jews among us, if only they can stop viewing Israel through the lenses of their private problems—are now in duty bound to turn our attention.

8   Jewish interests and the new left

NATHAN GLAZER

Are there conflicts between what we might call Jewish interests and the interests of people in general? Should Jewish interests be subordinated or ignored in favor of national interests? Should they be subordinated to class interests or to the interests of the future, as derived, let us say, from Marxist theory? Is there any obligation for Jews to support Jewish interests—and for what reason?

    Nathan Glazer concludes that Jews, like all men, have an interest in ending the war in Vietnam, ensuring employment and prosperity, and ending poverty and hunger in the United States and throughout the world, whether they are directly affected or not. He further argues that the specific Jewish interests that all Jews share because they are Jews and the interests that Jews develop because of their economic and occupational distribution do not contradict the interests of other people and do not lead to Jewish opposition to policies necessary to all—despite claims to the contrary.

    He goes on to demonstrate that the New Left's programs would do nothing to assuage the real and terrible evils of our society and others, and that its aims in one area contradict its aims in others.

I have placed prominently in the title the words *Jewish interests,* and I plan to speak directly to some of the following questions: What *are* Jewish interests? Are there conflicts between what we might call Jewish interests and the interests of people in general? Should Jewish interests be subordinated or ignored in favor of national interests (American, Russian, or what have you)?

NATHAN GLAZER *is Professor of Education and Social Structure, Graduate School of Education, Harvard University.*

Should Jewish interests be subordinated to class interests or to the interests of the future, as derived, let us say, from Marxist theory? Is there any obligation for Jews to support Jewish interests—and for what reason?

It is not a comfortable role for a social scientist or a liberal to discuss such questions, but unfortunately it is an essential one. In considering Jewish youth and the New Left, we are divided between various positions. Some of us believe that Jewish youth upholds the finest traditions of Jewish history by supporting the aims and objectives of the New Left, as it does disproportionately when compared to other youth. For others, Jewish youth in effect supports the interests of humanity—and therefore by necessity the interests of Jews, included within humanity—when it supports the objectives of the New Left. Or, alternatively, some of us believe that the Jewish youth that supports the New Left has betrayed the Jewish people. Some of us may even believe that it hardly matters whether Jewish youth betrays the Jewish people by supporting the New Left or betrays humanity by supporting the interests of Jews because to speak of Jewish interests in an age when all national identities are limited and suspect is illegitimate.

Obviously I have not formulated all the necessary questions or all the possibilities, nor have I formulated them well. But I believe it is necessary for us to begin to talk of these matters, because otherwise our positions are poorly grounded and confused. I believe in particular it is necessary to talk of these matters because, although we all believe that interest is at the base of all political position taking and action, we are uncomfortable with the concept of interest unless it is formulated in terms of the largest possible *legitimate* interest, and undoubtedly the two most prominent ideological interests today are national interests and class interests. Thus, if we have laws that favor the oil industry (as we do), we all know and may say publicly at some level that this favoritism exists because of the political power of the oil industry. At the highest level, however, we will express our support for these policies (if indeed we support them) in national terms. We will say that the oil depletion allowance leads to greater oil exploration and more oil reserves and thus strengthens the national defense. Or we might argue in simpler, nonnational humanitarian terms. We might, for example, argue for high tariffs on imported shoes by saying that we must support a healthy shoe industry for the benefit of the workers employed in it and for the town they live in. This in the end is a defense in terms of national interests too, for presumably other workers and towns in other countries will be hurt by the higher tariffs; implicitly we accept the fact that the interests of *American* workers should be of greater concern to American policy makers.

Alternatively, our ultimate judgment to defend policies and actions may be stated in class terms. Because the Russians belong to a socialist state concerned for the ultimate victory of socialist revolution, they will argue that whatever increases the military strength of Russia advances the interests of the world working class. The Chinese will play with other variants of this central theory, incorporating all poor countries into an international proletarian and deprived class and thus ingeniously linking class and national interests, at least partially and temporarily (for within those poor countries not all people form part of the world deprived class, and many are slated for liquidation).

We are all uncomfortable with the idea of interest, no matter how we formulate it, but it is necessary to begin directly with this question if we are to come to any position on Jewish youth and the New Left that is not immoral and illogical. This general discomfort with the idea of interest—whether we take as our ultimate ground for justification national or class interests—is clearly demonstrated by my examples. Russians and Chinese will couch national interests in class terms, no matter how distorted, and Americans will couch class interests in national terms, no matter how distorted. And yet, as we know, we cannot accept either of these ultimate grounds without question. All Russians suffered from the terrible invasion and slaughter and destruction by Germans, whether they were rich peasants, poor, honest workers, or black-market operators. There *was* a national interest involved as well as a class interest. Even such a derided symbol of the effort to turn class interest into national interest as the famous statement, "What's good for General Motors is good for the country," cannot be categorically rejected as simply a defense of class privilege. A few hundred thousand General Motors workers might well agree with the statement. Interest thus appears to us not in the unambiguous and hard-edged forms that national and class theorists would insist upon. Interests are varied and contradictory, they merge and diverge, and whatever general theory we adopt as to what is a right or proper interest is not likely to give us guidance in any concrete situation.

Difficult as it is to determine what are the interests that *should* guide actions—in terms of some moral position—it is even more difficult to determine what should be the relationship between the individual and any general interest. We try to base political arguments on a statement of interests that can be applied as universally as possible, because we believe that under those circumstances we can make a claim for the commitment or action of individuals. To ask people to fight for General Motors is hard; to ask them to fight for the United States is better; to ask them to fight for the interests of democracy and freedom and humanity as aspired to by the United States is best of all. Similarly, it is difficult to ask people to defend the interests of the ruling circles of the Communist party, easier to ask them to fight for the nation, and best to ask them to fight for the international working class which itself incorporates the interest of humanity.

I am not comfortable with these remarks—I am sure many people have put them better elsewhere or perhaps demonstrated their inadequacy—but I begin with them because I want to ask what Jewish interests are and what we can demand or claim from Jews and Jewish youth in defense of those interests. Clearly, if the term *Jewish interests* means the interests of an imperialistic, even if small, state in the Middle East which dominates its neighbors and oppresses its minorities, we can ask nothing in defense of Jewish interests; if it means the interests of exploitative landlords, businessmen, and civil servants who oppress black tenants, workers, and clients, we can ask nothing in defense of Jewish interests. There is no question that this is the point of view of a substantial segment of Jewish youth.

Having set forth these general points, I will state my thesis: there is, intertwined with New Left theories, orientations, and policies, a set of positions that in various ways contradict Jewish interests, and these interests are legitimate interests that do not contradict the interests of humanity in general. The term *contradict Jewish interests* is of course one that makes some of us uncomfortable. We do not like to think in terms of specific Jewish interests. Perhaps if I said that there are positions and orientations in some general political outlook that contradict black, or Negro, interests, we would be less uncomfortable. We are by now used to the idea that there are black interests, that they are legitimate and in harmony with human interests, and there are political positions that are contradictory to them or that oppose them. Perhaps I am wrong, but I think that Jews would be more uncomfortable about a discussion of Jewish interests than of black interests, and yet whatever problems exist in dealing with one exist in dealing with the other.

Thus, there are social classes in black communities just as there are in Jewish communities. Their interests may diverge: the worker with seniority does not have the same interests as the unemployed ghetto man or the black professional. There are varied black states, and the divergence of their interests has just been demonstrated by the sanguinary war in Nigeria. Blacks are capable of crimes against humanity just as whites are; just recently I read in *Le Monde* of the situation of the Central

African Republic, where the ruler had subjected his ministers to unspeakable tortures and had the eyes of one man torn out before his own children.

I do not suggest that this is typical of black rulers, but on the other hand we must not leap to the conclusion that overcharging in the ghetto or exploitation of black workers is typical of Jewish businessmen. My point is that we may speak of Jewish interests; we may determine whether they contradict the interests of humanity; we may come to some conclusion as to whether we can with a clear mind, or with as clear a mind as human complexity permits, demand of Jewish youth that they at least refuse to work *against* Jewish interests.

There are three questions we must settle before we can make any claims for Jewish interests. First of all there are the varied interests of all those who are called Jews in many countries, classes, and occupations. How can there then be so-called Jewish interests?

Second, there is the question of whether there are truly Jewish interests as such or only the interests of groups among whom Jews are heavily overrepresented—teachers in New York City, shopkeepers, businessmen, students in elite colleges.

Third, there is the most basic question concerning Jewish or any group interests: whether and to what extent they themselves may contradict or be made to harmonize with the interests of all men. Can the interests of humanity be in conflict with the interests of any given group? Very often this question can be posed in reference to short-term versus long-term interests. Conceivably, the average German or Japanese was better off because of the German or Japanese conquests. But since the conquests were not allowed to remain permanent, then in the end they were worse off. It would have been better to have thought of the interests of a world system to begin with.

I will argue that there are Jewish interests, in all three senses suggested by these questions, and that the thrust of the New Left is to oppose them. And since these three senses range from the most particularistic to the most universalistic, it is in the interests of Jews, not only as Jews, but as men who prefer—as all rational men should—a humane and democratic society, to weaken and limit the power of the New Left.

When we think of the interests of Jews in general, it may appear that there are no interests which bind Jews everywhere, regardless of class or condition or religion. I would argue that there are two such interests that bind Jews everywhere: one is the existence of the State of Israel, and the other is the decline of anti-Semitism. Of course there can be no argument that Jews of all kinds should be against anti-Semitism; by definition anti-Semitism is against Jews.

There is considerably more argument about Israel. For a long time, many Jews have tried to make a sharp distinction between a Jew and a Zionist. Such a distinction can be maintained legitimately. Arabs too make such a distinction, so that their desire to destroy the State of Israel and their violent antipathy to all Jews who support it can be seen as anti-Zionist, not as anti-Jewish. This effort is less and less sucessful, however, because all but tiny minorities of Jews now see their interests fully bound up with the existence of the State of Israel. How would their interests be affected if Arabs had the military power to overwhelm the state? Perhaps we can best understand how by trying to sense what passion can be aroused in American Negroes by the now old story of black slavery. Such indignities and outrages to people with whom one identifies are indignities and outrages to oneself. One can scarcely imagine what pain was stored up in the hearts of American Negroes—even if the pain is now repressed or unconscious—by the civil war in Nigeria and the starvation of the Biafrans. It affects one's sense of worth to have one's people butchered. I am convinced that all Jews suffer from the holocaust in the Middle East, and all Jews would suffer further if Israel were to go under. This is to my mind a primal Jewish interest, and it is an interest to which the New Left is in general indifferent or opposed.

I believe we are aware of the general line of political argument along which the New Left supports the Arabs against Israel. First, the Arabs are seen as a people in rebellion against Western imperialism. The Jews are seen as a people allied with Western imperialism. The United States supports the Israelis against the communist world, included in which are the peoples of "national liberation," such as North Vietnam and Cuba, as well as the more placid bureaucratic states to which the New Left is less friendly, such as Russia. Therefore, this is evidence of the Israeli alliance with imperialism, since the United States is imperialistic. (It would be too subtle to see U.S. support as a result of the political pressure of 6 million Jews rather than as a result of common imperialistic interest.)

Another reason why the New Left supports the Arabs is because the most militant blacks do. And they do so because of a similar argument (the United States supports Israel; the United States is imperialistic; ergo Israel is imperialistic) and because of some peculiar historical accidents: the fact that Arab and Negro states became allied in the United Nations against Western states and the even odder fact of the rise of the Black Muslims. (Suppose, instead, that the *Black Jews* had become the important sect?)

Now, I consider this line of argument worthless, but without going into the reasons why I think so, it is clear that the New Left has an overwhelming and unbendable tendency to support the Arabs and to oppose Israel. I think there is another important reason for this that I have not mentioned. This is simply style; Arab *irrationality* appeals to them more than Israeli sobriety. It is closer to their own rhetoric. Israeli language is closer to the gray rhetoric of the Establishment. This matter of style is related to the New Left passion for the apocalypse and the millennium. Obviously the continuance of Israel is in no sense apocalyptic or millennial. It is a state like other states, with problems of employment, minority integration, balance of payments, and the like, and, of course, permanent problems of defense; it is, in other words, a bore. The State of Israel cannot envisage any final victory or any ultimate resolutions. The Arabs can, and I think the New Left likes final victories and ultimate resolutions and is impatient with anything that is merely long-sustained trouble with no promise of a final mind-blowing disaster or victory.

And finally another linked theme of New Left feeling—we can scarcely say thinking—tends to put it against Israel: it is against efficiency, just as it is against sobriety and for apocalypse and millennium. Efficiency means capitalism, order, discipline. Even in the states it admires—Cuba and China, for example— the New Left will tend to play down the important role of efficiency, discipline, and order in order to emphasize, in opposition, spontaneity. Its cultural style also moves in that direction, as exhibited in art, music, and clothes. Certainly there is nothing in Israeli styles of life, as created by a situation demanding a defense that can never lose and a national discipline that supports it, that would appeal to this cultural style, which, we have so often been told, is an essential part of the whole New Left, intimately bound up with its politics.

Even on the second Jewish issue, that of anti-Semitism, we can expect nothing from the New Left. The New Left is not anti-Semitic. On the other hand, I cannot recall a single statement by any New Left leader or in any New Left publication that has ever attacked anti-Semitism. It is considered a nonissue. One of the reasons that anti-Semitism is considered a nonissue is the perfectly legitimate one that it really is not much of a threat. Yet, another of the reasons that it is a nonissue is the vigilance of those who find it abhorrent and who fight it.

It is understandable why, in the budget of issues with which the New Left deals—racism, university government, and, overwhelmingly, Vietnam—anti-Semitism should not be high on the agenda. What is less understandable is the distinct aversion of New Left types for even bothering to criticize someone who uses anti-Semitism. Those who use anti-Semitism or who are anti-Semitic can be punished politically in this country. Political costs, and severe ones, are exacted for anti-Semitism, which is one reason why anti-Semitism has become a minor issue. But the New Left does not participate in that broad spectrum of political positions that exact costs and apply sanctions for anti-Semitism. I think this inaction is based on sycophancy toward the blacks. If a white politician were to be anti-Semitic, I suspect the New Left *might* include this in the catalog of his sins, no matter how unimportant the trait was considered. When blacks are anti-Semitic—as some occasionally are—such anti-Semitism cannot be criticized. Certainly the New Left is no shield against anti-Semitism. Insofar as anti-Semitism is an issue that must always be of concern to Jews—though, I would add, not their chief concern, certainly not at a time like this—New Left interests and Jewish interests diverge.

There is a second chief class of Jewish interests: Jews have been affected because they are disproportionately represented in certain professions or jobs. We know that more than half of New York City's teachers are Jews. We know there is heavy Jewish overrepresentation in ghetto business. We know there is heavy Jewish overrepresentation in elite colleges. We know that disproportionate numbers of Jews are professors, writers, editors, and so forth.

Here we deal with a really complex set of issues. In the New York City teachers' strikes, teachers' interests and Jewish interests became hopelessly entwined. This was inevitable. It is very hard to attack the role without also attacking the person who fills it. Defending their interests, teachers insisted they were being attacked as Jews. Attacking these interests, blacks on occasion insisted on seizing political advantage by identifying them as Jews. Both sides brought in the Jewish issue. It became impossible to view the situation as merely a fight between teachers and militant community leaders rather than between Jews and blacks. What are people but the roles they play? If Jews play teachers' roles, it becomes very hard to distinguish the one from the other in passionate conflicts.

But to recur to the New Left, *all* the roles that Jews play are roles that the New Left disapproves of and wishes to reduce. It attacks civil service bureaucracies. It attacks the principles of merit and nondiscrimination on which they are based. It attacks scholastic bases for entry into college. It attacks the role and authority of professors as well as teachers. It is critical, of course, of all private business and of its whole associated institutional complex—lawyers, stockbrokers, accountants, and such —in which Jews are prominent.

The kinds of society the New Left admires have no place for Jews in their historic roles. Thus, almost all the Jews left Cuba after the revolution. Only Jewish intellectuals could adapt to that kind of state; certainly Jewish businessmen, lawyers, doctors, and shopkeepers could not. Many Jews who are radical may find it unpleasant that the roles in which Jews predominate must be eliminated or reduced in what they consider the good society. Nevertheless, they believe such eliminations or reductions to be a historic inevitability if justice is to prevail.

I believe it is just and prudent for any society to see that all major groups are represented in all the major institutions of the society. It is also prudent for any society to do what it can to combat the feeling that some groups are unfairly favored and others exploited. These necessities in part justify some of the positions the New Left has taken. Where I would disagree is in attacking the value or the legitimacy of the roles that Jews fill and the bases on which Jews fill them.

Thus, I think that any society will find certain kinds of civil bureaucracies necessary. It will find merchants or their equivalents necessary. It will find landlords or their equivalents necessary. It will have to make investments, and someone will have to decide how. I do not find in most of these endeavors that socialist societies do a *better* job than free-market societies in which Jews, owing to their history and resultant skills and values, tend to play a large functional role. I am not sure that state distribution systems do a better job than private ones— from all accounts, they do worse—that state landlords do a better job than private ones, that state investors necessarily reflect

public and popular desires and tastes better than private investors, or that appointments to bureaucracies on the basis of political loyalty enable them to operate better than appointments on
the basis of objective examination do. Thus, I disagree with the
New Left in that I do not see any inherent injustice necessarily
attached to the roles of merchant, landlord, school teacher, or
professor, even though any individual filling these roles may be
unjust or evil. I do see issues of prudence that may arise because
of the number of Jews that fill such roles, and I might support
efforts to redirect Jews out of such tension-producing roles and
to give relocation aid to them just as we give aid to those who
lose their homes to public purposes.

Finally, I would like to speak of the relationship of Jewish
interests to the interests of any men and all men—universal
human interests. Jews, like all men, have an interest in ending
the war in Vietnam, ensuring employment and prosperity, and
ending poverty and hunger, whether they are affected directly
or not, in the United States and throughout the world. But do the
specific Jewish interests I have discussed—the interests that I
believe all Jews share because they are Jews, and the interests
that Jews develop because of their economic and occupational
distribution—do they contradict the interests of all people?
Would such Jewish interest lead Jews to oppose policies necessary to all because of their partial interests as Jews? The New
Left believes this and I disagree completely.

In order to support my position I would have to go through
the catalog of the real and terrible evils of our society and others
and demonstrate that the New Left's programs would do nothing
to assuage them, that its aims in one area contradict its aims in
others. I have made this argument in various writings, and so I
will only review briefly six of these contradictions within the
New Left.

1. On the one hand the New Left demands better material
conditions for the poor; on the other it demands the kind of
education and the kind of economic arrangements that would

make it difficult or impossible to achieve a higher production of goods and services.

2. On the one hand it insists that the most intense and committed should play the largest role in determining policies (this is the meaning of participatory democracy and the reason for the opposition to "formal" democracy); on the other it ignores the reality that on various occasions the most intense and committed have wanted to adopt repressive and authoritarian policies and that the relatively passive majority have made it possible for democracy to survive.

3. On the one hand it demands spontaneity and freedom for all; on the other it demands policies (for example, preserving the environment) that must involve some restriction on freedom and spontaneity.

4. On the one hand it applauds the demand of the poor for material goods; on the other it derides the state of material comfort that the working and the lower middle classes have achieved.

5. On the one hand it attacks the violence of American forces in Vietnam and of the police at home; on the other it seeks to break down the institutions and restraints—governmental, legal, and social—which still, to some extent, control this violence and prevent it from becoming even more frightful.

6. On the one hand it insists that all nations deserve their freedom and independence; on the other it excludes certain nations (Israel among them) from this general grant.

This is only a brief catalog of the contradictions which the stance of the New Left presents and with which it has seized the imagination and commitment of a good part of Jewish youth.

Among those groups that have found in the complex and ambiguous structure of American society physical security, cultural and religious freedom, and material comfort, are American Jews. It will take a good deal of argument, I hope, to convince them that this system is totally corrupt, that those who oppose it must be our friends, that it is worthy only of derision, sabotage, and destruction.

A substantial part of our youth is convinced—or acts as if it is. Those of us who know how bad bad can be and how much most Americans have gained have a good deal of work cut out for us. Our job is to moderate the excesses of New Left rhetoric and analysis so that we can improve our society without destroying it.[1]

1. Nathan Glazer's new volume *Remembering the Answers: Essays on the American Student Revolt* expands upon a number of points made in the foregoing article.

9   The new left
and the newer leftists

MORDECAI S. CHERTOFF

Exercising what may be a moot point of editorial privilege, the editor exploits his position to have a few words at the expense of those with whom he disagrees. He deals with some of the causes of the youth revolt, the generation gap, law and order, Jewish self-hatred, the Black Panther party, the recrudescence of anti-Semitism in America, and the transformation of the image of the Jew in his own and in others' eyes since the Six-Day War. He also answers some of the points raised by New Leftists in their criticism of Israel and Israeli policy.

Most important, perhaps, is his brief sketch of the emerging Jewish radical movements which affirm Zionism and Judaism and whose members react as socialists and radicals to the social ills of the country and of the world. Although his listing of these groups and of the underground press they are producing is, of necessity, imcomplete, it indicates the direction in which at least some new winds are blowing and perhaps even justifies a measure of optimism in the future of the American Jewish community.

Violence in the cities and on campus has spawned an almost endless series of investigations. Federal, state, and municipal authorities, university trustees, and ad hoc faculty committees have variously attempted to discern the underlying causes of the current unrest and, in some cases, to prescribe for it, and the analyses have focused on a variety of causes: Vietnam, affluence, oppression, overextended adolescence and dependency, the generation gap, the credibility gap, and the breakdown of law and order. Some writers combine the social and psychological

MORDECAI S. CHERTOFF *is executive director of the American Histadrut Cultural Exchange Institute.*

elements and emphasize the conflict between permissive, child-centered, idea-oriented environments (such as are to be found in the prosperous middle classes) and the bureaucratic environments of high schools and colleges. The clash that results when a child with an enlightened upbringing enters a restrictive organization may be a factor in developing leftist attitudes in young people, whose experience will appear to them to contradict the claims of the society to be free and open. Many Jewish children fall into this pattern.

Other writers emphasize historical factors. Nathan Glazer goes back to the emancipation.[1] At that time, the right was identified with "romanticism, monarchy, hierarchy, tradition, nationalism, and generally anti-Semitism. The left . . . emphasized rationality and science, parliamentary democracy, social equality, internationalism, and of course freedom and equality for the Jews." All in all, the Jews in Europe were better off with the left than with the right, particularly when the left was more liberal than radical. And this political bias was carried over to America. Despite manifestations of anti-Semitism in the left, there was little question that the bulk of Jewish sympathies lay in that direction. Jewish identification with the left today stems not a little from the fact that the parents of the Jews are generally liberals and many of them were radicals in their youth.

> If the fathers are liberals, the young Jews often share their disillusionment concerning recent political developments and carry this disillusionment further. They do not become radical by reacting against their parents; rather they become radical by seeing themselves as carrying their parents' position to its logical conclusion. In their minds they overcome the hypocrisy of their parents whose thinking is not translated into action.

Glazer points out that perhaps half of the American Communist party in the 1950s and the 1960s was Jewish. Although

1. Nathan Glazer, "The New Left and the Jews," *Jewish Journal of Sociology* (London: December 1969), pp. 121-132.

the party never had more than 50,000 members, the turnover was so rapid that perhaps ten times that number were members at least for a time. This makes a substantial reservoir of present-day parents for whose children being radical is not something shocking or strange, but rather may be a means of fulfilling what they see as the best drives of their parents. And to parents who were communists, we must add those who were socialists of sorts.

In his contribution to this volume, Glazer shows how today, for the first time in some decades, to be left is to contradict some strongly held Jewish interests.

Bruno Bettelheim takes Melville's classic, *Moby Dick,* as his text, pointing out that its hero, Ishmael, is "the outsider *par excellence,"* and that, inevitably, Melville expected his reader to be aware of the biblical description of Ishmael as one whose "hand will be against every man and every man's hand [will be] against him."[2] And he goes on to adduce Melville's description of his protagonist's state of mind:

> Whenever I find myself growing grim about the mouth; whenever it is a damp, drizzly November in my soul; whenever I find myself involuntarily pausing before coffin ware-houses, and bringing up the rear of every funeral I meet; and especially whenever my hypos get such an upper hand of me, that it requires a strong moral principle to prevent me from deliberately stepping into the street and method-ically knocking people's hats off—then, I account it high time to get to sea as soon as I can. This is my substitute for pistol and ball.

For the adolescent in crisis, the only way of avoiding either senseless violence or destruction has always been "to change the environment *in toto*—to 'escape the Establishment,' as we now say." Going to sea was one way, going West was another; there are many frontiers. What distinguishes Melville's time from

2. Bruno Bettelheim, "Obsolete Youth, Towards a Psychograph of Adolescent Rebellion," *Encounter* (September 1969), pp. 29-42.

our own is that, as Bettelheim sees it, "the goal was not to break up the established order, but to return to it from one's wanderings, find one's rightful place in society, and there improve it by virtue of the manhood one had gained."

Without Melville's frontiers, today's adolescents turn to the alternatives Ishmael was able to escape: senseless violence or self-destruction. However, even with adolescence unduly prolonged, adolescent malaise does not account for current discontent. Nor do Vietnam or the Negro problem (which neither German nor Japanese nor French students share with their peers in the United States). What Bettelheim sees as the common core of worldwide student discontent is the feeling that youth has no future. This feeling arises from their fears that

> modern technology has made them obsolete—that they have become socially irrelevant and, as persons, insignificant. . . . Their anxiety is not (as they claim) about an impending atomic war. It is not that society has no future. Their existential anxiety is that *they* have no future in a society that does not need them to go on existing. . . .they think they have been classified as "waste material," and they feel compelled to "reject a system that rejects us."

Hence the violence; the Luddite tendencies to destroy the "machine"—in one university it was an attack on the computer, in another destruction of the Mathematics Research Center and physics building—hence the mindlessness and the reliance upon "gut" reaction rather than reason.

Daniel Bell sees the changed educational requirements in society as crucial to the malaise—the alienation—of youth today.[3] "An educational system which used to reflect the status structure of the society now becomes the *determinant* of class position in the society." Since there is an increase of about one third in the number of young there is "a consequent sense of increased competition for place. There is a reduction of the status of the college. Today, in the elite schools, more than 85

3. Daniel Bell, "Unstable America," *Encounter* (June 1970), pp. 11-26.

percent of the graduates go on to some postgraduate work, so that in these places the college becomes simply a waystation. . . . In the nature of the modern technological revolution, there is an awareness that a college degree, even an advanced one, is no longer the means of stepping on to the high plateau of society. Rather, advancement involves a continual process of professional training and retraining in order to keep up with the new techniques and new knowledge being produced." In short, Bell sees much of the alienation of the young as a reaction to the social revolution that has taken place in their own status.

This social revolution, a product of the postindustrial society, has been intensified by the Vietnam war, which many analysts see, with Bell, as "the catalyst of all social tensions in the United States." Even were the war to end immediately, the tensions would not be resolved, but there would be a release of funds and perhaps even leadership talent sufficient for at least an attempt to ameliorate the tensions.

Other causes of the current unrest already alluded to—the credibility gap (initially a product of the Vietnam war) and the breakdown of law and order—are ascribed all too often to the generation gap. Any number of surveys have adduced enough evidence to support Joseph Adelson's aperçu that the very concept of the generation gap may well be one of those false ideas whose time has come and can, therefore, no more be resisted, though it is false, than if it were true. [4]

The prophets of ancient Israel longed for the time when conflict between generations would come to an end. But although Abraham, the biblical idol breaker, was aeons removed from his idol-worshipping father, only an excessively modern commentator would speak of a generation gap in their relationship. To bring the question closer to our own universe of experience, neither the American, French, nor Russian revolutions were explained so simplistically. Indeed, the surveys have shown

4. Joseph Adelson, *New York Times Magazine* (18 January 1970).

that, if anything, the young today may very well be more guilty of political docility than of rebelliousness; with very few exceptions, they share the political opinions and attitudes of their parents, so that a former left sympathizer boasts of "my son, the revolutionary," while a leading Bircher is apparently pleased with his daughter, who was cited in one survey as an extreme rightist.

Without the frontiers of Melville's days against which to prove their manhood, today's youth are in revolt against society. But it is a mindless revolt, without plan or program, without a guiding ideal beyond the fervor to destroy the evil they claim to see about them. A symposium on domestic and foreign policy problems in New York was disrupted by SDS elements who refused to let Arthur Goldberg, the Establishment man, have his say. After he had left the rostrum in disgust, the meeting broke up into groups of angry debaters, each with an SDSer at its focal point. I heard one middle-aged member of the audience challenge the angry young rebel in his group: "Granted," he said, "we've made a mess of things; you want to set them straight. What would you do, given the power; what is your program?" The answer was in character: "Program! What do you mean program? How should I have a program? I'm only 26."

And it is these young people that Margaret Mead sees as the first generation of the new, better society. She tells us that most children are unable to learn at all from the parents and elders they will never be, which implies that there is really nothing for them to learn from us.

In the early forties, college students were constantly being warned that the left aimed to subvert the American way and destroy our democracy; today's college generation feels itself threatened by the right—a right that they are stimulating to backlash by their violence, their contempt for democratic processes, and the elitism inherent in the New Left stance. And while the over-thirty, "obsolescent" generation looks warily to both right and left, Margaret Mead advises us that the real threat to adult hegemony is from neither of these extremes but from below, from the young.[5] The young protest that they can have no blueprint for the better society because they are too young; the left talks, without goal or plan, of revolution for the sake of revolution; it is the obsolescent generation which must struggle to minimize the right backlash and deal with racial strife, the high cost of living, pollution, crime and, yes, Vietnam, Cambodia, Laos, Thailand, and the Middle East.

The young are disenchanted with Western culture and its institutions. They despise American society and its values, which, along with an admitted materialism, include such positive virtues as respect for law and the democratic process, tolerance, strong family life, patriotism, and hard work. They reject the very promise of the American dream. They therefore despise American Jewish culture, which accepts these values, and the Jews themselves, whose upward mobility testifies to the validity of the dream. In fact, Jewish tradition itself is a threat to totalitarianism and collectivism and has been recognized and fought as such, both from the right (Nazi Germany) and from the left (Soviet Russia). What has become so fashionable on the left—elitism, hedonism, the all-powerful state, and the cult of irreverence—are directly antithetical to everything Judaism stands for. For many leftists, American Jewish support of Israel is enough to damn Israel, too, along with the United States, even if Israel's guilt is only by association.

One hundred and thirty years ago de Tocqueville could enthuse over American virtues such as respect for law:

> . . .in the United States, everyone is personally interested in enforcing the obedience of the whole community to the law. . . . However irksome an enactment may be, the citizen . . . complies with it, not only because it is the work of the majority, but because it is his own. . . . that numerous and turbulent multitude does not exist who, regarding the law

5. Margaret Mead, Lecture at the Museum of Natural History, as reported in the *New York Times* (16 March 1969).

as their natural enemy, look upon it with fear and distrust
. . . . all classes display the utmost reliance upon the legislation of their country. . . .[6]

Too much of what passes for law today, including the proliferation of rulings extending the areas of permissible invasion
of privacy—wiretapping and bugging, the recent and abomi-
nable "no-knock enter-and-search" law and preventive detention, and police harassment of students illustrated by the kill-
ings at Kent State, Ohio, and Jackson, Mississippi, and the
persecution of the Black Panthers—makes it difficult for any
serious analyst to describe the United States today in de Tocqueville's terms. Unfortunately, the average citizen is not aware
of the threat that these aberrations constitute until they impinge
directly upon his own life.

It is all too easy to dismiss repression of dissidents as emer-
gency measures called forth by the current crisis, but police
high-handedness spills over into every area of our daily lives.
Under these circumstances it was, perhaps, inevitable that a
distinguished citizen was arrested while jogging with his son
around the reservoir in the park of one of our major cities moments before the park curfew went into effect. Because he lec-
tured the police on his rights, wagging a finger at them in pro-
fessorial fashion, the charge was assault and battery with a finger!
After spending half the night in jail and being released on bail
(which he was not permitted to post himself and had to do
through the agency of a bail bondsman), he was released miles
from home in the early predawn hours, still dressed in shorts
and without taxi fare for the trip home. Although the charge
was dismissed, apparently to protect the police from a lawsuit
for false arrest, he was fined on the lesser charge of curfew violation and is now the proud possessor of a police record, complete with fingerprints. Minor? A petty incident? Perhaps. But
it was enough to radicalize his impressionable young son and

6. Alexis de Tocqueville, *Democracy in America*, vol. 2 (New York:
Knopf, 1946), pp. 247-248.

shake his own faith in the law and its upholders. An interesting aftermath to the incident was the flood of letters and phone calls he received from all over the city, recounting similar adventures including that of a local university professor who, while playing ball with his son, was arrested for loitering in front of his own home.

For young people who have not had any personal experience with overzealous upholders of the law, there are the fascinating accounts of Prince Crazy, George Demerle, an agent provocateur who moved among the hippie and East Village (New York City) circles, outtalking the wildest among them about the needs for bombs and burnings. He had his counterpart on the university scene in Tommy the Traveler, M. L. Singkata Thomas Tongyai, a self-proclaimed roving "radical" who had been a key figure in planning the firebombing of ROTC offices and other incendiary operations at Hobart College and other institutions that seemed to need a little stirring up to discredit dissent. There were reports of Tommy's agitational presence in such episodes as Chicago's Days of Rage and the diversionary, turbulent march on the South Vietnamese embassy in Washington, which marred the otherwise orderly peace demonstration. He and his counterparts may well show up again in new areas of tension.

Furthermore, de Tocqueville's "fundamental identity in political principle—the democratic faith of the people" may well be in danger of no longer serving as one of the primary forces holding the union together. It obviously does not apply to many of the younger generation and certainly has no relevance to the most articulate of them, the New Left.

The New Left, of course, is far from a monolithic unit. At a recent New Left meeting in New York, among those represented or taking part were the following: the Yippies, the Black Panthers, the Young Lords party, the Committee of Returned Volunteers (mostly from the Peace Corps), the Women's Liberation Movement, the Gay Liberation Front, the Venceremos

Brigade (volunteers who cut sugar cane in Cuba), MAN (Make-A-Nation—a black militant group), NOW (the National Organization for Women), the Revolutionary Antiwar Movement, SDS (Students for a Democratic Society), the Weathermen, and other organizations. According to the *New York Times* report, a visitor from Uganda was puzzled by what he saw and shocked to learn that a New Left petition with 300 signers represented 164 organizations.

Tom Milstein, in his contribution to this volume, presents an overview of the New Left in which he sketches its development and the major elements of which it is composed. He makes the point that despite the almost bewildering number of groups calling themselves New Leftists, the New Left is, nevertheless, a "fairly coherent social movement, with a well-defined subculture . . . distinctive social bases, and an ideology which, beneath the many disputes, is surprisingly consistent and widely shared."

They are, for example, disenchanted with the so-called wishy-washy liberals and the complacent working class. They identify with underdogs all over the world and are scathingly critical of American affluence, which, they assume, has been achieved by exploitation of underdeveloped countries everywhere. America, in their view, is responsible for most of the world's political and social problems.

The same equation is applied to the Middle East, where Israel is more highly industrialized and better off than any of her neighbours. Israel is blamed for differences in economic level and social development in the Middle East in much the same way that the United States is blamed for the poverty in Latin America or Africa. Israel is guilty, too, of having been the victor in three wars against the Arabs. The genesis of these wars is not considered relevant; the Arabs, as the economic and military underdogs, are assured automatically of New Left sympathy and support. The Jewish community in the United States and Israel in the Middle East are seen as part of the affluent Establishment and hence as legitimate targets of New Left obloquy.

The essential consistency of New Left attitudes emerges from within the movement, too. Carl Oglesby, an early SDS leader and editor of the *New Left Reader,* writes that "there only *seems* to be a profusion of conflicting radical positions in the New Left. In fact, there is just one position and it is very main line in its elements. . . ."[7]

To say, then, that *the* New Left is anti-Zionist and contemptuous of Jewish values is not to confuse the whole with individual parts; it is a justified characterization of the movement, a characterization which holds for most Jews within the movement as well as for non-Jews.

It is a truism—for reasons which Seymour Martin Lipset gives us in his essay in this volume—that the Jews were an important source of mass support for the various radical movements in Eastern Europe, although they were not the prime movers of either yesterday's left or today's New Left movements. The old left Jews fought Zionism as a counterrevolutionary force and as an obstacle, too, to their ready escape from their Jewishness and their integration into the promised brave new world of the communist revolution. In this respect there has been no change in the left; there is no generation gap between the old and the new. An important difference between the radicals of the twenties and thirties, however, and those of the sixties and seventies is that the earlier Jewish radicals were prepared to sacrifice their Jewish identity—and Zionism—on the altar of party discipline and party loyalty, and they were the most outspoken damners of their own people's interests. Today there is a growing Jewish radical movement which does not feel that its radical purity is sullied by defense of Israel and a commitment to Jewish values.

7. Carl Oglesby, "Notes of an Old Leftist," *Center Magazine* of the Center for the Study of Democratic Institutions, Santa Barbara, California (May 1970), pp. 84-87.

We have our self-haters today, too, of course. The most extreme expression of this hatred has come, perhaps, from Michael Lerner of Berkeley, who puts Marx ahead of the prophets, since it was Marx who "took their inspiration and began to deal with the social world."[8] But apparently before even Marxism will be able to reach the young, "the synagogue as currently established will have to be smashed." He goes on to a sweeping indictment of the entire religious establishment: "Anyone who is familiar with the internal politics of the United Synagogue, the Union of American Hebrew Congregations, the Synagogue Council of America, etc., knows that they are sewers which allow of no significant reform. The demand of the Jewish radical must be: 'Shut down the synagogue, so that Judaism may have a chance.'" Similarly, disbanding the orchestras would perhaps give music a chance. But there is worse to come: Jewish community institutions have within them no saving remnant, and the Jewish community itself "is racist, internally corrupt, and an apologist for the worst aspects of American capitalism and materialism." Can blind self-hatred go any further? It can, indeed, and does. Turning his attention to black anti-Semitism, Lerner teaches us that

> no matter how inappropriate a response [it is] from the black community, [it] is nevertheless a disgrace to Jews: for this is not an anti-Semitism rooted in a long tradition of irrational hatred of the Christ-killers but rather rooted in the concrete fact of oppression by Jews of blacks in the ghetto. In short, this anti-Semitism is in part an earned anti-Semitism.

This, despite the fact than an overwhelming proportion of ghetto slumlords today are not Jews but blacks themselves, and in the face of the testimony of James Baldwin, a black who should know the black mind somewhat more intimately than a Jewish professor in Berkeley can: Baldwin sees the roots of black anti-

8. Michael P. Lerner, "Jewish New Leftism at Berkeley," *Judaism* (Fall 1969), pp. 473–478.

Semitism not in the conflict with Jewish slumlords or Jewish school teachers, but in Christianity.

Nor does Lerner spare American Zionists, who "are out-and-out tools of the U.S. State Department, switching their line on almost every question to suit U.S. needs." And it is not only religion and Zionism which they corrupt: "The hypocrisy and self-delusion of the Jewish community are not limited to its approach to Zionism. In almost every area the young Jew finds little but the stink of moral decay. Issues and concerns that have intrinsic merit are completely spoiled and dirtied by the handling they receive from Jewish organizations." Fortunately, Lerner speaks only for himself and the New Left splinter group he formed, the Committee for a Progressive Middle East.

Still another splinter group, the Radical Jewish Union of Columbia University, disrupted services at Temple Emanu-El in New York, demanding help to raise a $100,000 defense fund for Black Panther leaders, lest these young radicals move "from demonstration to demolition." But the Black Panthers, to judge from their own magazine, are more interested in demolition—if not of Temple Emanu-El, of Israel. A caption in their own magazine (August 30, 1969) reads: "Panthers, vanguard supporters of Arab liberation," and in another issue the *Black Panther* ran a cartoon depicting a dead pig riddled with bullets, labeled "world Zionism."

Richard C. Hottelet, CBS radio network news commentator, reported on Friday, January 30, 1970, that the Fatah "guerrilla organization is discussing training Black Panthers in actual combat against Israel to prepare them for a sabotage assassination campaign in the United States." Warm statements of support for the communist-armed Arab terrorists are often found in the official publications of the Black Panther party. Lest it be thought that the Black Panthers are merely anti-Israel, the June 1967 issue of *Black Power,* the forerunner of the Panther's official publication, the *Black Panther,* ran the following:

We're gonna burn their towns and that ain't all
We're gonna piss upon the Wailing Wall
And then we'll get Kosygin and de Gaulle
That will be ecstasy, killing every Jew we see in Jewland.

Stokely Carmichael was given prime time on such programs as the "David Frost Show." Speaking at the convention of the Organization of Arab Students on August 31, 1968, he said: "We have begun to see the evil of Zionism, and we will fight to wipe it out wherever it exists, be it in the Ghetto of the United States or in the Middle East."

Another issue of the *Black Panther* contains an admiring story about Al Fatah, which "pioneered . . . the road of armed struggle which brooks no false solutions, does not recognize the so-called peaceful solution, and knows only the gun as the sole means to achieve victory." Al Fatah is nothing if not consistent: it rejected the U.S. cease-fire proposals and the ensuing attempts to arrive at a peaceful solution of the Middle East conflict, and Palestinian guerrillas kidnapped a Jordanian newspaper editor known to be in favor of a negotiated peace. Al Fatah's program for Israel, as enunciated in the official Palestine National Covenant, bases itself on the assertion that Israeli Jews are neither a nation nor even a people and thus have no right to national self-determination (Article 20).[9] Only those Jews who were living permanently in Palestine "until the beginning of the Zionist invasion" will be considered Palestinians and permitted to remain (Article 6). The date of that invasion, according to the 1968 Covenant, was 1917, when the Jewish population was 40,000, as compared to two and a half million today. Al Fatah, then, is calling for the extermination or expulsion of almost 99 percent of the Israeli Jews. Against this background, any talk of Al Fatah wanting a binational state is delusory. Yasir

9. The full text of the Palestine National Covenant appeared most recently in *Jewish Frontier* (October 1970), pp. 7-10; and in *Midstream* (March 1970), pp. 14-18, with brief comments.

Arafat, the Fatah leader, made the Palestinian position clear enough when he said, "Peace for us means Israel's destruction and nothing else. Palestine is only a small drop in the great Arab ocean. Our nation is the Arab nation, extending from the Atlantic to the Red Sea, and beyond."

While Al Fatah's English propaganda calls for "a democratic, nonsectarian [or secular] Palestine where Jews, Muslims, and Christians will work, worship, and live peacefully together while enjoying equal rights and obligations," their Arabic pamphlets take a somewhat different approach. A Fatah publication, "Tahrir Al Aktar al Muhtala Wauslub Alfikah Dhid Al Istiimar Almubashar" (The Liberation of the Occupied Lands and the Struggle Against Direct Imperialism) includes the following points:

> The liberation action is not only the removal of an armed imperialist base; but, more important, *it is the destruction of a society*. [Our] armed violence will be expressed in many ways. In addition to the destruction of the military force of the Zionist occupying state, it will also be turned towards the *destruction of the means of life* of Zionist society in all their forms—industrial, agricultural, and financial. The armed violence must seek to *destroy the military, political, economic, financial, and ideological institutions* of the Zionist occupying state, so as to prevent any possibility of the growth of a new Zionist society.
>
> The aim of the Palestine Liberation War is not only to inflict a military defeat but also *to destroy* the Zionist character of the occupied land, *whether it is human or social*.

This is Al Fatah's program; English-language pamphlets and statements to the world press are simply tactical ploys intended to lull opposition to Al Fatah's planned genocide. That Arab guerrillas identify *Jew* with *Zionist* or *Israeli* was dramatized during the four-plane hijacking of last September, when they permitted non-Jewish women and children to leave the planes for hotels in Amman, while all Jews—Israeli and American alike—were lumped together and forced to remain in the planes.

The same issue of the *Black Panther* which paid high tribute to Al Fatah carried a full-page ad of the International Committee to Support Eldridge Cleaver, then head of the Ministry of Information of the Black Panthers. It was signed by a group of sponsors including Allen Ginsberg, Herbert Gold, Norman Mailer, Paul Jacobs, Nat Rentoff, Susan Sontag, Arthur Waskow, Jules Feiffer, Maurice Zeitlin, Noam Chomsky, Theodore Soltaroff, and others. Cleaver was quoted in the *New York Times* (31 December 1969) as saying, "The Black Panther party in the United States fully supports Arab guerrillas in the Middle East." The *Times* further reported that Cleaver, in an interview with an Algerian newspaper, maintained that "Zionists wherever they may be, are our enemies. . . ."

A more recent issue of the *Black Panther* (24 October 1970) hailed Leila Khaled, the PFLP (Popular Front for the Liberation of Palestine) guerrilla hijacker (whose effort to hijack an El-Al airliner on September 6 was foiled) as a "revolutionary sister." And in an interview which appeared in the Fall 1970 issue of *Leviathan*, a leftist magazine, Khaled declared:

> The Black Panther party has come out in support of the Popular Front and the Al Fatah resistance movement, and I am with the black revolutionaries because they are defending their rights as human beings. And I'm with them in their revolutions against what is called a democratic government in the United States. It is not at all a democratic government. I hope they can have their rights, and they can't have their rights except by force. Force is the only way they can be had.

In an advertisement in the *New York Times* (1 November 1970), a group of 50 black Americans lashed out at United States support of Israel and expressed their solidarity with their "Palestinian brothers and sisters." Many of them are supporters, sympathizers, and well-known activists connected with the left-wing movement. They demanded "that all military aid or assistance of any kind to Israel must stop. Imperialism and Zionism must and will get out of the Middle East. We call for Afro-American solidarity with the Palestinian people's struggle for national liberation and to regain all of their stolen land." A number of signatories were identified as members of the Socialist Workers party, a Trotskyist organization which expresses the most virulent anti-Zionist, anti-Israel views in the left-wing movement. Several other signatories are leaders in the civil rights movement, including Phil Hutchings, former chairman of the Student Nonviolent Coordinating Committee (SNCC); the Reverend Albert B. Cleague of Detroit; Robert Williams, who returned recently from several years of exile in Cuba and China after fleeing his home in Monroe, North Carolina, where he had been involved in organizing the self-defense of the black community; Florence R. Kennedy, a New York attorney; and Florence Beal, a leader of the Third World Women's Alliance.

The statement expressed solidarity with the three major Arab guerrilla groups and singled out an anti-Zionist group within Israel as proof that anti-Zionism exists even among Jews. This group is the Israeli Socialist Organization, or Matzpen, which calls for the dismantling of the Israeli state and hews to the line of the Democratic Popular Front for the Liberation of Palestine, led by Dr. Nayef Hawetmeh.

The signatories, who call themselves the Committee of Black Americans for Truth About the Middle East,[10] also claimed that the United States was responsible for "the slaughter of Palestinian refugees and freedom fighters" because of its financial and moral support of the Hussein government during the Jordanian civil war. Moreover, they asserted, without giving any facts or proof to back their statement, that

> Israel supported the United States in the Korean War; aided
> France and the Terrorist Secret Army Organization in

10. This is an ad hoc group, which does not represent any significant segment of the black community. It was reportedly set up by the predominantly white Socialist Workers party.

Algeria against the Algerian revolution; opposed the anticolonial independence movements in Morocco, Tunisia, Indonesia and elsewhere; trained the counterrevolutionary paracommandos of General Mobuto, who was one of the persons responsible for the murder of Patrice Lumumba in the Congo; and presently provides arms and equipment to the Portuguese troops fighting against the Angolan and Mozambican freedom fighters.

In striking contrast, Whitney Young, Jr., executive director of the National Urban League, rejected "the myth of Arab-black friendship" in a letter reiterating his support of American military aid to Israel. "I know of no real aid oil-rich Arab countries have given the struggling new nations of black Africa, although the Israelis have a very impressive program of technical assistance of the no-strings-attached variety, even in nations that take the Arab line in the UN," he wrote in reply to a critic objecting to his signature on a *New York Times* advertisement in support of Israel.[11] Until peace comes to the Middle East, he wrote, "I would continue to favor providing Israel with the weapons she needs to defend herself against those who have sworn to destroy her." Young further asserted, "Arab history and culture is replete with instances of racial prejudice. Today, the Arab rulers of the Sudan are waging a merciless war against the black people of the southern region of that country, and Arabs in Chad are at war with the black government of that country."

Young said he was unaware of what his critic called the "Arab Revolution." He wrote: "If the Arab nations had really been concerned with improving 'the social, economic, and political existences' of their people, they would long ago have ceased threatening to push Israel into the sea and concentrated their energies on improving the lives of their people." In his letter, Young contrasted the situation in the Arab countries as well as institutional racism in America with Israeli efforts on behalf

11. Young's letter, dated 7 October 1970, was released by the American Jewish Congress, which reprinted it for distribution among its members.

of its growing population of Oriental Jews: "My 1969 visit to Israel impressed upon me the fact that Israelis are acutely conscious of the gap afflicting their Oriental population and are taking steps—educational and economic—to close it." He observed that the Oriental Jews of Israel came to that country to flee "the most brutal kind of religious oppression and social and economic discrimination."

The advertisement signed by Young in the *New York Times* (28 June 1970) was sponsored by the A. Philip Randolph Institute. It was also signed by 64 Negro leaders of organizations, elected officials, educators, and businessmen. It urged "our government to take steps to help guarantee Israel's right to exist as a nation." In his letter explaining his stand, Young sharply rejected criticism of Israel's occupation of former Arab territories. He noted that the Israeli occupation of the West Bank has been "the most lenient armed occupation in history. Despite the repeated acts of armed terrorism, West Bank Arabs enjoy self-government under the leaders appointed by the Jordanians, publish anti-Israeli newspapers, and freely propagandize against the Israelis, an extraordinary situation." He added that West Bank Arabs have found jobs and higher pay within Israel itself, have joined the Histadrut, and receive equal pay in employment and other benefits. Young observed that in the years preceding the Israeli occupation, Arab citizens were "brutalized and mercilessly exploited by the Jordanian ruling classes."

Despite the sentiment in the June advertisement and in Young's letter, a leading black newspaperman, Howard B. Woods, editor and publisher of the *St. Louis Sentinel*, warned that although black Americans are generally sympathetic to Israel, a "rising tide of pro-Arab feeling rooted in a variety of causes is becoming increasingly evident among segments of black militants, intellectuals, and persons living in the inner cities." The popular pattern of most black militants, he said, "is to be antiestablishment. Since they view the establishment as being pro-Israel, they feel they must be pro-Arab." Woods said that anti-Israel feelings among black people in underdeveloped urban areas could possibly be attributed to "long-dormant attitudes on domestic conditions rather than being based on international situations." Whatever the causes, they do not mitigate the dangers inherent in this sentiment, both for Israel and for Israel's supporters, Jewish or otherwise.

At the time of this writing, there has been no reaction from Jewish Panther supporters to a *New York Times* report of a visit to Amman by a Black Panther delegation which declared its full support to the guerrillas, rejected the Rogers-proposed peace talks then scheduled to begin, and reiterated the by now familiar call for elimination of the "Zionist entity."

Some time ago a group of 145 left-wing students from Europe, Asia, and Africa attended a five-week summer camp run by Al Fatah near Amman. They included about 20 Germans, 30 Britons, 20 Frenchmen, and a mixed company from America, Scandinavia, Holland, Switzerland, and Italy. SDS headquarters in Frankfurt wanted "to clear up the differences of opinion amongst us on the correct assessment of the several liberation movements." When asked why they did not, in all fairness, also send some of their people to Tel Aviv, the reply was: "We'll go to Israel only when it has become socialist."

Discussing this "pilgrimage" to Amman and the strange figures that socialist Germans cut among Arab terrorists, C. C. Aronsfeld refers to the "no less bizarre" group of Jews who came with them to do their stint in the anti-Zionist campaign.

> They offered a pathetic spectacle as they strove to justify themselves before the refugees. They had come, they averred, despite their Jewish origin, animated by the very highest ideals of the class struggle which made them allies of the Arab enemies of Israel. The gesture of dialectical self-mutilation went sadly unappreciated. The Arabs, confirming the suspicions of their ideological inadequacy, shook angry fists as these incredible "anti-Zionists," treating them to what an earwitness called "the outdated categories of religion and nationalism."[12]

12. C. C. Aronsfeld, "New Left Germans and El Fatah," *Jewish Frontier* (October 1969), pp. 21-23.

Here is an appalling instance of self-hatred not simply in word, but in deed.

Non-Jewish leftists have not waited for either Lerner or the Radical Jewish Union to provide their cue, although Jewish self-hatred has certainly not discouraged them from developing their own line of anti-Jewish propaganda. The Anti-Defamation League of B'nai B'rith—one of Lerner's sewers of corruption— has pointed to new major manifestations of anti-Jewish attitudes among minority extremist elements within the black community, which have reacted to white racism with a black racism all their own, and "among extreme left groups which eschew the racist forms of anti-Semitism but, taking their cue from the Soviet and Chinese worlds, nevertheless heap virulent abuse on Israel and all who look with favor on the Jewish State."

Concerning the reference to blacks, the ADL report specified the Black Panthers, the Black Muslims, and the African-American Student Association. These groups have all assumed strong pro-Arab positions. They equate their own racial, social, and economic status in the United States with that of the Palestinians in the Middle East. Since the United States supports Israel, Israel is, "objectively speaking," the agent of white Western imperialism. Among New Left groups sharing these attitudes the ADL listed the Weathermen faction of SDS, Revolutionary Movement II, the Young Workers Liberation League (Communist party), the Young Socialist Alliance (Trotskyist Socialist Workers party), and the Maoist Progressive Labor party.

The ADL report went on to describe the three black groups as among those "which have become purveyors of pro-Arab, anti-Israel propaganda of the most blatant variety and often with a zeal that can only be compared with the worst gutter-level anti-Semitism." And it emphasizes the point that "on the extreme left . . . there is a concerted, energetic campaign of intense hostility towards Israel, and active support of Al Fatah and other guerrilla groups." The ADL singles out the Young Socialist Alliance as the most active anti-Israel organization on campus today.

As we know from the Soviet example on the left and from anti-Semites such as Gerald L. K. Smith on the right, the identification of Jews as Zionists is a hoary and transparent device to mask what might otherwise be an anti-Semitism too blatant for a generally tolerant American society. The *Black Panther*, for example, has repeatedly referred to a slumlord as a "racist Zionist." But even that mask is dropping as permissiveness comes to include acceptance of extremes in language and ideas as well as in clothing and hairstyles, and the anti-Semitism is becoming more openly and more brutally expressed. A well-informed source within the black community predicts an upsurge in black anti-Semitism even beyond the levels it has already reached.

The ADL report seems to have missed identifying an interesting group—The Committee on New Alternatives in the Middle East, an umbrella organization for left-wing opposition to Israel. Its first activity was to bring Aryeh Bober to the United States on a national speaking tour. Bober is the leader of a miniscule (one hundred-member) Israeli New Left student group, the Israel Socialist Organization, a splinter of the Israeli Communist party, which itself split into two separate organizations, Maki and Rakah. The ISO is often referred to as Matzpen (Compass), after the name of the periodical it publishes.

Carl Gershman, writing in *Commentary*, reports on Bober's appearance at Columbia and on the formation of the committee which sponsored him.[13] Noam Chomsky's letter to a list of distinguished intellectuals, inviting them to join, stated that the group would "take no specific stand on the Middle East." He described Matzpen as "a small, non-Zionist, Jewish-Arab organization which recognizes the national rights of both Jews and Arabs in Palestine" and believes that reconciliation between them depends upon "a profound social transformation" of the entire area. Gershman reports that Bober delivered himself of a "sweeping, unsparing, and at times virulent . . . indictment

13. Carl Gershman, "'Matzpen' and Its Sponsors," *Commentary* (August 1970), pp. 52-53.

of Israel. He described Israel as 'National Socialist,' declared that she was like any oppressor throughout history, and associated Zionism with the crimes of fascism, colonialism, and imperialism." Bober was neutral, according to Gershman, on the subject of the Arab governments, but "he ardently endorsed the Palestinian guerrillas. 'We must support the Palestinian revolution without any precondition,' he said. 'It is the right of oppressed people to fight against oppression by any means they see fit.'"

Barry Gray interviewed Bober on radio and, after listening to a half hour of anti-Israel, proterrorist rantings, wondered aloud how he had been "suckered" into inviting Bober to begin with. Bober's intemperate attack on Israel and his claim that most of his Matzpen membership had been imprisoned by the Israeli government for their political views were rejected out of hand by Gray's panel, one member of which dismissed Bober's views as being essentially irrelevant.

This is the spokesman for a group Chomsky described as "non-Zionist." It is that, of course, but it is, first of all, anti-Zionist and opposes the very existence of "a Zionist Israel." Gershman put his finger on the semantic sleight of hand displayed in the invitation: "Chomsky noted in his letter that Matzpen advocates a 'profound transformation' of the Middle East. What he neglected to mention was that this transformation involves the dissolution of the State of Israel." Chomsky's modest footnote 5, on page 207 of this volume, to the contrary notwithstanding, it would seem that "any rational observer" who claims Matzpen supports the Arabs is neither fabricating nor falsifying.

Chomsky's references to a secular state is a popular New Left ploy and has become a cliché of New Left and Palestinian propaganda. The advertisement of the Committee of Black Americans for Truth About the Middle East includes in its diatribe what purports to be a statement made by Al Fatah's Yasir Arafat in January, 1969, describing his political vision of a free Palestine as "a democratic, secular, nonracial state. . . ."

But is that what Arafat and his friends really want? In an interview with the Cairo newspaper *Al-Gumhuriya*[14] on January 6, 1970, exactly one year later, Arafat rejected at least part of the vision imputed to him. He stated:

> We have raised our slogan of establishing a democratic state in Palestine in which Muslims, Christians, and Jews will live together . . . but we have not raised the slogan calling for the establishment of a secular state. What happened was that the French writer Ania Francos, authoress of the book *The Palestinians*, in several articles she published, spread, in the name of the Palestinian revolution, the slogan calling for the establishment of a secular state, but I believe this to be a distortion of the term *democracy* as we embrace it.

However, a resolution introduced to the Palestine National Congress in 1969 by the Democratic Popular Front for the Liberation of Palestine uses the term *democratic* but does not include *secular*. That resolution and Arafat's statement to the Cairo paper were for Arab consumption and certainly reflect their real sentiments; English-language statements are obviously for propaganda purposes. Score another red herring.

Nor should there by any lingering doubts as to Chomsky's own stand. He described himself as a "non-Zionist socialist" when he addressed a convention of the Arab-American University Graduates in Evanston, Illinois. Seth King, in the *New York Times* (2 November 1970), reported that Chomsky said that he believed there were Israelis who were willing to consider creating a secular state in which both the Palestinians and the Israelis would share in the federal government and all Palestinian Arabs would have the right to return to their old homes. "Certainly it would mean some abandonment of independence," he said, "but this would be a small price compared with the loss Israel and the Palestinians are now suffering through their grow-

---

14. Quoted by Menachem S. Arnoni in an unpublished manuscript, *A Leftist Re-Examination of the Arab-Israeli Conflict.*

ing dependence on other groups, including the great powers."

If there is any question as to what he means by "some abandonment of independence" (is he "just a little pregnant" with a solution?), it is clarified by the requirement that all Palestinian Arabs be permitted to return. This is precisely what Al Fatah proposes. Chomsky's solution, in fact, is similar to that proposed by Al Fatah and, as reported by both the *New York Times* and the *Jewish Telegraphic Agency*, far more extreme than the kind of settlement that Arab states such as Jordan and Egypt profess to favor. No wonder the convention delegates were unanimous in supporting it!

But, as mentioned previously, there are other Jewish radicals as well—young men and women who shared in "the shock of recognition" which swept over the entire Jewish world just prior to the Six-Day War of June, 1967, and were appalled by the sudden about-face of friends and colleagues who decided that their sympathies belonged with Goliath after all. The proliferation of young Jewish radical groups comes just when there is a growing disillusionment with the New Left, as detailed in the League for Industrial Democracy report of an extensive survey of student leaders in the late spring of 1970.[15]

M. Jay Rosenberg is credited by Bill Novak, editor of *Response* (one of the leading journals produced by college students) with having sparked the growth of the underground Jewish press.[16] Writing in New York's *Village Voice*, Rosenberg, then a senior at the State University of New York in Albany, lashed out at those American leftists "who put down everything Jewish," and who are willing to fight everybody else's struggle for liberation while denying their own:

> . . . All those Jewish students . . . who are prepared to die for the Vietnamese, the Biafrans, the Greeks, and the Czechs

15. See Tom Kahn's article in this volume.
16. Bill Novak, "The Underground Jewish Press—A Look at the New Jewish Student Newspapers," unpublished manuscript.

yet who reject Israel—these are our . . . shame. The Jew must accept his identity; he's not just another white man. It's time he realizes he's a Jew, and he'd better accept it. . . . A man who cannot accept his own identity is a hypocrite and a liar when he pretends to accept someone else's.

And Rosenberg goes on to state his own position:

From this point on I shall join no movement that does not accept and support my people's struggle. If I must choose between the Jewish cause and a "progressive" anti-Israel SDS, I shall choose the Jewish cause. If barricades are erected, I will fight as a Jew.[17]

In a recent issue of *Midstream* Rosenberg outlines his evolution as a Jew, from his "most superficial" Jewish education as a boy in upstate New York, growing up in a left-liberal home, to what he sees as his political coming of age in the days immediately before and following the Six-Day War. What he emerged with is a philosophy he shares with thousands of other young Jews, who, as he says, "will not surrender their identity just so they can be accepted by their 'revolutionary peers.' Nor will they give up their radicalism to accommodate the Jewish establishment." He continues:

What we say is this: We are radicals. We actively oppose the war in Vietnam. We support the black liberation movement as we endorse all genuine movements of liberation. And thus, first and foremost, we support our own. We will march with our brothers on the left. We will support them.

But when they call for the death of Israel, when they acquiesce in plans for the liquidation of the Jewish state, we then have no choice but to fight them. We shall denounce anti-Semitism whether it emanates from the right or the left. There is no such thing as "progressive anti-Semitism." And we shall not allow the "revolutionaries" to escape our indictment of racism by claiming that they are "anti-Zionist but not anti-Semitic." If they can reconcile themselves to the existence of every nation on the planet but Israel, if they

17. M. Jay Rosenberg, "To Uncle Tom and Other Such Jews," *Village Voice* (13 February 1969).

call for revolution in every country but only death for
Israel, then they are clearly against the Jewish people. One
may call them what he will.[18]

The radical Zionism reflected in Rosenberg's credo is that
of a growing movement. While affirming Zionism—and Judaism
—they react to the social ills of the country and of the world
as socialists and radicals. Among the activist groups which have
arisen on American campuses to reinterpret Jewish concerns
both in America and Israel are: the Jewish Student Movement
(Northwestern); the Jewish Action Committee (Wayne State);
Kadimah (Columbia); the Jewish Student Union (LIU, CCNY,
Indiana, Philadelphia, and Berkeley); the Maccabees (University
of Florida); and many others which call themselves simply
American Students for Israel.

The Jewish Students Unions at Berkeley and at Philadelphia
are affiliated—directly, since there is no countrywide Jewish
student union in the United States—to the World Union of
Jewish Students (WUJS), which in most countries coordinates
Jewish student activities and speaks in the name of the Jewish
students.

Students have also created major intellectual forums for
the discussion of issues vital to the Middle East at Harvard,
Yale, Boston University, and Brandeis, among others.

Off-campus groups have proliferated, too. Some are primarily
concerned with social action, such as Na'aseh (Philadelphia),
Jews for Urban Justice (Washington, D.C.), and the New
Jewish Committee (Minneapolis). Others, like the Havurat
Shalom (Boston) and the Havurah (New York) are concerned
with religious questions.

To these must be added the Jewish Liberation Project (centered
in New York), the Youth Committee for Peace and Democracy
in the Middle East (New York), and the Committee for
Social Justice in the Middle East (Canada).

18. M. Jay Rosenberg, "My Evolution as a Jew," *Midstream* (August/
September 1970) pp. 50–53.

Most of these publish their own newspapers, some more and some less regularly. There are presently at least 20—some claim 40—such periodicals with a combined circulation of well over three hundred thousand, and new ones are constantly being born.[19]

Although the quality of these publications varies, some of them are well written indeed, and among them they cover a broad spectrum of subjects ranging from the Middle East to the American scene and Soviet Jewry. They include articles on Al Fatah and the Palestinians; the New Left and the Black Panthers; the state of Jewish education and Jewish community life and institutions; Martin Buber; Moshe Dayan; Isaac Luria; and Rabbi Nahman of Bratslav. One publication offers an Uncle Jake Award—the recipient being roughly the Jewish equivalent of the classic Uncle Tom—while another excoriates the Jewish Defense League as a rightist, vigilante excresence. They are all distinguished by forthright, uninhibited writing and sometimes an eagerness to belabor even the obvious.

19. The youngest is probably the *Jewish Free Press*, published by the Council of Jewish Organizations at Columbia University. Their first—rather modest— issue appeared only last December (1970).

Among the better-known of these "underground" student newspapers are: *Genesis 2* (Cambridge, Mass.); *ACIID* (A Call for Insight Into Israel's Dilemmas, Washington University, St. Louis); the *Jewish Liberation Journal* (New York); *Other Stand* (McGill University, Montreal); *Mosaic* (Concerned Jewish Students, Harvard-Radcliffe Hillel, Cambridge, Mass.); the *Source* (University of Hartford); *Doreinu* (Our Generation, the Washington-Baltimore Union of Jewish Students); the *Jewish Radical* (Berkeley Union of Jewish Students, University of California); *Ha-Orah* (The Light, a "National" Jewish student paper, California); the *Flame* (Jewish Student Union, CCNY, New York); *Dawn* (Long Island University, New York); *Irgun* (Duke University); the *New England Free Press; Masada* (Progressive Students for Israel, York University, Toronto); *Coalescence* (University of Toronto); *House 4-Rum* (Michigan); *Ha-Peh* (The Mouth, Northeastern); *Hashomer* (The Watchman, Durham).

Network (North American Jewish Students Network—affiliated with the WUJS) was changed from a mimeographed, sporadically appearing publication to a well-printed information and reference service, a "transcontinental bulletin board and informational channel" to supplement—and assist—the independent local papers.

On a considerably more ambitious scale—and on a more professional level—is *Response, A Contemporary Jewish Review.* Originally published at Columbia "to examine the vitality and relevance of Judaism to personal development and community progress," it has grown from a two-dozen page semi-annual to an 80 or more page quarterly. Now located on the campus of Brandeis University, it remains an independent journal. *Davka* (Exactly!), launched by the Hillel Organizing Project in Los Angeles "to explore those problems which cast their weight on the hearts and minds of the Jewish people," devoted its first issue (November/December 1970) to "The Ills of American Jewry," and will focus each issue on one theme (the second issue is to deal with alternative "Jewish Life Styles" in the United States and in Israel). Both of these journals include articles and poetry, and the first has included fiction as well.

Internationally, the World Union of Jewish Students publishes its own journal, *Forum,* over a hundred double-column pages of rather weighty material and news of Union activities.

That the new radical groups are having an affect upon the student scene may be reflected by the fact that at the SDS conference in Austin, Texas, SDSers themselves rejected an attempt by their former national secretary to push through a resolution condemning Israel and supporting Al Fatah. At the same time, new Jewish radicals have successfully demanded courses in Jewish studies at many of their universities; these demands have been so successful that there are now more posts available than qualified men to fill them.

This contemporary Jewish college student is far removed from his predecessor of the pre-Israel era both in his attitudes toward Zionism and towards his Jewishness. He is no longer impressed by the sterile and destructive attitudes of the New Left. He is impressed by the differences between the United States and tiny Israel, fighting in the fourth year of its Six-Day War, with 25 percent and more of its Gross National Product committed to defense needs and every able-bodied male up to the age of fifty-six subject to call-up in the reserves. Yet, Israel finds the funds and the manpower for other projects too: a growing network of universities; encouragement of the intellectual life generally; constant improvement in health services; and a vastly expanded housing program. To support all of these advances, Israelis willingly pay higher and higher taxes and do with fewer and fewer consumer goods.

In the United States, on the other hand, the young Jewish radical is part of an affluent community where there is a complete absence of any war drain—where there is no one who cannot buy a suit or take a vacation because of any war-imposed belt tightening. Nevertheless, the president vetos housing, health, and education bills, and there is a cutting back of essential services to those who need them most.

New Left denigration of Israel and extravagant praise of Arab socialism no longer blind this young radical to the political realities in the Middle East either, and he is developing a point of view and an approach based on his newly rediscovered Jewish values and ideals rather than on outmoded slogans and self-hatred. For him, in the changing American-Jewish scene and in Israel he may well, with Bettelheim, find the frontiers where he can test his manhood and feel needed, or, with Bell, lose his sense of alienation by participating in a social revolution in which he is essential rather than peripheral.

Many of those who have undergone this historic evolution or transformation attribute it to Israel's victory in the Six-Day War and to the fear of another holocaust, which preceded it. Robert Alter, one of the contributors to this volume, summed up the new Jew in *Commentary*, just four months after the war:

> . . . the Jews of Israel have chosen definitively to enter into a new relationship as collectively responsible agents in history, with all the complicated burden of practical and moral choices, all the tensions between values and actions, ideals and actuality, implied by such involvement in the mixed stuff of reality. The founding of the state has introduced a

qualitative change in the facts of existence for every Jew, whether or not he chooses to be a Zionist. Israel's very presence among the nations is an affirmation that the Jews are not symbols, witnesses, ghostly emissaries of some obscure mission, but men like other men who need to occupy physical space in a real world before they can fulfill whatever loftier aspirations they may have.[20]

Israel's victory was a profoundly unsettling experience for a good many Jewish intellectuals, almost as unsettling as the creation of the state itself. And the changes required of them by both events are being made slowly and often painfully. There are still those who are impressed by what seems to be the New Left concern for all of mankind, but more and more of the present college generation are discovering that for concern to have meaning, it must be translated into action, and that there is a limit to the number of trumpets to which one can respond. They are responding, in growing numbers, to their own.

20. Robert Alter, "Israel and the Jewish Intellectuals," *Commentary* (October 1967), p. 51.

10   Israel and the new left

*Who speaks for the New Left? The best we can say is
that although each leftist claims to speak for himself
only, there are those who are, in the view of outsiders,
considered New Left spokesmen. One of these is Noam
Chomsky, who denies that the New Left is anti-Israel.
There is no movement doctrine on Israel, he writes,
but there is a lot of confusion, a lot of unhappiness, and
some, though rather limited, debate. There is a great
deal of sympathy for the socialist elements within the
Jewish and Arab national movements, and this is combined with a genuine fear that national movements can
do enormous harm if they subordinate the struggle for
social reconstruction to national aims. The New Left
includes Zionist critics, says Chomsky, but this does
not imply that they are self-hating Jews.*

*Chomsky believes that American hardliners would
like nothing better than to be able to identify the New
Left as totally pro-Arab and anti-Israel—in favor of
sweeping the Jews into the sea and supporting or
applauding Russian-backed genocide in the Middle
East. This would be a marvelous way to discredit the
rising challenge to American militarism. And at this
point, unfortunately, he sees Western Zionism as lend-
ing a helping hand.*

When I accepted the invitation to speak on the topic "Israel and
the New Left," I made it clear that I cannot speak as an expert
on the Middle East or the New Left, and that I of course do not
appear as a "spokesman" for the New Left, whatever this might
mean. In fact, as anyone who has the slightest familiarity with
the New Left would understand at once, it is quite impossible
to identify a definite New Left doctrine on this, as on most other

NOAM CHOMSKY *is Professor of Modern Language and Linguistics,
Massachusetts Institute of Technology.*

197

matters. The New Left is a highly decentralized, very loose grouping of mostly young people who share certain points of view, but on most matters are quite divided in their opinions. Someone who speaks of the "New Left position" on the Middle East at once betrays his ignorance of the character and activities of the New Left.

My only qualifications to speak on this subject are a good deal of sympathy with much that has been done by the so-called "New Left" and some degree of involvement in its activities, and a deep concern with the problems of Palestine and Israel that goes back to early childhood, but that I have hesitated to express or discuss in any public manner, for reasons to which I will return.

I would like to discuss four topics:

1. New Left attitudes toward Israel.

2. The reactions among many Western intellectuals and political commentators to what they claim to be the New Left attitudes towards Israel.

3. What the likely evolution of this problem—and a severe problem it is—may be in the next few years.

4. What a group such as this might do that would be constructive, in terms of certain values that I suspect many of us more or less share.

I would like to begin by saying that I think that the topic of this symposium is somewhat misconceived. There is, I will suggest, very little to say about attitudes of the New Left to Israel. However, there is a great deal to say about how these attitudes have been depicted and, in my opinion, grossly distorted. This question is one that deserves serious thought and analysis. I believe that in part the reasons for this distortion have more to do with domestic American problems than with the Israel-Arab crisis itself. I will also mention a few examples of irresponsible journalism, the reasons for which I will not attempt to analyze, though I think this matter too deserves attention. I will try to justify and elaborate these conclusions as I proceed.

Consider the first topic: New Left attitudes towards Israel. I will limit myself in this discussion to the student movement, omitting reference to the Black Liberation movement, whose attitudes towards the Middle East must be interpreted in terms of domestic American problems and developments. I will merely say, in this connection, that the widely-voiced claims regarding the alleged anti-Semitism of the Panthers and other groups seem to me severely distorted and misleading, and the thinly-veiled suggestion that they advocate something like genocide or that they can be compared in this respect to Nazis is so ignorant as to deserve no further comment.

There is no New Left doctrine on the Middle East. Rather, there is confusion, unhappiness, some—though limited—debate, and a great deal of sympathy, often at a rather intuitive and barely articulated level, for socialist elements within the Jewish and Arab national movements, combined with a general fear that national movements can do enormous harm if they subordinate the struggle for social reconstruction to purely national aims.

In preparing this discussion, I looked through several New Left anthologies and discovered practically nothing on the Middle East. In most of them, there is no reference at all. One recent anthology, intended primarily as an internal movement document, does contain several comments on the Middle East, specifically about the Kibbutz movement.[1] One comment is in an article of mine, which notes that "an example of major importance [for radicals] is provided by the Palestinian (later Israeli) Kibbutzim," an example that was largely overlooked and undervalued by the "radical centralizers" of the old left. In addition, there are several pages of highly favorable comment on the kibbutz as a model for activists by Rick Margolies, who is con-

1. Priscilla Long, ed., *The New Left* (Boston: Porter Sargent, 1969).

cerned with community organizing and the development of urban cooperatives. Margolies singles out Martin Buber's *Paths in Utopia* as must reading—and indeed, this is a book that ranks high on New Left reading lists.

As a side comment, I might add that there are Zionist critics of the New Left, some even who call themselves socialists, who, if they were to be consistent in the style of their argument, would be forced to consider Buber an anti-Zionist or even an anti-Semite, or perhaps afflicted with "Jewish self-hatred." I return to such criticism in a moment.

I also checked the pamphlet collection put out by the New England Free Press, a major New Left literature center. In a listing of some 200 pamphlets on various topics, there are two on the Middle East. One is by members of the Israeli Socialist Organization (the Matzpen group), which is anti-Zionist and also opposed to all of the Arab states as well as to the position of Al Fatah. A second pamphlet, by Larry Hochman, is highly critical of Zionism and Israeli policy. The author raises the "complicated question of how Israel, as a state, can act so as to bring about the eventual federation which I regard as the best, if not the only possibility for long-term peace." After discussing various possibilities, he concludes:

> It may well be that the price of the continued existence of a state that was born unnaturally is extreme patience in the face of threats and provocations, and great political skill in the face of hostility. It is an historic sorrow that such difficult efforts should be required of the Jews, of all people. It was with great emotion and deep feelings (which I shared) that the survivors of the European horror viewed the birth of Israel only three years later. But only such patience and skill can possibly lead to the survival of a Jewish community in Southwest Asia.

The Africa Research Group has written quite critically of Israeli support for counterinsurgency in Africa. I recall also one series of articles in SDS *New Left Notes,* published shortly before the demise of SDS. It was violently anti-Israel and so extreme that it passed virtually unnoticed, at least among the New Left groups that I had any personal contact with.

To my knowledge, there has been only one issue of a New Left journal that was devoted to an exploration of the problems of the Middle East, namely, the symposium that appeared in *Liberation* in November, 1969. There were four contributors: Gebran Majdalany, Amos Kenan, Paul Jacobs, and myself. Majdalany is a left-wing Beirut intellectual associated with Al Fatah. Kenan is a leftist Israeli journalist, critical of Israeli policy in certain respects and a courageous defender of Arab rights; he is strongly pro-Israel, by any reasonable standards. Jacobs is a radical American writer whose views are rather similar to Kenan's. Thus he concludes by stating that if there is to be peace, Israel must make clear that the "occupation of the territories acquired in June, 1967, will end at that point in the future when the threat of their state being wiped out has ceased to be a daily problem" and "must make public serious proposals for dealing with the rights of the Palestinian Arabs," while the Palestinians "must, minimally, renounce the concept of eliminating the State of Israel." My article discusses possibilities for Arab-Jewish cooperation and suggests that there might "be room for fruitful discussion and perhaps eventual cooperative effort between the Arab and Israeli left"; specifically, "the goal of a democratic socialist community with equal rights for all citizens [a position articulated on the Arab left] and the goal of 'a federative framework with the Kingdom of Jordan and the Palestinian people, based on cooperation in the fields of security and economics' [the formulation of the Israeli writer Haim Darin-Drabkin] do not, on the face of it, appear to be incompatible." Obviously, however, there are many problems and obstacles to be overcome and, equally obviously, "Israel cannot hope to achieve peace on its terms by force," whereas the Palestinians must come to accept the fact that "there is no possibility that the Jewish population of Israel will give up its cultural autonomy, or freely leave or abandon a high degree of self-government."[2]

I would urge the reader who is interested in the actual content of these articles to disregard comments that have appeared in the Israeli and American-Zionist press as well as the reports that have been circulated orally, and turn to the originals. The reports that I have read and heard are quite amazing in their distortion and misrepresentation.

After the Six-Day War a number of articles appeared in various journals by people who are associated, in some fashion, with the New Left. I. F. Stone wrote in the *New York Review* (3 August 1967), speaking from the point of view of someone "closely bound emotionally with the birth of Israel." In words that recall those of the Israeli writer Amos Oz, he speaks of the conflict as a "tragedy," "a struggle of right against right." He expresses great faith in Israeli "zeal and intelligence" and accepts, without question, the right of existence of Israel, while giving no word of support to the Palestinian Arab movements. "Jewry [he writes] can no more turn its back on Israel than Israel on Jewry. The ideal solution would allow the Jews to make their contributions as citizens in the diverse societies and nations which are their homes while Israel finds acceptance as a Jewish state in a renascent Arab civilization." I again urge the reader who may be interested to turn to the original, since Stone's views too have been subjected to the most incredible distortion.[3] I will return to some examples presently.

In the Arden House discussions I heard several references to *Ramparts* as an example of a New Left journal that had taken a militant and uncompromising anti-Israel and pro-Arab position. Since this did not accord with my recollections, I decided

2. My essay appears in full in H. Mason, ed., *Reflections on the Middle East Crisis* (The Hague: Mouton, 1969).
3. It is readily available in Walter Laqueur, ed., *The Israel-Arab Reader* (New York: Bantam, 1969).

to check for myself — and I urge the interested reader to do like-wise.

The July 1967 issue of *Ramparts* was devoted largely to the Israeli-Arab Crisis. An editorial comment observed:

> While there can be no doubt as to the basic legitimacy of the State of Israel, it is tragic that this small nation, which was to be a haven from war's violence, should now be forced to rely for its existence on preemptive military power.

If there is any analogy between the Middle East and Vietnam, the editorial continued, it is

> between the Israelis and the Viet Cong — two fiercely in-dependent nationalist groups, totally convinced of the right-ness of their causes and therefore willing to fight brilliantly and effectively for them. . . .
>
> As it is unreasonable to deny the absolute right of the State of Israel to exist and use international waterways, it is equally unprincipled to maintain that all Arab claims are irrational and that they have no legitimate grievances in the Holy Land.

The editorial denied that "the clash is between Arab socialism and Israel as a tool of American imperialism" (a simplistic view held, according to this editorial, by many in the American left).

There were three contributions to the symposium. In the first, Paul Jacobs presented a general pro-Israel position, com-bined with a warning that military force alone will not bring peace. Michael Walzer and Martin Peretz then presented a justification of Israeli policy against critics of the right and the left. Finally, I. F. Stone spoke of the necessity to search for re-conciliation and urged that "some kind of confederation" should not be beyond the range of ingenuity, with "a predominantly Jewish state, but one linked fraternally with one or two Arab states, one Palestinian, one Jordanian." He also urged that funds from the world Jewish community be diverted to resettlement of refugees, to right the wrong of Palestinian homelessness. "This alone," he wrote, "can make Israel secure." He also argued that in the long run this would be cheaper, as well as far more humane, than an approach through military strength. His article was, as always, pro-Israel and, in this case, highly critical of Nasser (who, he said, ran a police state), though Stone then regarded Nasser as probably the best hope for Egypt.

In September, 1967, Robert Scheer reported from Cairo, arguing that after the Israeli victory, major responsibility for peace rested with Israel, which had an obligation (of an unspecified nature) to the refugees. Israel, he urged, should "initiate a settlement through a third party which will try to return the occupied lands, while at the same time guaranteeing the peace of her borders." He believed that Israel should not try to bring down Nasser, since the alternative was likely to be a far more militaristic Egypt ruled by the Moslem Brotherhood.

In the November issue, Scheer presented a descriptive historical account which, as I read it, expressed no particular political position or sympathies. With respect to the Six-Day War, he held that "Nasser entered the trap of Arab nationalist rhetoric" and that his "irrational Israel policy" cost him dearly.

Robert Scheer had an article in the January 1968 issue, extending his earlier remarks. Here he concentrated on the problem of oil. He formulated the "central thesis" of his two essays of November and January as follows: "The great powers cannot be expected to be concerned, on any consistent basis, with the interests and needs of the Arabs and Jews who live in the Mideast." He wrote:

> The Arab denial of legitimate Jewish nationhood as the basis of Israel is the subject of deserved ridicule. But that the mainstream of Zionism has, in like fashion, denied the existence of a legitimate Arab quest for nationhood is not commonly admitted. . . . The Arab nation and the Jewish nation are both legitimate concepts which can survive together only if they exist as part of the same social revolution to meet the needs of the people of the Mideast. But,

as competing nationalisms of the old model, neither is viable, and the histrionics of a Ben-Gurion or a Nasser cannot alter that fact.

Maurice Zeitlin continued the discussion in the same issue, with an article on the postwar Israeli left. His position was very sympathetic to Israel, which he described as "an egalitarian and democratic society."

I found no other articles in *Ramparts* dealing with the Arab-Israel conflict.

There are, in addition, various radical Jewish groups, in part student-based, in part initiated by well-known New Left activists such as Arthur Waskow. Invariably, to my knowledge, these groups accept the existence of the State of Israel as a predominantly Jewish state without question, though they are generally critical of one or another aspect of Israeli policy.

Herbert Marcuse expressed his views on the problem in an article that appeared in the *New Outlook* (July/August 1968). He begins by speaking of his "personal, though not only personal feelings of solidarity and identification with Israel." He declares his sympathy with the goal of creating for the Jews "a place . . . where they will not need to fear persecution and oppression," and expresses his pleasure that Jean-Paul Sartre "has said that under all circumstances a new war of annihilation against Israel must be prevented. . . . The state [of Israel] is here and an understanding with its inimical neighbors must be found; that is the only solution." He urges that "we all must do what we can to help the representatives of Israel and the Arab states finally to sit down together and discuss their own problems . . . and to try to solve them," and he urges as well that Israel and the Arab states "form a united front against the attacks of the imperialist powers." He also suggests that the "leftist trends" among the Arabs and Israelis are not too far apart, and that perhaps this means that there is "a basis for a direct understanding between these two forces."

Probably a more careful search would unearth other items.

I doubt that it would change the conclusion that I have already formulated and that I now repeat:

> There is no New Left doctrine on the Middle East. Rather, there is confusion, unhappiness, some—though limited—debate, and a great deal of sympathy . . . for the socialist elements within the Jewish and Arab national movements, combined with a general fear that national movements can do enormous harm if they subordinate the struggle for social reconstruction to purely national aims.

Some segments of the New Left support views rather like those of the Israeli group SIAH (Smol Yisreeli Hadash, Israeli New Left) and the related Movement for Peace and Security; others—in particular, the Trotskyite groups—are close to Matzpen; still others support Al Fatah and other Palestinian groups. Most remain silent, unhappy with the situation, but unable to see any hopeful way out.

The introduction to the November 1969 issue of *Liberation*, already mentioned, gives some insight into what I think are rather general attitudes. The editor writes:

> The peace movement and the American left have generally adopted a stance of pained indifference to the conflict in the Middle East. The apparent hopelessness of finding a just resolution is almost overwhelming. Moreover, many of us, without necessarily supporting the Arab or Palestinian position, have recoiled from the pro-Israeli chauvinism of the American Jewish community. The strenuous efforts by Zionist fund-raisers to picture Israel as a "free-world bastion" exploits and reinforces cold war idiocies. The celebration of the "fighting Jew" further alienates those of us who are not thrilled by Prussian efficiency.

These remarks, in my opinion, are also accurate, in pointing out that, to the extent that there is anti-Israel feeling in the New Left, it is in part in reaction to the behavior of the American Jewish community—to its extolling of the martial and chauvinistic elements in Israeli society, which are by no means dominant there, but which tend to occupy the center of attention in the

United States. In fact, American Zionism has always been predominantly on the right, in the spectrum of world Zionism. Little has changed in that respect.

The mixture of confusion and concern that is typical of New Left attitudes towards the Middle East crisis is by no means surprising, considering the composition, character, and ideals of the loosely organized, disparate groups that are identified with the New Left. What I do find surprising, however, is the way in which these facts are presented by others. For example, in the Arden House discussion, Nathan Glazer repeatedly referred to the "overwhelming and unbendable tendency [of the New Left] to support the Arabs and to oppose Israel." This phrase appeared in his talk and was reiterated several times in his discussion.[4] This characterization applies to some elements in the New Left. It is, however, beyond dispute that it is false as a general characterization. For example, it does not apply to those groups whose position is rather like that of SIAH or to the groups that identify more or less with Matzpen.[5] It does not, of course, apply to those—the great majority, in my opinion—who have taken no stand. It is not true of the authors and journals that I mentioned in this review.

These facts are important, and I want to stress them. The repeated claims that one reads in the press that, in Professor Glazer's words, "the New Left has an overwhelming and unbendable tendency to support the Arabs and to oppose Israel" are demonstrably false. Whatever one's attitude may be towards the Israeli-Arab conflict or towards the New Left, there is little

4. I quote from the tape transcript supplied to me by Mordecai S. Chertoff, which accords with my notes. Professor Glazer's paper, in the form in which it appears in this volume, is not available to me. I hope that he has modified his formulation in the light of the Arden House discussion.
5. I repeat that the position of Matzpen cannot be described by any rational observer as illustrating an unbendable tendency to support the Arabs. It is necessary to emphasize this fact because of the great distortions of their position that commonly appear. One may or may not agree with their position, but there is little point in fabrication and falsehood.

point in proceeding on the basis of easily refutable claims. In
particular, it is simply irrational to "prove" that the New Left
is pro-Arab and anti-Israel by citing a list of pro-Fatah statements, exactly as it would be irrational to "prove" that the New
Left is pro-Zionist by citing only Stone, Marcuse, Waskow,
articles that have appeared in *Ramparts,* and so on.

Let me now turn to the second and, I think, more interesting
point: the response to what is imagined to be the New Left doctrine on Israel. I cannot survey the full range of reactions, but I
will mention a few examples which are, I believe, representative
of important, if not dominant, tendencies.

On the day before the Arden House meeting I received in
the mail the February 1970 issue of the *New Middle East.* It contains a letter by T. R. Fyvel on the New Left and Israel. He
writes:

> My impression from conversations last year was that quite
> a few Jewish Americans of the Jewish New Left thought
> roughly like this: "I profoundly oppose President Johnson
> for pursuing an unjust war in Vietnam. President Johnson
> is Israel's leading supporter. Aligned with such support,
> Israel cannot be right."

I cannot, of course, deny that Mr. Fyvel heard such an argument.
I can only say that in my own experience with the New Left,
which is fairly extensive, I have never heard anything remotely
resembling it. Of course, such an argument would be totally
irrational. For example, pursuing such reasoning, these alleged
New Leftists should support the Israeli occupation of Jerusalem,
since President Johnson expressed his opposition to it — and they
should support the Russian invasion of Czechoslovakia, since
it was also denounced by President Johnson. If there are people
who actually present such arguments, their views can safely be
dismissed on grounds of irrationality.

I am inclined to suspect that Fyvel's impression is based on a
serious misunderstanding. My suspicions are aroused still

further when I read on in his letter, as he criticizes American Jewish academics. Why, he asks, "have they not produced working groups, formulated programmes, turned out studies in binationalism designed to help solve this Middle East conflict?"

The question strikes me as perhaps disingenuous. Those who even raise such questions are likely to be denounced by T. R. Fyvel, among others, as people who "say without any nuances that Arabs are good, Arabs are right—and Israel is wrong and must be liquidated." Given the likelihood of such a response, it is not surprising that many are discouraged from formulating programs that do not support the more nationalist and hawkish elements of Israeli opinion. The response that I quoted, incidentally, is from T. R. Fyvel himself.[6] It is his characterization of my position, which can only be based on the one article that I wrote on the Middle East, namely, the essay in *Liberation* cited earlier.

But Fyvel is on target when he relates the Middle East to Vietnam. I believe that for the New Left itself, these matters are quite separate; but for critics of the New Left, the issues are related in a significant way, which does not have much to do with the Middle East, though it has a great deal to do with the United States.

To explain, let me turn to a second example of the response to what is claimed to be the New Left position on Israel: a recent series of columns by Joseph Alsop.[7] I will not waste the reader's time discussing in detail the "facts" he reports, in his characteristically imaginative fashion. What is of considerable interest, however, is the way that Alsop tries to exploit the very strong and quite natural support that exists for Israel in an effort to discredit the growing domestic opposition to American militarism.

6. T. R. Fyvel, "Problems of an Israeli Intellectual," *New Middle East* (January 1970). In a later issue (March 1970), Mr. Fyvel acknowledges that this characterization was quite false, as I pointed out in a letter in the February issue, and attributes it to carelessness in editing a tape.
7. *Boston Globe* (12-13 February 1970).

His line of argument is quite simple. Those who attack "America's will and America's power"—I am cited as the prime, though extreme, example—are virtually inviting the Russians to move in and launch an attack on Israel. It is only American force and the American martial spirit that are warding off a genocidal Russian assault on Israel. To round out this fanciful thesis, it would be useful if opponents of the Vietnam war—more generally, opponents of American militarism—could also be depicted as believing that Israel "must be liquidated," to use Fyvel's phrase. Without saying it in so many words, Alsop tries to convey the impression that this is true in my case. He even invents a meeting between me and an unofficial emissary of the Israeli government to enliven this image.[8] Alsop then turns to that other notorious anti-Semite, I. F. Stone, who, he claims, "hurled the first stone at Israel from the New Left, in a slimy article on the Six-Day War that was closely comparable to his book on the Korean war." The reference is to the article in the *New York Review* that I have already cited. Note, incidentally, the last phrase. Not even Alsop's fevered imagination could conjure up a comparison between Stone's article on the Six-Day War and his book on the Korean War. The point, of course, is not to attempt a rational argument, but rather to plant a useful association: slimy attack on Israel; skepticism about the Korean War; assault on America's national will and power. With a skillful exploitation of the natural sympathy for Israel and a few well-chosen

8. I can only guess what private fancy may have led Alsop to claim that "some time ago, the Israelis sent an unofficial emissary to Professor Noam Chomsky, to try to explain to him that the defense of the United States was not absolutely disconnected from the defense of Israel." Conceivably, he is referring to an interview with the Israeli journalist Shabtai Tevet in my office at MIT. I do not recall discussing with him the "defense of the United States," although when I drove him to a Cambridge restaurant afterwards, we did discuss the cold war and disagreed in our interpretation of it. I find it hard to believe that Mr. Tevet was an unofficial emissary of the Israeli government. If this is not Alsop's source, then one must attribute his comment to pure invention, instead of the grotesque misrepresentation that is his usual style.

innuendos and misrepresentations, Alsop can finally end by warning Senator Javits to stop "whacking away at our own national defense."

Alsop is merely a spokesman for the military, and it would therefore be tempting to dismiss all of this as a rather clumsy Pentagon propaganda effort. But that, I believe, would be a mistake. The cold war consensus is eroding, and the effects of this on American society may be profound. The cold war has provided effective ideological support for American intervention overseas and for the growing system of military state capitalism at home. It is almost certain that there will be powerful resistance to the challenge to the prevailing American ideology, with its conservative cast and demonization of the "Sino-Soviet military bloc" that has caused the forces of freedom such pain from Vietnam to the Dominican Republic. For such purposes, the Middle East crisis is most convenient. Apologists for American intervention abroad and militarized state capitalism at home would like nothing better than to be able to identify the New Left as in favor of sweeping the Jews into the sea and applauding Russian-backed genocide (or, at the very least, as entirely unconcerned with the fate of the people of Israel, if that is the best that propagandists can achieve). What a marvelous way to discredit the rising challenge to American militarism and to support the idea that America must be the gendarme of the world, the judge and executioner for world society. We will, I suspect, hear a good deal more of this in coming years.

At this point, I am sorry to say, Western Zionism sometimes lends a helping hand. A supporter of the peace forces in Israel or the Israeli left will, accordingly, be critical of certain aspects of Israeli government policy. The reaction, in American Zionist circles, is likely to be that such a man has no concern for the welfare or security of the Jews of Israel. If he goes as far as Fyvel suggests and actually discusses binationalism as a long-range goal, thus challenging the concept of a Jewish state as a desirable end, then he can confidently expect to be denounced as virtually in favor of Auschwitz—and if he happens to be Jewish, as a "traitor to his people." There are many reasons for such hysterical reactions, and I do not intend to explore them or speculate about them. However, the effect is to play right into the hands of the Alsops. It is easy enough to begin by accusing the left, or the peace movement, of tolerance for genocide in Israel and then to proceed, using Alsopian techniques of free association, to discredit the opposition to American aggression in Vietnam, domestic militarism, and the ideology that supports it.

I mentioned earlier that I have personally been reluctant to write or speak about the Middle East, though I have been asked to for a long time—in particular, by a number of Israeli doves who point out that the absence of American support for their position is used as a weapon against them in Israel. The reason for this reluctance is simple. It has always been quite predictable that if anyone associated with the peace movement or the American left were to be critical of Israeli government policy, this would be used as a means to bolster American militarism, in the manner that I have just indicated.

These considerations explain in part why there has been such great interest and exaggerated concern over New Left doctrine on Israel and the Arabs. When a prowar enthusiast such as William Griffith writes articles critical of Israel in the *Reader's Digest,* no one cares. But if I. F. Stone were to write similar things in the *New York Review,* with less than 1 percent of the *Digest's* circulation, you can be certain that the bruised cold warriors would seize upon it happily and leap into the fray.

Let me now turn to a third example of reactions to alleged New Left attitudes with regard to the Middle East. In *Encounter* (December 1969), Seymour Martin Lipset has an article on the left, Jews, and Israel, called "The Socialism of Fools." He begins by quoting a statement he claims to have heard from Martin Luther King, equating criticism of Zionism with anti-Semitism. Instead of pointing out the absurdity of such a statement, he appears to accept it. Then follows a long discussion of left-wing anti-Semitism and anti-Zionism. Finally, Lipset turns to the New Left. He writes: "The most important political event affecting Israel in Western politics in recent years has been the rise of the New Left."

This statement seems to me a bit of an exaggeration, but compared to what follows, it is remarkable for its sobriety. Lipset then goes on to claim that "the New Left, particularly since June 1967, has identified Israel with the American Establishment." Citing no evidence to support this alleged fact, Lipset moves on at once to an explanation for it. In particular, he is interested in explaining the alleged attitudes of Jews on the left. Many of them, he says, "exhibit familiar forms of Jewish self-hatred, of so-called Jewish anti-Semitism, of the sort which were widespread within the left before the Nazi holocaust and the creation of the State of Israel." He goes on to assert that "self-hatred is becoming a major problem for the American Jewish community."

Lipset seems to feel that arguments or evidence to support these judgments would be quite superfluous. In any event, he offers none—literally, none whatsoever.

This kind of amateur psychoanalysis is quite fashionable and of course is particularly useful as a way of avoiding issues and side-stepping arguments. Perhaps I am lacking in perceptiveness, but I detect no signs of Jewish self-hatred on the part of the many radical Jewish students I know. But there is no question that if they can be dismissed in this manner, then there is no need to try to deal with the difficult questions they raise about war, imperialism, and problems of industrial society.

Next, Lipset states that the New Left is unaware of the kibbutz. Again, this is news to me. As I have already mentioned, Buber's *Paths in Utopia* is widely read and often discussed, and the kibbutz has been an explicit model for New Left activists. In fact, it is Lipset's generation of socialists who were contemptuous of the kibbutz and of libertarian socialism in general.

Finally, Lipset turns again to the familiar duo, I. F. Stone and Noam Chomsky, the "older left-wing critics of Israel [who] cannot be accused of ignorance concerning the Israeli socialist movement or its radical institutions":

> Chomsky, in fact, was a long time member of Hashomer Hatzair, the left-wing Zionist youth movement, which prided itself on its Marxism-Leninism and its loyalty to communist ideals.

In fact, I was never a member of Hashomer Hatzair, precisely because I was opposed to the Bolshevist doctrines that it accepted and, in the American movement, to its dominant Stalinist tendencies.

Lipset then goes on to assert that Stone and I have

> a commitment which currently involves defining the Al Fatah terrorists as "left-wing guerrillas" and Israel as "a collaborator with imperialism," if not worse. One doubts whether even the most sophisticated presentation of Israel's case could ever regain their support.

Notice, incidentally, the quotation marks around the phrases "left-wing guerrillas" and "a collaborator with imperialism," the implication being, presumably, that these were taken from some of our writings.

All of this is complete fabrication. The alleged quotations do not exist, nor have I ever expressed anything that could even be misinterpreted by a careless reader as expressing the "commitment" that Lipset attributes to me. As to Al Fatah, I have never identified it as a left-wing movement, which would be nonsensical, though I have pointed out that it contains left-wing elements, as of course it does. In the article that appeared in *Reflections on the Middle East Crisis* (see footnote 2, page 202), I referred to Gerard Chaliand's observation that Al Fatah appears to be analogous to the early Kuomintang—a broad coalition of many political tendencies—and that it may be supplanted by more revolutionary groups, as in China, if it fails. I find it difficult to believe that I. F. Stone has ever written anything remotely resembling what Lipset attributes to him (without reference), though it is easy enough to find explicit refutations of such views, as in the articles of his that I cited earlier—to my knowledge, his only recent articles on Israel.

The interesting question is: why the irresponsible allegations, the falsification, and the unsubstantiated—indeed, unargued—accusations of "Jewish self-hatred?" Whatever the answer may be, I merely note two consequences. First, Lipset's irresponsibility contributes to the Alsopian effort to rebuild the cold war consensus and buttress American militarism. Second, it harms the efforts to support the Israel left or the Israeli peace movement or to try to facilitate contacts, which might be useful, between Arabs and Israelis who are sometimes not too far removed from one another in their formulation of the basic issues and expression of hope for the future.

In a letter published in *Encounter* I pointed out a number of the falsifications just noted, and Lipset duly revised his article, in an interesting way (see p. 103 of this volume). He states, in the revision, that Stone and I "now write harshly about Israel" and adds:

> But Stone, Chomsky, and Cohn-Bendit are today committed supporters of the international revolutionary left. And that left currently defines the Al Fatah terrorists as "left-wing guerrillas," and Israel as "a collaborator with imperialism," if not worse. One doubts whether even the most sophisticated presentation of Israel's case could ever regain their support.

In his revision, Lipset again gives no reference or citation to support his claims. The falsifications that appeared in the original article might have simply been the result of carelessness. The revisions introduced in response to my letter, however, cannot be explained in this way. Knowing that he cannot support his original claims by actual documentary evidence, Lipset attempts instead to insinuate the same conclusions indirectly. Thus if Stone and I are committed supporters of the international

revolutionary left which defines Al Fatah as "left-wing guerrillas" and Israel as "a collaborator with imperialism," if not
worse, then it will be concluded by Lipset's readers that Stone
and I accept these positions of the movement to which he claims
we are committed. The avoidance of citation and reference is,
no doubt, intended to overcome the difficulty that Stone and I
have taken quite a different stand, as Lipset knows very well.

Before turning to other matters, I would like to make an
observation about Lipset's discussion of "the anti-Semitism,
'the socialism of fools,' occasionally voiced by groups such as
the Black Panthers, SNCC . . . and other black militant organizations. . . ." To illustrate anti-Semitism on the part of SNCC he
cites a quotation in a SNCC newsletter which asks readers
whether they know

> *that* the famous European Jews, the Rothschilds, who have
> long controlled the wealth of many European nations, were
> involved in the original conspiracy with the British to create
> the "State of Israel" and are still among Israel's chief sup-
> porters? *That the Rothschilds also control much of Africa's
> mineral wealth?*

To illustrate Black Panther anti-Semitism, he cites an attack on
Zionism, as well as a definitely anti-Semitic poem that he found
in the June 1967 issue of the paper of the Black Panther party
of Northern California.

The quotation from the SNCC newsletter, whatever one may
think of it, is hardly an illustration of anti-Semitism. Similarly,
anti-Zionist statements of the Panthers or anyone else are not,
in themselves, expressions of anti-Semitism. There is no doubt
that an assiduous search would reveal anti-Semitic statements
by black militants, just as there is no doubt that the black movements have always welcomed support by Jews and other whites.
There is also no doubt that by applying the same technique, one
could "prove" that Israel is a racist state bent on genocide. Suppose, for example, that someone were to document this claim by
quoting remarks that appear in *Machanaim* (April 1969) by

Shraga Gafni, who cites biblical authorization for driving the
"Canaanite peoples" from the land of Israel and who explains
that "not every enemy deserves peace." Specifically:

> As to the Arabs—the element that now resides in the land
> but is foreign in its essence to the land and its promise—
> their sentence must be that of all previous foreign elements.
> Our wars with them have been inevitable, just as in the days
> of the conquest of our possessions in antiquity, our wars
> with the people who ruled our land for their own benefit
> were inevitable. . . . In the case of enemies who, in the
> nature of their being, have only one single goal, to destroy
> you, there is no remedy but for them to be destroyed. This
> was the judgment of Amalek.[9]

For details of the judgment of Amalek, see 1 Samuel, chapter 15.

Suppose, then, that someone were to cite such statements in
a discussion of Jewish anti-Arabism, as illustrating the commitment to a war of extermination "occasionally voiced" by the
Israelis. Some might interpret this as rather cynical and even
deceitful. What is true in one case is no less true in the other.

Let me add several words of clarification. I have not suggested, nor would I, that it is unfair to criticize the New Left.
On the contrary, rational criticism is to be welcomed. Nor am I
suggesting that, say, my remarks on the Middle East are beyond
criticism. Again, serious criticism is to be welcomed.[10] What
I think is quite interesting, however, is the irrationality and
fabrication that has been so characteristic of the response to the
New Left. It is this fact that requires explanation, and I suspect
that the basic explanation is the one I suggested.

9. This is the journal of the Israeli Army rabbinate. The Israeli scientist who sent me this article comments that "Shraga Gafni" is probably the literary pseudonym of Rabbi Shlomo Goren, the chief rabbi
of Tel Aviv and the chief rabbi of the Israeli Army. The same correspon-
dent accused me, with some justification, of hypocrisy for my unwillingness to criticize the Israeli Establishment in the same terms that
I use in discussion of the Kennedy intellectuals and others.
10. For examples, see Shmuel B'ari, "Let's Not Make Bi-Nationalism
an Escape," *New Outlook* (December 1969); Shlomo Avineri in "The
Crisis in the Middle East: An Exchange," *Columbia Forum* (Spring
1970).

Notice that many of those responsible for these hopelessly distorted and irrational attacks on the New Left will, of course, express their opposition to the war in Vietnam. This expression of opposition in itself is quite meaningless. By now, opposition to the war is widespread in every sector of American society. Unfortunately, this opposition is, for the most part, entirely unprincipled. It is based on the cost to the United States, the failure of American policy, the "tragic mistakes" that occurred through failure to comprehend the realities of Southeast Asia or the limitations of American power. People who are opposed to the war on such grounds may very well support the principle of extending American power, the principle of forceful intervention in the internal affairs of other nations (where we can get away with it), and the rebuilding of the cold war consensus or some functional equivalent. My impression is that those who invent these fables about the New Left and Israel are, predominantly, people who have not dissociated themselves from such policies in any meaningful way or who actively support them— whatever their attitude may be to the catastrophe in Vietnam.

To conclude this discussion of reactions to the imagined position of the New Left, I would like to mention the response within Israel. I do not read the Israeli press or Israeli journals regularly, and my information is extremely limited. I can, therefore, make only the most tentative observations, based on what I have seen. I will limit these comments to the reporting of my own contributions to this conference.[11]

In the *Ha-Aretz* weekend edition, in early June,[12] Refael Rothstein has an article entitled "Ha-Dibbuk shel Ha-Smol He-Hadash be-Artzot Ha-Brit" ("The Dybbuk of the New Left in the United States"). Rothstein was present at the Arden House Conference and wrote a largely accurate, factual report

11. As is evident, these remarks were added after the Arden House Conference.
12. My copy of this article is unfortunately undated.

in *Ha-Aretz* immediately afterward.[13] His article in the weekend edition contains a number of errors and, more important, descends to a level of personal insult that, regrettably, I have observed before in *Ha-Aretz*.

According to Rothstein, I am "the man who astonishes Zionists with his articles and speeches that are full of sharp criticism of the politics of security of Israel. . . ." In fact, prior to the Arden House Conference I had given exactly one talk on the subject in a series of open lectures sponsored by the Arab Students Club (the other two speakers, so far, have been the Zionist rabbi of the Hillel Foundation and Simha Flapan of Givat Haviva) and written one article, in essence, the text of that talk. Next, Rothstein observes that at the Arden House Conference, I was the "Dybbuk" to be exorcised, the new reincarnation of "Jewish self-hatred." How can one account for this strange phenomenon of Jewish self-hatred (the existence of which is axiomatic and therefore requires neither argument nor evidence)? Rothstein quotes a young Israeli girl who offers what he apparently regards as a satisfactory explanation: she has perceived that the great problem of American Jewish males is that "they lack security in their manhood." "I am certain," she says, "that they lack manliness—all of these Chomskys, supporters of Fatah."

Reading this ingenious explanation of why we "support Fatah"—an allegation which, needless to say, also requires no evidence—I am reminded of a remark by Rothstein's colleague Shabtai Tevet, who commented, with reference to my opinions:

13. In this article (19 February 1970), Rothstein quotes Professor Rotenstreich as claiming that I and other "New Leftists" distort the historical record. He cites one example: that it is a mistake to depict Martin Buber as opposed to the idea of a Jewish state or as an anti-Zionist. For the record, I have never so much as mentioned Martin Buber in anything I have written on this subject, and my only reference to Buber in the Arden House Conference, prior to Professor Rotenstreich's remarks, is the one given above.

The custom with drunkards is to deprive them of rights, so that they will not harm people. But what can one do to a man with academic credentials whose mind has been impaired.[14]

Next Rothstein reports a discussion we had about the Panthers, in which I expressed my opinion that their position on the Middle East relates more to domestic issues than to Middle Eastern realities. He writes:

I could only recall to mind those young Jews, intelligent and good-looking, who resided in Germany in the thirties. They too interpreted the speeches of the Nazis as "mere rhetoric." I only hope that my meditations are baseless, an expression of what is called among our young Jews and free men "Jewish paranoia."

In this conversation Rothstein asked whether anyone among the Arabs is prepared to recognize Jewish national rights in Palestine. As he correctly reports, I mentioned the Democratic Front of Hawatmeh, which has been widely reported to have put forth such a program.[15] He adds: "This declaration was presented, apparently, shortly after the 'Front' acknowledged the terrorist attack on the cafeteria of the Hebrew University." I do not know whether this assertion is true. Let us assume that it is. With similar logic, one might discount all statements of the Israeli government, noting that they occur after such incidents as the virtual destruction of the city of Suez by bombardment

14. This appears at the end of a column that must be read in its entirety for its style and intellectual level to be appreciated fully. In *Ha-Aretz*, in November, 1969, Tevet wrote an article purportedly based on an interview with me. In a letter that was apparently published (I have seen no copy), I pointed out a long list of falsehoods and misrepresentations. The quotation just given is from Tevet's answer (10 December 1969).

15. See, for example, Gérard Chaliand, *La résistance Palestinienne* (Paris: Seuil, 1970). According to the "usually well-informed paper" *Al-Sayyad* of Beirut, the Democratic Front advocates a "binational Palestinian state," *New Middle East* (April 1970) review of the Arab press.

or the attack on the metal works at Abu Za'bal, where dozens of Arab workers were killed.

Rothstein then asserts, correctly, that I believe that the Jews will not and should not relinquish their national rights. Then follow some sarcastic remarks about the "third world" which have no bearing on our discussion at all and are just as well left unmentioned.

At this point, Rothstein moves to fabrication of a sort that is by now familiar. He claims that I "define Fatah as 'left-wing guerrilla fighters.'" As a matter of fact, in a lengthy interview I explained to Rothstein over and over again that Al Fatah cannot be regarded as a left-wing organization and that I was persuaded by Chaliand's characterization of it as somewhat like the early Kuomintang, a broad national front including many tendencies. I was quite insistent about this point, and I am sure that Rothstein understood it. In fact, in his factual report of the conference cited earlier he quotes me more accurately as emphasizing the internal splits within the Palestinian movements, which are far from monolithic (and surely include a wide range of political tendencies from left to right); in particular, as is well known, this is true of Al Fatah. I can only assume, then, that the distortion in the article in the *Ha-Aretz* weekend edition was conscious. For the fantasies Rothstein wishes to spin, it is necessary that the Dybbuk of the New Left regard Al Fatah as left-wing guerrillas. Ergo, it is a fact, whatever the real facts may be.

Continuing, Rothstein writes that "one of the contributions of Professor Chomsky to peace in the Middle East is the financing of a lecture series here [in the United States] by Aryeh Bober, a spokesman of 'Matzpen,'" and he goes on to talk about the other well-known anti-Zionists on the American left who financed this trip. This is complete invention. I haven't the slightest idea how Bober's trip was financed; it is a certainty that neither I nor any group that I am involved in financed it. Bober did receive an invitation from a group of Americans of which I am a member. The group intends to invite many speakers who represent something other than the official positions of Middle Eastern governments and Palestinian organizations, in an effort to broaden the scope of discussion here. My relation to this committee, which has not a cent to its name and no defined political position, is that I wrote a letter inviting people who might be interested in such an enterprise to join, making clear that it is not my group, that I am not its leader or organizer, and that the group would take no position in support of the specific policies of the people invited.

Perhaps this is enough to convey the tone and accuracy of Rothstein's report. I might add a personal comment. During the past few years I have taken rather unpopular positions on a number of subjects, and reports of my activities and statements, as well as interviews with me, have appeared frequently in the American and foreign press. Much of the press comment has, naturally, been quite hostile. However, there is nothing in my personal experience that surpasses the reporting in *Ha-Aretz* in distortion or petty and childish insults. Shabtai Tevet's articles, in particular, set something of a journalistic record in these respects. This surprised me, since I had regarded *Ha-Aretz* as a newspaper that met international standards and avoided gutter journalism. I do not know whether what I have seen is in any sense representative. It is the people of Israel, of course, who will suffer from this irresponsible journalism. Presumably, they believe much of what they read in the Israeli press. Given the critical situation in which Israel finds itself, it is extremely important that Israelis have an accurate and clear understanding of what is happening in the world. If they believe that the American New Left consists of perverts and self-hating Jews who have lost their senses, and that the Black Panthers—who are barely able to maintain their existence in the face of harsh judicial repression, not to speak of police assassination, as in the case of Fred Hampton and Mark Clark—are a threat to the Jews that can be compared with the Nazis in the thirties, then they will be living in a world of fantasy and nightmare that has little relation to reality, and their response to events is likely to be irrational and ultimately suicidal.

The only other discussion I have seen of the Arden House Conference is in an article by Yaacov Sharett called "An Israeli View of Noam Chomsky," in the *Jewish Frontier* (May 1970). Sharett begins by explaining that "one could build a whole structure rebutting Chomsky and the Al Fatah propagandists," but instead of bothering with this, he will restrict himself to explaining the attitudes he claims I share with the propagandists of Al Fatah.[16] According to Sharett, I argue "that the idea of the kibbutz as a solution to universal social evils . . . was the mainspring of Zionism." He goes on to imply that I "justify Arab terror, and espouse the-worse-the-better theory," and writes: "The expectation, indeed, the sinister hope of an Arab revolt on the West Bank and in the Gaza Strip, resulting in terrible bloodbaths, is to be detected in Chomsky's pronouncements." This vision, he explains, is very satisfying to the "American New Left non-Jewish Jew" because it "fulfills deep-rooted urges to sadism, masochism, cannibalism (of both father and mother), and fratricide."

16. To be precise, he mentions one actual statement of mine ("the only quotation I shall permit myself to select from Chomsky's writings"), namely, that "the concept of a Jewish state is not so deeply rooted in the history of the Jewish settlement of Palestine as one might be led to believe, *judging by the temperament that has prevailed in recent years.*" (Sharett omits the italicized words.) I go on to quote the conclusion of the careful Esco Foundation study that from 1921 to 1939 "the position of the Zionist leadership . . . was strongly tinctured with binationalism," and I point out that "the first official formulation of the demand for a Jewish state was in 1942." These remarks are quite unexceptionable, so far as I can see. Sharett's only comment is this: "Herzl's *Der Judenstadt* was conveniently overlooked—or perhaps it was not included in the Hashomer Hatzair educational literature." Herzl's *Der Judenstadt* was not overlooked, but was rather irrelevant. It was not an official formulation of the Zionist movement, and its existence relates in no way to the misconceptions that result from the temperament that has prevailed in recent years.

Notice that as he states, this is the only reference Sharett makes to any actual quotations (or other facts, for that matter). All the rest is allegation, without reference.

Next, Sharett claims that "Noam Chomsky still dares to equate Israeli response to terror and attack with the Nazi Holocaust," and he claims that I hold to "the nonsensical idea that Palestinian binationalism is popular with the Arabs." He then proceeds with his explanation of this "adolescent daydreaming":

> There is still a very important factor missing, one essential for making Professor Chomsky's outlook understood. Shattered youthful dreams of joining the idealistic kibbutz way of life, which would ultimately redeem humanity; disillusionment with the narrow, nationalistic Jewish state in view of the stresses and price involved; criticism of Israel's inevitable commitment to the Western world, to old-fashioned democracy, to "square" American Jewry, to Jewish tradition with all its contradictions with modern life; the easy and simplistic equating of the Jews returning to their homeland with the Crusader invasions and with Western modern colonialism; the false equation of Arab enmity to Israel with all which is just and "progressive" in today's world; the "Vietnamization" of the Arab-Jewish conflict and the transformation of Zionism into Nazism; the ease with which a clever Jewish philologist can swallow Arab propaganda — are all these enough to explain Noam Chomsky's attitude towards Israel?

One can see, reading this list and the comments quoted before, that Sharett was quite wise to state in the beginning of his article that he was not going to bother with citing quotations from my writing or with any other reference to fact. I would suggest that the reader who is interested try to find some source, in my writings, for Sharett's assertions and allegations. His other interpretations are as fanciful as his formulation of the invented views that he attributes to me.

However, Sharett is not interested in documenting what he takes to be my views but rather in explaining them. He thinks he has found the key in my remark, which for once he has actually succeeded in recording correctly, that, in my opinion, for Israel to lose a battle just once means annihilation. The light dawns. Perhaps the reason for my attitude is that the "mild Noam, the hero of verbal battles, is perhaps just scared."

Here Sharett has at last succeeded in touching the real world of fact. I do think that Israel is following a policy that may, ultimately, prove suicidal, and annihilation of Israel—which, in fact, can only lose once—is a prospect that gives me no pleasure. It also gives me no pleasure to see that an Israeli writer such as Yaakov Sharett is incapable of distinguishing courage from bravado. Surely any rational person will be concerned with the possibility that the present policies may be suicidal in the long run, will attempt to analyze this possibility in a serious way, and if, indeed, there exist alternatives—as is at least arguable— will be interested in exploring them.

What is most interesting about Sharett's comments is that they are based on total ignorance. He knows nothing about my personal background and has apparently made no attempt to find out what I have actually written about Israel. Therefore it is not at all surprising that most of the statements that he makes are demonstrably false; they are, after all, merely stabs in the dark. It is for this reason, of course, that he avoids documentation and cites no references to support his allegations—they simply do not exist. Like Lipset, he skips over the small problem of producing evidence and proceeds at once to offering explanations for what he imagines to be the case. I will not speculate on what may motivate this curious behavior. These rather silly forays succeed only in discrediting their authors and, perhaps unfortunately, in deluding those who may be so naive as to have some trust in what such authors write. Again, it is worth mentioning that if this is any sample of the kind of analysis or "information" that is being presented to Israelis, then the situation may be rather serious, for they cannot afford to live in such a dream world.

Let me now turn to the third topic: the question of what the future may hold, insofar as relations of the New Left to Israel are concerned. In the fall of 1969, Golda Meir wrote a letter to

President Nixon expressing her support for his efforts in Vietnam. In the correspondence columns of *Ha-Aretz,* Professor Y. Bar-Hillel, who has been active in the Israeli peace movement, wrote a brief letter in which he said that if Israeli policy continues along these lines, Israel's only friends will be Joseph Alsop and the John Birch Society. Of course, he was consciously overstating the point, but there is a point that he was overstating. Space does not permit elaboration here, but Israel is, in fact, being impelled, step by step, into the extremely unfortunate position of dependence on the United States,[17] combined with harshness in its domestic policies. These tendencies, if they continue, may ultimately lead to the situation that Lipset, Fyvel, and others incorrectly claim to exist today and that Alsop looks forward to with such eagerness: estrangement between Israel and the international left, including left-wing groups in the United States.

The matter of Vietnam may be indicative, in this regard. In a thoughtful article on the New Left and Israel, Yochanan Peres quotes a young American:

> . . . Some of us are almost nomads, we like to travel. Everywhere we arrive we find young people with whom we have a common language. The very least is that everyone condemns Vietnam. Only in Israel do we find an "understanding" for the imperialist intervention and indifference to the suffering of the Vietnamese.[18]

I do not know whether this is an accurate perception. Peres seems to believe that it is; at least, he makes no comment to suggest otherwise. He warns of the danger that Israel might lose

17. A weak reed at best. Recall that from 1960 to 1965, "United States aid expenditures [to Egypt] amounted to a sum of about $970 million, double those of the Soviet Union and the Eastern Bloc," and that while President Johnson was "entertaining Levi Eshkol 'at the ranch' in June of 1964, Egyptian officers were being trained in Chemical Warfare at Fort McClellan . . . ," Warren Young, "American Interests in the UAR," *New Outlook* (January 1970), pp. 26–39.
18. Yochanan Peres, "The New Left and Israel," *New Outlook* (February 1970), pp. 18–27.

touch "with advanced Western society and culture." Again, I am in no position to judge whether this danger is real. There is no doubt in my mind, however, that those who do have an "understanding" for the vicious American attack on the peasants of Indochina and who are indifferent to their suffering will, in the long run, be unable to maintain contact with whatever is decent in Western society.

These possibilities are more than disturbing. Even if they are still remote, they are sad, tragic—and avoidable.

Let me finally turn briefly to the fourth topic I mentioned: the question of what might be done in the United States to prevent the realization of the fears of some, the hopes of others, with regard to hostility between Israel and the New Left. First and most important, it is necessary to stop equating criticism of Israeli government policy with anti-Semitism, to put an end to the silly talk about Jewish self-hatred (or else, to provide some evidence to substantiate what have, so far, been simply wild charges), and to pay some attention to what people are actually saying and thinking. Irresponsible and malicious commentary of the sort I have reviewed will have the effect of presenting American youth with only two alternatives: either support Israeli policy totally or support the Palestinians. If the only way to relate to Israel, without enduring insults and falsification, is by supporting the settlement of Hebron, the bombardment of the city of Suez, the imprisonment of Arabs on political charges, and so on, then it is predictable that many young people will choose to reject Israel entirely and without qualification, will choose to develop the "unbendable tendency to oppose Israel and support the Arabs" that some critics claim to perceive right now and may, by their efforts, bring to realization.

It is important to tolerate and, in fact, to encourage contacts with and support for the Israeli left and the peace forces within Israel, groups that include sharp critics of government policy.

It is of critical importance that debate and discussion and exploration of the issues be undertaken in the United States, far beyond anything that exists today. And it would be quite helpful if this can be free of the exaggeration, distortion, insult, and sheer hysteria that has, unfortunately, characterized much of the response to such efforts.

Personally, I think that Israel has suffered, and will continue to suffer, from efforts in the United States to stifle discussion, slander critics, and exploit Israel's problems cynically in order to bolster American militarism, as well as from the general tendency in the United States to support automatically the more chauvinistic and militaristic elements in Israeli society. We should, at the very least, be able to duplicate here the range of discussion and debate that exists in Israel itself. In Israel, the "peace list" (Reshimat Shalom) group was known as "the Professors' party." In the United States, the American Professors for Peace in the Middle East recently published an ad that, to me at least, suggests the rhetoric of the Greater Israel movement. I couldn't sign such a statement and face my Israeli friends.

This, I think, is an unfortunate situation, and in the long run it will also prove harmful to Israeli society, and even to its independence and security.

11 The new left and the right to exist

NATHAN ROTENSTREICH

New Left approaches to Israel and the Middle East were surveyed by Noam Chomsky in his Arden House Conference paper, to which he added comments for publication in this volume. More direct explication of Chomsky's views has appeared in Liberation *(November 1969) and subsequently in the* Columbia Forum *(Winter 1969).*

In a wide-ranging response to Chomsky, Nathan Rotenstreich draws on the former's spoken word as well as his writings. He dissects the Liberation *article and takes issue with Chomsky's interpretation of Buber, of binationalism, and of Zionist ideology generally. Rotenstreich charges Chomsky with invoking a double standard in questions of national interest: one standard for Israel, another for everyone else. This he calls a "philanthropic" approach which ignores human realities and, therefore, is irrelevant to the situation.*

Arab nationalism, he points out, is not a result of the Six-Day War or the "occupation" of Arab territory, although these intensified Arab nationalism. To compare Israel in the Middle East with the United States in Vietnam is to claim that Israel is an outsider with no rights in the Middle East and, therefore, no right to exist.

He excoriates Chomsky's claim, in Liberation, *that ". . . The Nazi massacre, though unforgettable in its horror, no longer determines the choice of action. Rather, it is the living death of the refugee camps and the steady drift towards further misery yet to come that set the policy." Putting the two in the same context, says Rotenstreich, is a "defiance of reality," a "deceiving device." "Are we to forget the Nazi massacre?*

NATHAN ROTENSTREICH *is Professor of Philosophy, Hebrew University, Jerusalem.*

. . . or is this an experience which will never be erased from the memory of mankind?" He concludes that the whole raison d'être of Zionism was to create a new pattern of existence—and that this remains the motivation behind Israel's insistence on retaining its identity and its independence today.

I

Professor Chomsky has presented a bibliographic map of that literature of the New Left which addresses itself to what he calls the Middle East situation or to what I would prefer to describe —calling a spade a spade—as the problem of Israel. I am not an expert on the New Left, but I am deeply interested in the subject and in its ideological undertones. I am in no position either to deny or to affirm the variety of positions Chomsky has put forward. However, we need more than a bibliography to cover the various substantive positions taken by persons close to the New Left, including Chomsky himself. Before attempting to analyze Chomsky on the subject of Israel's ideology and "national interest," let me first mention a statement of Paul Goodman's in his essay "Objective Values":

> Buber felt, rightly or wrongly, that for historical reasons the Jews had to occupy Palestine and affirm their national identity with their own land. But then, once the state was established, he urged them to dissolve it, to become binational and enter into fraternity with the Arabs at whatever cost, to spend the money sent by American Jews to create Arab-Israel cooperation.[1]

The statement is totally false. Two of my senior colleagues, close to Buber both personally and ideologically—Professor Samuel Hugo Bergman and Professor Ernst Akiba Simon— wrote to the publisher of Penguin Books denying the substance

1. Paul Goodman, "Objective Values," in David Cooper, ed., *The Dialectics of Liberation* (Middlesex: Penguin, 1968), p. 12.

of Goodman's statement and putting things straight. Before the establishment of the State of Israel, Buber supported the concept of a binational state in Palestine, and he always supported Arab-Israeli cooperation. But Buber never—as Mr. Goodman asserts and as Professor Chomsky urges in his own analysis of the problem—suggested the dissolution of the State of Israel. In fact, Goodman is even wrong in saying that Buber summed up the return of the Jews to the Land of Israel by saying, "The Jews had to occupy Palestine"; Buber, like the rest of us, conceived of the return to Palestine as a settlement and not as an occupation. I am afraid that the choice of words reveals an underlying negative insinuation.

Be that as it may, within the variety of views mentioned by Chomsky, there seems to be a leitmotiv, a constant or recurrent theme urging the dissolution of the State of Israel and the establishment of a binational state. In the paper he presented to us at Arden House, Chomsky does not mention this intent, but he has elaborated it clearly enough in the essay "Nationalism and Conflict in Palestine," which has appeared in several publications. I shall take the liberty of addressing myself to this paper rather than limit myself to Chomsky's contribution to the conference.[2]

II

It seems to me that Chomsky makes light of New Left opposition to the existence of the State of Israel. He did so at the Arden House Conference, and he did so more explicitly at the forum of the Arab club of MIT, when he spoke on "Nationalism and Conflict in Palestine." Obviously, the term *Palestine* as used by the Arabs has a definite political meaning. To take another example, Chomsky wrote a letter on behalf of a member of the

2. Noam Chomsky, "Nationalism and Conflict in Palestine," in Herbert Mason, ed., *Reflections on the Middle East Crisis* (The Hague: Mouton, 1969).

Matzpen group who came to the United States on a speaking tour. In this letter, Chomsky describes Matzpen as a *non*-Zionist group, whereas in "Israel and the New Left," his contribution to this volume, he refers to Matzpen as *anti*-Zionist. What is his rationale for thus evading a clear definition of Matzpen? Why was Chomsky's sponsorship of an anti-Zionist not revealed by him in that letter?

I do not question Chomsky's deep interest in Israel's present very difficult situation. I simply wish to point out that there is an attempt, in which Chomsky participates, to keep things artificially balanced, to present nationalist and antinationalist on both sides of the controversy, to play down fundamental differences, in order to be able to claim a climate of conciliation where unfortunately there is none.

III

In a letter to *Encounter,* Chomsky refers to left-wing elements in the Al Fatah movement.[3] The leitmotiv I mentioned above emerges here too. What is the meaning of *left* in this context? If there is a basic principle of the left, that principle can be expressed in the following way: human evil springs from injustice, and the greatest injustice is caused by the dominance over man by men; economic dominance seems to be one of the most prominent manifestations of that injustice. This principle also provides the main philosophical basis of socialism. Where, except in their constant quoting from Che Guevara and Mao Tse Tung, are there traces of left ideology in Al Fatah? Is there any such principle revealed in their human, day-to-day behavior? Let us not forget that the most vocal pseudoleftist group among the Arab guerrillas is the Popular Liberation Front. Is this a movement shaped by a leftist orientation or is it merely using a leftist rhetoric? The most we can say is that Al Fatah takes the

3. *Encounter* (February 1970), p. 94.

view that until national liberation, as they see it, is achieved, everything else must be postponed. National liberation takes primacy over any other issue.

To suggest that there is a leftist character to some elements of Al Fatah is to create it out of whole cloth. This fabrication does not help Al Fatah understand its own position, nor does it help the promotion of radical social thought or international cooperation. It is my conviction that persons of the caliber of Chomsky, who have access to Arab groups, should try to show them that they must direct at least part of their energy to social reconstruction—to, let us say, a revolution in the social base of the Arab world.

One more preliminary comment: we are not concerned here with specific acts or policies of the government of Israel. I myself have often taken exception to both. We are concerned with the right of Israel to exist as an independent state and as the homeland of the Jews.

IV

In his article Chomsky makes the following broad statement:

> I am thinking of an international movement that could challenge the destructive concept of "national interest" which in practice means the interest of the ruling groups of the various societies of the world and which creates insoluble conflicts over issues that in no way reflect the needs and the aspirations of the people of these societies. . . .[4]

In the traditional pre-New Left manner, Chomsky identifies "national interests" with the ruling groups of society and suggests a lack of validity and moral justification in all national aspirations, holding that these aspirations do not reflect the needs and wishes of the masses in these societies. To be sure, this is offered as a general statement, but in its immediate appli-

4. Chomsky, op. cit., p. 94.

cation it refers to Zionist ideology and thereby questions the right of Israel to exist as a nation. Who is the ruling group of Israel which oppresses the majority of the people, imposing on them an adherence to nationalist aspirations, though these aspirations do not reflect the real needs of the society and the real aspirations of the people? This sounds like a typical doctrinaire pronouncement of Radio Moscow.

Nor does Chomsky hesitate to make sweeping statements: "With all the differences that have so often been stressed, there still remains an analogy to Vietnam where American force applied on an enormous and horrifying scale led to a tremendous upsurge of Vietcong strength."[5] It may be that Chomsky is not aware of the fact that in spite of his vaguely qualifying statement as to the differences between Israel in the Middle East and the American force in Vietnam, he makes us guilty by association. The American forces came to Vietnam from the outside; they are there as a result of a variety of political and strategic considerations on the part of the United States. But we Jews are in Israel because this is our destiny. There are those individuals who may try to escape this destiny, but, historically, we as a people do not want to escape it and are indeed not able to escape it. By suggesting a similarity between Israel and Vietnam, Chomsky, again possibly without realizing it, strengthens the image of our apartness from the Arab world; we are, he implies, strangers there, like the Americans in Vietnam, who can extricate themselves and who, even if they do not want to extricate themselves, will eventually be forced to do so. A foreign force has, after all, a place to return to.

Chomsky's argument is inadequate both historically and factually and obviously does not serve the cause of international cooperation. Later in his paper, where he presents what he calls the "Arab case" and the "Jewish case," we are faced again with a spurious "even-handed" tolerance. What does emerge from

5. Ibid., p. 80.

his presentation is that Zionism never intended to uproot the Arabs, even though segments of the Arab population did find themselves in a predicament both as individuals and as a people, as a result of Zionist activity. The Arab liberation movement, on the other hand, as represented by the Arab guerrillas, aims deliberately and programmatically to annihilate the State of Israel and to negate the identification of the Jews with their homeland. This Arab antagonism is deep-seated, tragic, and disastrous, and it did not grow out of the so-called occupation following the Six-Day War, though the occupation gave it added momentum. There is no point in concealing that antagonism, and there is no way out of the current impasse but a reasonable and dignified compromise. The concept of two separate states— which underlies the original United Nations partition program —was intended as just such a compromise, and I myself do not see any other possibility but partition. I will return to this point presently.

V

In his presentation already referred to, Chomsky speaks on the one hand about hundreds of thousands of Arab refugees in exile and on the other about the Jews exposed to the savage Nazi persecutions which culminated in the most fantastic outburst of collective insanity in human history. Again, to mention my own articles of belief, I think that the State of Israel should have been more imaginative in suggesting possibilities for the amelioration of the plight of the Arab refugees. But I am afraid that here, too, the tendency to present things as if they were equal is all too obvious. To place on the same level the catastrophe of the Jewish people brought about by the implementation of an ideology according to which Jews were simply not members of the human race and the plight of the Arab refugees, whose situation is the result of a war in which they have actively participated, is to defy facts and to blur moral considerations. We encounter here again the inclination to force things together, the tendency to identify internationalism with a falsely balanced view of reality.

Somehow one cannot suppress the feeling that Jews involved in the New Left and its various branches have to prove their internationalism by giving away the lamb of the poor man. This engenders misgivings, since we see people of stature and influence who do not exercise their potential impact for the sake of a real reconciliation but are obsessed, like tacticians and politicians, with the perpetual attempt to strike a balance.

VI

This brings me to what is possibly the central and, indeed, the most repugnant issue in Chomsky's presentation. He says:

> In 1947 the Palestinian Jewish community was traumatized by the holocaust. . . . Today the situation is very different. The Nazi massacre, though unforgettable in its horror, no longer determines the choice of action. Rather, it is the living death of the refugee camps and the steady drift towards further misery yet to come that sets the terms for policy.[6]

When I argued about this statement with Chomsky at Arden House, he replied (according to the tape) as follows: "Nothing that we do today in Israel or elsewhere is going to save the people who were in refugee camps in Europe in 1945. . . . I do not think we should forget it [the Nazi massacre] but it does not set the terms of action."

Let me point out first this further manifestation of a falsely balanced equation: the Nazi massacre, on the one hand, and the "living death of the refugee camps," which means camps for the Arab refugees, on the other. Now let us come back to the main issue. Should not the Nazi massacre set the line of action?

6. Ibid., p. 88.

The Nazi massacre is the most recent and the most extreme manifestation of the continued hostility toward and persecution of the Jewish people, which led in that case to annihilation. How could and how should a people possibly forget the Nazi massacre, its background in history, and its warning, which is not only crucial for the Jews but for the world as well?

Perhaps Chomsky's statement should be reversed: immediately after the war we were simply concerned with rescuing the remnants of the concentration camps; now, however, we may be in a position to see the historical dimensions of the holocaust and to take the predicament of the Jews as a guide, a directive for action, and a reminder of our responsibility for continued efforts to safeguard the position of the Jews throughout the world. What Chomsky is suggesting is that we relegate the Nazi experience to the limbo of history. Perhaps he does not see how close he comes to all those whose attitude to politics is *realpolitisch,* neither utopian nor historical nor humanistic. This is but one of the results of the approach taken by Chomsky, which aims to cut off the close and concrete relationship between the State of Israel and the Jewish people, both as a matter of historical development and as a phenomenon manifest in the Middle East crisis today.

VII

Chomsky writes:

> The concept of a Jewish state is not so deeply rooted in the history of the Jewish settlement in Palestine as one might be led to believe, judging by the temperament that has prevailed in recent years. . . . The first official formulation of the demand for a Jewish state was in 1942. . . .[7]

He is invoking Ahad Ha'am as quoted by Moshe Smilanski,[8] who was voicing his opposition to the American Zionist pro-

7. Ibid., p. 88.
8. Ibid., p. 81.

gram—known as the Biltmore Program—to establish a Jewish state. It would be out of place to deal here with the history of the idea of the Jewish state in modern Zionism. But let me make a few very brief comments.

First, I refer to Ahad Ha'am, who is quoted by Chomsky, because of his well-known attitude to Herzl, the author of *The Jewish State*. But in one of his major theoretical articles, "Flesh and Spirit," first published in 1904, Ahad Ha'am concludes with these words:

> And if, as we hope, the future holds for Israel yet a third national existence, the fundamental principle of individual as of national life will be neither the sovereignty of the flesh over the spirit, nor the annihilation of the flesh for the spirit's sake, but the uplifting of the flesh by the spirit.[9]

Now, during the thirties a controversy about the Jewish state was carried on within the Zionist movement. What was the nature of that controversy? It did not deal with the question of whether or not the concept of a Jewish state lay within the scope of Zionist aspirations, but rather with whether or not to make this concept a concrete and immediate goal of the Zionist movement. One of the strong points of Zionism was that it managed to maintain utopian vistas on the one hand and to cling to concrete action, here and now, on the other. This constructive utopianism, so to speak, is the real background of the controversy of the thirties, which aroused reservations such as those voiced in the Zionist Labor movement when it came to formulating a Jewish state as the goal of a concrete program of action. But *pari passu,* when the time was ripe, after World War II, for international and Jewish reasons Zionism seized the opportunity and established the Jewish state.

Chomsky opposes the existence of the State of Israel and mentions his sympathy with those who opposed a Jewish state. He was, and is, against a Jewish state because he opposes "na-

9. Ahad Ha'am "Bassar Va-Ruah" (Flesh and Spirit), *Al Parashat Derahim,* vol. 3 (Berlin: Jüdischer Verlag, 1921), p. 232.

tional interests," and he advocates both for Arabs and Israelis extrication from a national movement in which the goals of social reconstruction are subordinated to the demand for national self-determination. He advocates a revival of the concept of a binational state (to put his view positively) and the elimination of any legal ties between Israel and the Jewish people as well as between Palestinian Arabs and the Arab world. More specifically, in his oral presentation at Arden House he advocated the abolition both of the Law of Return and of legal ownership of land in Israel by the world Jewish community. With reference to the Law of Return he mentions his opposition to the Australian immigration laws since they are racist laws, permitting only white people to emigrate to Australia. Concerning the Law of Return, we should recall that he mentions that law in his summary presentation of the "Arab case": "There are hundreds of thousands of Arab refugees in exile, while the 'Law of Return' of the Jewish state confers citizenship, automatically, on any Jew who chooses to settle in [their] former homes."

It is significant that Chomsky, who opposes "national interests," does accept the national interest of the Arabs or of the Arab Liberation movement. After all, what the Arabs want is the abolition of Israel as a Jewish state, and it is of no significance at this point to debate whether the slogan "Abolish the State of Israel" in lieu of the slogan "Annihilate the Jews in Israel" is sincere or not. Here, at least, Chomsky accepts Arab aspirations and even uses the same language; he sees the Law of Return as analogous to the racist Australian immigration laws. This surely implies that the Law of Return is a racist law too, and this is, of course, an Arab slogan.

But what is the theoretical background of the Law of Return? It is not a law regulating immigration or restricting it to any one group—though, of course, it manifests itself in immigration directives. It is a law which asserts that Jews alone are in the category of those who *return* to the land of Israel. Are those emigrating to Australia *returning* to Australia? Again we see that the propensity to use analogies, even when there are substantive differences involved, is a recurring one in this discussion and culminates in an intellectual blunder and a moral misrepresentation. The same applies *mutatis mutandis* to comments on the ownership of the land. The Jewish people at large, and not the community of Israel, built Israel in the past and is rebuilding Israel today. This is not an expansionist impulse; it is an attempt to bestow concreteness and tangibility on the Jewish aspiration to have roots in the world by striking root in the land of Israel. Thus, there is a difference between ownership of the land by the Jewish people and ownership of land by individuals. For individuals, ownership is possession; for the Jewish people, ownership is realization.

As I have already said, Chomsky recognizes Arab national interests and accepts them. There is a kind of philanthropy inherent here, in the sense that philanthropy applies different standards to different peoples: Arab national interests are recognized, at least in terms of Arab opposition to the existence of the State of Israel; Jewish national interests, certainly in terms of efforts to maintain the State of Israel, are denied. Virtually, there seems to be at least post factum agreement between the view presented by Chomsky and the views propagated by different Arab groups, such as, for instance, the Arabs for Semitic Brotherhood. In a pamphlet of theirs, this latter group says: "There is no place for a racist, exclusive Israel in the Arab world. But there is a place for a Jewish community which is ready to identify with Palestinian Arabs in Palestine." This means that there is a place for Jews who will develop a *kehila,* who will be Arabs of Mosaic faith.

We have had this before; the raison d'être of Zionism—which has not been obviated by events—was to create and to safeguard a new pattern of Jewish existence, to bring about a situation in which our convictions and our faith are integrated in institutional expressions and manifestations. An identification with Palestinian Arabs in Palestine would dissolve the present and historic fusion between the Jew and the Jewish public realm and manifest existence and relegate him to a purely individual status.

VIII

Chomsky advocates the establishment of a binational state in Palestine. He consciously uses this term, which originally derives from a notion discussed and advocated by some people prior to the establishment of the State of Israel and prior to the UN resolution on the partition of Palestine. Let us look more closely, both conceptually and historically, at the notion of the binational state. When, in the thirties, Buber, Magnes, and their followers, as well as Hashomer Hatzair, advocated the establishment of a binational state, I never supported them. I thought then that as a matter of principle the concept of the binational state would never do even elementary justice to the idea of a Jewish homeland, with its symbolic, historic, and practical meanings. Yet, for Magnes, Buber, and Hashomer Hatzair the concept of a binational state was nevertheless intimately connected with the Jewishness of that state. It was not meant to be a state just for those who happened to live in it. In his letter to Ghandi, Buber says, among other things, ". . . our Jewish destiny is indissolubly bound up with this possibility of gathering, and this in Palestine." And even more strongly, "We cannot renounce the Jewish claim; something even higher than the life of our people is bound up in the Land, namely, the work, which is their divine mission."[10] Hashomer Hatzair, advocating the establishment of a binational state, very emphatically stressed *aliyah* as a right of the Jews.

It would be pointless to dwell on past controversies, except for the fact that Chomsky returns to them when he suggests the

10. Martin Buber and J. L. Magnes, *The Bond*, Two Letters to Ghandi from Martin Buber and J. L. Magnes (Jerusalem: Rubin Mass, 1939), p. 7, pp. 12-13.

establishment of a binational state as a solution of the present conflict between Jews and Arabs. For him, however, the binational state loses the worldwide Jewish dimension and becomes an entity for those who happen to live within its proposed boundaries. This is what logicians call *quaternio terminorum*—that is, using a single term to refer to matters or objects with different meanings.

But there is to all this a historical or, if you like, a practical aspect as well. The concept of partition embodied, essentially, an attempt to translate the binational character of what was Palestine into geographical and political terms. The two states envisaged, Jewish and Arab, would have had to be separate political and geographical entities, leaving the Jewish state free to define its own Jewish character within the boundaries of Palestine. Unfortunately, the Palestinian Arabs did not sieze the opportunity granted them in 1948 of establishing a state of their own and may possibly have missed the historical bus. The frustration of the Palestinian Arabs—what may be described as the late-adolescent character of their nationalism now—is to be explained by that late arrival at the struggle for national independence.

Let us, for the sake of argument, grant that the partition plan was a mistake. But we live here, we live now. The State of Israel is a fact, and a tremendous amount of energy, devotion, hope, and blood has been invested in the creation of the state and in the safeguarding of its future. How can a humanist suggest giving all of this away, disregarding those who do lay claim to the State of Israel and for whom the existence of the State of Israel is a major human commitment? This is to impose a doctrinaire scheme on reality, and not on an impersonal reality but rather on a reality which engenders identification and engagement. Why do we have to yield to Arab national interests by erasing ourselves—yield to schematic programming which imposes pseudouniversalistic patterns on living human beings?

Furthermore, are existing binational states so edifying, so

encouraging as models to follow? Look in our own area at Cyprus and Lebanon. Look at what goes on in Belgium. What are the Walloons and the Flemish segment of the population after? French culture is very well established in France, and Dutch culture is deeply rooted in the Netherlands. But apparently nationalism has its own momentum, and it strives for political expression even when this expression does not seem essential to an outsider. And we are in an even more precarious situation. The hostility of the Arab world to Zionism, to the settlement of Jews in the land of Israel, to the State of Israel, a hostility which extends to Jews generally—all these make binational coexistence not only contradictory to our aspirations but impractical and self-defeating as well.

Our problem is the recognition of our existence, if not a priori, then at least post factum. The left, when it is faithful to its ideological origin, propounds the notion that being human carries with it legitimate, inalienable rights, and one of those rights is self-determination. This self-determination is concomitant with the concept of freedom. I am entitled to determine my freedom, and my determination is, in turn, a manifestation of freedom. To be sure, my determination has to be checked and evaluated according to whether or not it encroaches on the freedom of other human beings. Because we recognize the rights of other human beings, in some empirical situations we must compromise. This is what we Jews must do in relation to the Arab world. But to deny the very right of self-determination written large in societal and ethnic terms, insofar as this right applies to the Jews and to their foothold in the world, the State of Israel, is to forego a basic principle of the left's, even when this denial is propagated explicitly or implicitly by sincere protagonists of the left. To be sincere is at best to be true to oneself; it is not necessarily to be consistent. Protagonists of the left should exercise their better judgment by calling the Arab world to acknowledge the principle of recognition. Certainly, they should not be led astray by the overwhelming power of linguistic or conceptual associations. I believe that in this matter the New Left could and should serve better objectives than it presently does.

Let me offer one final example of the method used to make a scapegoat, if this term may be permitted me, of Israel:

> One of the consequences of the partition—to my mind an extremely unfortunate one—has been the relative decline in importance of the collectives within Israel. Perhaps this trend could be reversed if the national struggle were to be transcended by a movement for social reconstruction of a revitalized Arab-Jewish left.[11]

A few points must be made here. First, what Chomsky is talking about is the consequence, not of the partition, but of the creation of the State of Israel. Is it, to use a philosophical formula, post hoc or propter hoc? Is it *because* of the creation of the State of Israel that the kibbutz movement has lost some of its importance, or is it that since the founding of the State of Israel the kibbutz movement has not gained in strength, relative to the general increase of the population of Israel?

Second, was there in existence, before the founding of the State of Israel, an Arab-Jewish left identified with the kibbutz movement? Did this left lose its importance when the State of Israel came into existence, and must it be revitalized? After all, revitalization is revival, and *revival* connotes that something was vital before and must now be resurrected. This is not the place to dwell on the role of the kibbutz in Israeli society, its importance, and its relative strength. But one thing must be said: the kibbutz movement, unlike many communal attempts, is not composed of people running away from the mainstream of society and from an overriding responsibility to society. On the contrary, one of the major characteristics of the kibbutz movement, and one of the major sources of its vitality, is the

11. Chomsky, op. cit., p. 84.

sense of broad social responsibility felt by its members, individually and collectively.

Let me close with some general comments on the phenomenon of the New Left and its attitude to Israel, particularly the extent to which Jews are involved in the New Left and take positions against Israel. Let me emphasize that I mean *a position against Israel* and not a critical attitude toward this or that decision of the government of Israel. It is a continuing feature of Jewish history that Jews have been and are today engaged in apologetics. First, they had to defend themselves by denying responsibility for deicide. Then they moved on to declare that the Gospel was themselves, that they produced the Gospel. Now, we must justify ourselves against an accusation of secular deicide, or genocide—the notion that we have uprooted the Arabs, that we have done them harm, like the harm the Nazis did to the Jews. In this argument Arnold Toynbee and the New Left stand on common ground. To be a leftist—and I stand second to none in being a leftist—is to be radical, that is to say, to go to the roots of a situation. There are historical roots to this kind of apologetics. One of the major legitimations of Zionism is that Jews may cease their apologetics and live on the assumption that to exist implies the right to exist.

I do not deny that many persons close to the New Left are deeply concerned with the fate of the Jews and with the future of Israel, or at least with the future of the Jews who have found refuge in Israel—whether as a matter of choice, a matter of necessity, or both. But this does not mean that their concern motivates them in the direction of adequate or proper action. Perhaps out of concern they overcome the concern. And perhaps they become prey to what may be called "the sacrifice of Isaac syndrome"—the compulsion to sacrifice one's dearest. If this is so, the readiness to offer such a sacrifice is a questionable virtue, not only in terms of theological ethics but in terms of human ethics as well.

12 *The claim*
of the Palestinian Arabs

MARIE SYRKIN

*Another response to New Left views—and to Chomsky
—comes from Marie Syrkin. In her rebuttal, she takes
issue with attempts to minimize the extent of anti-
Semitism among black militants and disproves ingen-
uous claims that all the Palestinians want is a "democratic, secular Palestine."*

*Syrkin analyzes the relevant sections of the so-
called Palestinian National Covenant and goes on to a
thorough exploration of the background, history, and
meaning of the* Palestinian *concept, as applied in current
debate to the Arab guerrillas and the Arab refugees.*

In their attitude to Israel, the spokesmen of the left, New or
otherwise, display a disregard of facts, historic and social, which
exceeds in latitude even that permitted to self-styled visionaries.
Such nonchalance, to be expected in student rhetoric, is dismay-
ing when exhibited by men of scholarly training and reputation.
What is one to think of Noam Chomsky, for instance, who, while
admitting in his Arden House Conference address that "an
assiduous search would reveal anti-Semitic statements by black
militants," exculpates them from the charge of being anti-Jewish
as well as anti-Zionist. That is to say, even if some obscure crack-
pots among the blacks are anti-Semitic, it is unfair to dig up
unrepresentative quotations; yet, this is a technique with which
Chomsky appears to be familiar.

Are we to assume that special assiduity is required to scan
the pages of the *Black Panther,* in which attacks against "Zionist
exploitation here in Babylon" regularly go hand in hand with

MARIE SYRKIN *is Professor Emeritus of English Literature at Brandeis
University and editor of the* Jewish Frontier.

attacks against Israel? And surely Chomsky gets the point when the coordinator of the Black Panther party impartially attacks the "Zionist Judge Hoffman" of the Chicago conspiracy trial together with the "other Zionists," Yippie defendants Abbie Hoffman and Jerry Rubin, whose fervent espousal of the Palestine guerrillas provided them with no more immunity than did the anti-Israel declarations of Polish Jewish communists when they were branded as Zionists by the anti-Semitic regime in Poland.

The code word *Zionist,* a concession to radical ideology theoretically opposed to anti-Semitism, by this time deceives no one. If Chomsky wants the evidence straight, no assiduous investigation is required to discover the views of Negro spokesmen from Rap Brown to LeRoi Jones, who dispense with Zionist camouflage of their sentiments. LeRoi Jones, who, whatever his literary virtues, hardly qualifies as obscure, concludes a poem consisting of anti-Semitic obscenities in the Julius Streicher tradition with a simple, straightforward call to massacre the Jews:

. . . Selling fried potatoes
and people, the little arty bastards
talking arithmetic they sucked from the arab's
head.
Suck you pricks. The best is yet to come. On how
we beat you
and killed you
and tied you up.
And marked this specimen
"Dangerous Germ
Culture." And put you back
in a cold box.[1]

Just as Chomsky has apparently failed to note the well-publicized anti-Semitic utterances of the black militants, he is bewildered by the suggestion that the New Left is anti-Israel.

1. LeRoi Jones, "The Black Man Is Making New Gods," *Evergreen Review* (December 1967).

Where, he asks, do spokesmen of the left declare themselves against Israel? He points out that some, like I. F. Stone (who appears as a Zionist sympathizer in the Chomsky script), grant Israel's right to exist. This is too artless. From the time of the New Politics Convention of 1967, ritual support for the "national liberation movement of the Palestinians" has emanated from varied sectors of the left as piously as opposition to the war in Vietnam and imperialism. Since the avowed goal of the Palestinians is the destruction of Israel, the deduction in regard to leftist sentiment appears inescapable despite Chomsky's inability to find overt anti-Israel professions. By such reasoning, the Black Panthers, overwhelmingly committed to "killing pigs," might be considered antiporcine rather than antipolice.

This readiness to ignore inconvenient data is particularly visible in Chomsky's program for resolving the Arab-Israel conflict. His arguments, both in the Arden House address and particularly in his article, "Nationalism and Conflict in Palestine,"[2] like those of I. F. Stone in the article cited by Chomsky, follow a familiar line of the left. He deplores a chauvinistic concentration on "the national interest" of a people and the "monstrous historical injustice" done to the Palestinian Arabs. He advocates a "democratic, socialist Palestine—optimally, integrated into a broader federation—that preserves some degree of communal autonomy and self-government." And he points out correctly that such a program was originally envisaged by the socialist pioneers who came to Palestine at the turn of the century. But he declines to face why the dream failed, in what way the Palestinian Arabs suffered, and finally what would be the nature of the "democratic Palestine" envisaged by the Palestinian nationalists. In the following pages, I attempt the answers.

A democratic Palestine in place of Israel has become an appealing slogan. On November 2, 1969, the fifty-second anni-

2. Noam Chomsky, "Nationalism and Conflict in Palestine," *Liberation* (November 1969).

versary of the Balfour Declaration, the *New York Times* published a full-page advertisement calling for a "Nixon Declaration" which would view with favor the establishment of a Palestinian state in which Jews, Christians, and Moslems would live on the principle of "one man, one vote." The Arab sponsors of this advertisement urged President Nixon to assume the role of "peacemaker" and "reverse the process begun by the Balfour Declaration" by undoing the "dismemberment and mutilation of Palestine, its mutilation from a land sacred to and inhabited by Moslem, Christian, and Jew, to a land which is the exclusive domain of a few." Simultaneously, the Arab signatories called for the implementation of the United Nations resolutions regarding Palestine without specifying whether this demand included the 1947 Partition Resolution which set up a Jewish state in a part of Palestine because the Arabs and Jews were not living in peace with each other.

I am certain that many a good citizen, wearied by bloodshed and rumors of impending war in the Middle East, must have been favorably impressed by this apparent evidence of Arab moderation. Instead of the customary threats of extermination, civil offers of amity and coexistence were being publicly extended. That this offer was contingent on the dissolution of the Jewish state may not have immediately struck the casual reader, though the only difference between this proposal and the familiar Arab cries for the destruction of Israel lay in the failure to specify that Jews would be driven into the sea. After Israel ceased to exist, its citizens, or some of them, would be permitted to dwell as a minority in a hypothetical Palestinian state in which they would presumably be as safe and happy as the Jews of Egypt, Iraq, or Syria.

Obviously, Israel is unlikely to accede to a formula for its extinction, no matter how graciously phrased. A return to the status before 1947 will hardly commend itself to those for whom Jewish independence was both dream and necessity. From the Israel point of view, the only novelty in the latest Arab propaganda tactic is its resort to euphemisms. Taking a cue from public relations advisers who have deplored the sanguinary "rhetoric" which preceded the 1967 war, Arabs are determined to mute some of their pronouncements. The idea of a Nixon Declaration, bristling with good will, is a case in point. An ecumenical Palestine will obviously sit better with church groups and liberals than the prospect of another holocaust.

The more strident counterpart to the peace-loving Palestinians who simply invite Israel to disappear is the guerrilla force whose bombs inspire the revolutionaries of the left. In the current Middle East scenario, the pathetic Arab refugee has been replaced by the husky Palestinian commando; during the recent United Nations debate on refugees, Arab spokesmen made no secret of the change of emphasis. Instead of refugees maintained in constantly swelling numbers in UNRRA camps, the scene is dominated by organized guerrillas, well stocked with the ubiquitous Russian arms and supported by oil royalties from Saudi Arabia and Kuwait as well as by UNRRA rations.

The rallying cry has changed from "repatriation" to "liberation." Not bound by tenuous considerations of cease-fire lines, the terrorist groups can maintain tension along the northern and eastern borders, while Egypt wages its war of attrition across the Suez Canal. In addition to whatever military advantage may be gained from such harrassment of Israel in anticipation of the promised Fourth Round, the guerrillas play a significant part in the continuing political struggle against Israel. As a movement of "national liberation," they have captured the imagination of much of the left, who hail them as the Vietcong of the Middle East. Their slogans and acts of terror arouse instant sympathy among disciples of Fanon and devotees of the Third World. Even those not automatically turned on by revolutionary jargon are troubled by the vision the commandos raise of a lost Palestinian homeland, temporarily obscured by Zionist chicanery but now emerging into the light of day. The focus of the ideological debate has shifted. For the Palestinian refugee whose problems could eventually be solved by compensation, resettlement, and partial repatriation has been substituted a dispossessed Palestinian people whose aim is restoration.

Arab strategy may prove inimical to the best interests of the Middle East in terms of the welfare of its peoples, but it has shown itself unfailingly resourceful in keeping the pot boiling. The Arab states' political exploitation of the refugees by preventing their resettlement and absorption is too familiar to require comment. With the pretense to refugee status of a second and third generation born in the UNRRA camps growing thin, a new tactic has been devised. The substitution of the burly Palestinian exile for the frail refugee has changed the terms of the argument and disposed of any solution save through the elimination of Israel. Even the withdrawal of Israel to the 1967 borders would not lessen the force of the Palestinian's demand for his homeland. While the Arab states were reoccupying the territories they lost in 1967, the guerrillas would remain free to undo the evils of the Partition Resolution of 1947. Nasser made no secret of this strategy.

Though the immediate military success of this scheme may be limited, the emergence of the commandos has undoubtedly born fruit on the propaganda front. A reappraisal of the Zionist idea appears to be taking place ex post facto. Judging from articles and letters to the editor written by those who increasingly bolster their positions by references to the history of the Mandate, confidence in the moral validity of Israel's case has been shaken among people who formerly accepted the rise of Israel as the rectification of a historic wrong. Some are now disturbed not only by the endless warfare and its grim aftermath of human suffering but by the very existence of Israel itself. Despite all its wonders and achievements, should it be there? In this context the wrongs of the Arab refugees of 1948 merge with the fresh problems generated by the Six-Day War of 1967, particularly that of Palestinian nationalism.

Even such outrages as the recent hijacking and destruction of planes as well as the kidnapping of civilians has, among other things, served to publicize the guerrillas much in the way that the bombing of a college building publicizes the Weathermen. True, the public reacts in horror, but other reactions, more insidious, come into play, too. Like the gentlemen in the joke who, when informed that a man has thrown a burning lamp at his wife, exclaims, "What an awful wife!"—normal human beings seek justifying causes for the monstrous; the more monstrous, the more intent the search. This makes a rational examination of Palestinian demands all the more urgent.

The suffering of the Arabs who abandoned their homes and villages in 1948 and, in lesser measure, in 1967, is incontestable, and I do not propose to argue again whether they were the victims of Israel or of the failure of the Arab design to liquidate Israel. Whether they fled or were driven, whether the Israelis were savage or generous victors, is no longer of the essence of the debate. A refugee problem, given the will, can be settled in the Middle East as elsewhere in the world; an irredenta with all the profound passions it arouses is another matter. Hence the continuing debate on the rights and wrongs of the Arab-Israel conflict, particularly insofar as it presumes to question the continued existence of the Jewish state, must frankly face the new problem posed by the Palestinians.

Are we witnessing the synthetic creation of a Palestinian identity as a weapon in the anti-Israel arsenal? In the total evaluation of Arab and Jewish rights this question looms large. The Palestinian nationalist, whether in costume or true guise, is a new factor in the Arab-Jewish conflict—and one treated respectfully by Israeli commentators, many of whom argue that the origin of Palestinian nationalism is irrelevant to the issue. Supposing it did spring belatedly out of the head of Arab nationalism merely as a hostile response to Israel? The lad is alive and kicking, and calling him "bastard" will not exorcise him. But by the same token Israel is also there; if its ouster is demanded on the grounds of illegitimacy, then the counterclaims must be examined. Can the newcomer be fed only at the expense of the Jewish state or is there room elsewhere in the family domain for his natural development?

The question of origins is not merely academic. The Al Fatah terrorist who attacks an El Al plane in Zurich justifies his act on the grounds that the first Zionist Congress took place in Switzerland in 1897, so ushering in the "horror" of Zionism to the world scene. Commentators of all shades of the political spectrum seek to determine future policy according to their view of what actually took place in the last fifty years. Obviously, if the British sponsorship of the Zionist endeavor was a bad business to begin with—at best an error of judgment, as Dean Acheson discreetly indicates in his recent memoirs, or at worst a gross injustice, as Toynbee would have it—then the possible accommodations of the present must be made with such history in mind. Even those who believe that truth is best served by granting the clash of two wrongs or two rights will fit their prescription to their diagnosis of the cause of the trouble.

Any view of what should be done now to achieve a peaceful settlement between Arab and Jew is bound to be practically affected by a determination of the extent of the injury. A dispossessed Palestinian people, able to flourish only within the area of the Jewish state, would require compromises from Israel other than those to be made for the same number of dislocated refugees. For this reason a discussion of Palestinian nationalism is not a futile semantic exercise. There is little hope of devising a satisfactory territorial solution if the existence of Israel is really predicated on the ruthless dispossession of a people from its homeland—something radically different from the dislocation or resettlement of individuals as an aftermath of war, a familiar process in the Europe and Asia of the twentieth century.

The first point to be made is that the characterization of Palestinian nationalism as "artificial" does not come from Zionist adversaries but from classic Arab sources. In the period before and after the issuance of the Balfour Declaration, Arab nationalists consistently protested the use of the name *Palestine* or the adjective *Palestinian* to demark them from other Arabs in the region. All the declarations of the nascent Arab nationalist movement from 1880 on concentrated on "the unity of Syria" with no references to Palestine as other than "south Syria." Nothing could be more explicit than the statement of the General Syrian Congress in 1919:

> We ask that there should be no separation of the southern part of Syria, known as Palestine, nor of the littoral western zone which includes Lebanon, from the Syrian country. We desire that the unity of the country should be guaranteed against partition under whatever circumstances.

The Arab Congress meeting in Jerusalem in 1919 formulated an Arab Covenant whose first clause read:

> The Arab lands are a complete and indivisible whole, and the divisions of whatever nature to which they have been subjected are not approved nor recognized by the Arab nation.

George Antonius, the Arab historian, makes sure that there will be no misunderstanding on this score. In *The Arab Awakening*, first published in 1939, he writes:

> Except where otherwise specified the term Syria will be used to denote the whole of the country of that name which is now split up into mandated territories of (French) Syria and the Lebanon, and (British) Palestine and Transjordan.[3]

The extremist Mufti of Jerusalem originally opposed the Palestine Mandate on the grounds that it separated Palestine from Syria; he emphasized that there was no difference between Palestinian and Syrian Arabs in national characteristics or group life. As late as May, 1947, Arab representatives reminded the United Nations in a formal statement that "Palestine was . . . part of the Province of Syria. . . . Politically, the Arabs of Palestine were not independent in the sense of forming a separate political entity."

3. George Antonius, *The Arab Awakening* (New York: Putnam, 1965).

Before the creation of the Jewish state the whole thrust of Arab nationalism was directed against what its proponents viewed as the dismemberment of an ideal unitary Arab state. Even the setting up of several independent Arab states was viewed as a subtle thwarting of Arab nationalism, not its fulfillment. Nor was there a change after the establishment of Israel. In 1952, Charles Malik, the well-known Arab scholar and statesman, described the process dourly in *Foreign Affairs:* "Greater Syria was dismembered, the southern and northern parts being put under different administrations." And his demonstrative comment on the settlement "of countless Jews on Syrian [not Palestinian] soil" should be noted.

With an eye to the future, the Arab Ba'ath party, which describes itself as a "national, popular revolutionary movement fighting for Arab Unity, Freedom, and Socialism," declared in its constitution (1951): "The Arabs form one nation. This nation has the natural right to live in a single state and to be free to direct its own destiny." Moreover, the constitution equated the battle against colonialism with the "struggle to gather all the Arabs in a single, independent Arab state." No mention of Palestine, except as usurped Syrian territory, tainted any of these formulations. So rabid a figure as Ahmed Shukairy had no hesitation, while head of the Palestine Liberation Organization, in announcing on May 31, 1956, to the Security Council that "it is common knowledge that Palestine is nothing but southern Syria."

From the foregoing it is obvious that for Arabs *Palestine* was merely an inaccurate name for a sector of the Middle East whose separate designation was the result of imperialist plotting against Arab independence. Unlike its role in Jewish history and tradition, in Arab eyes Palestine was neither the cradle of a nation nor a holy land. It aroused none of the memories or special attachments given a homeland. Arab national passion was engaged by the concept of a greater Syria or an even larger united Arab state, not by this tiny segment which had become detached through the force majeure of foreign colonialism. In the lexicon of Arab nationalism the independent existence of a Palestine state, like the existence of an independent Lebanon, represented a violation of the Arab national will.

Historians have repeatedly pointed out that Palestine as a political unit ceased after the Roman conquest of the Jewish commonwealth, and that it was restored centuries later as a distinct political entity by the British Mandate for the specific purpose of establishing a Jewish National Home. Admittedly, this fact of ancient history would have little relevance to the present if, up to the Balfour Declaration, there had ever developed an Arab diaspora which, like the Jewish diaspora, had an emotional fixation on Palestine. Nothing of the kind took place. Even when the desert Arabs revolted against Turkish rule during World War I, the Arabs in Palestine were so little concerned with independence that they continued to fight alongside the Turks till liberated by the Allies.

The concept of Palestine as a separate national entity arose among Arabs as a purely negative reaction to Zionism after the Balfour Declaration. It is worth noting in this connection that those Arab spokesmen who originally welcomed the setting up of a Jewish homeland in a small portion of the territories freed from Ottoman rule made no pretense that they viewed the abstraction of Palestine from the total area assigned to the Arabs other than as the loss of a given number of square kilometers. Emir Feisal signed his celebrated agreement with Dr. Wiezmann (January, 1919) in behalf of the "Arab Kingdom of Hedjaz," and in his letter to Felix Frankfurter, then a member of the Zionist Delegation to the Peace Conference, the Emir wrote a few months later (1 March 1959):

> We are working together for a revived Near East, and our two movements complete one another. The Jewish movement is national and not imperialist. Our movement is national and not imperialist, and there is room in Syria for us both.

The Arab guerrillas who justify their demand for bases in Lebanon as in Jordan and Syria with the argument that the Arabs are one nation and therefore have the right to use each other's territories interchangeably, operate completely within the tradition of orthodox Arab nationalism. Some sophisticated Arab spokesmen have become aware of the pitfalls presented by Arab avowals that they are all one people with no difference between Jordanian, Palestinian, or Syrian. The editor of the Amman weekly, *Amman al Masa,* has warned that such reasoning might make the notion of the resettlement of Arab refugees "respectable," since its advocates could justly claim that the refugees were merely being moved to another part of their Arab fatherland, whatever its name. Such considerations, however, trouble neither the guerrillas, who move freely across the borders of the Arab states as citizens of the Arab nation, nor their sponsors. The same Syrian Ba'ath leaders whose program calls for one Arab state are the most zealous supporters of the terrorists whose purpose is to recover the "Palestine homeland."

The youth born in Lebanon or Jordan who is taught on the one hand that the Arabs are one people whose land was cut up by the imperialists and on the other that his family was thrust out of a Palestinian Eden whose allurements increase with each decade of Israeli achievement is not likely to be worried by logical niceties. Whatever the contradictions, current Arab strategy is not likely to renounce a successful technique. Nevertheless, in the face of the evidence no proponent of Arab nationalism would deny that the Palestinian variant is a very recent mutation.

Equally to the purpose is the fact that the absence of such a distinct Palestinian nationalism provided a rationale for the Balfour Declaration. In their various negotiations with the Arabs in regard to the territory liberated from the Turks, the British were faced with demands for a greater Syria, a kingdom of Hedjaz, an Arab state—but never for an independent Arab Palestine, for the reasons already indicated. The Arabs who opposed the Balfour Declaration and the Mandate objected to a foreign intruder in their midst and to the diminution in any measure of their vast holdings. All this is human and understandable. Just as understandable on another level is the not ignoble calculation which allotted 1 percent of the huge area freed by the Allies for the establishment of a Jewish National Home. Lord Balfour expressed the hope that the Arabs would recall that the Great Powers had liberated them from the "tyranny of a bestial conqueror" and had given them independent states. He trusted that

> remembering all that, they will not grudge that small notch—for it is no more geographically, whatever it may be historically—that small notch in what are now Arab territories being given to the people who for all these hundred of years have been separated from it.

It is necessary to repeat this statement because contemporary anti-Israel polemics—from the high-minded exhortations of Noam Chomsky to more primitive rantings—maintain the fiction that the British and the Jews proceeded with a total disregard of an Arab presence in Palestine. In support of this accusation, all kinds of stray bits from Herzl and lesser luminaries have been exhumed, though their bearing on the actual political deliberations which culminated in the Balfour Declaration was nil. The many pages devoted to analyzing the Sykes-Picot Agreement, the McMahon Letter, or the recommendations of the King-Crane Commission—all pre-Mandate documents—indicate that however proponents varied in the solutions or interpretations they offered, every aspect of the Arab case was weighed and considered; it did not go by default, as rewriters of history like to pretend.

The King-Crane Commission, appointed by President Wilson to study the question of the Palestine Mandate, brought in an outspokenly hostile report; it urged the abandonment of a Jewish National Home and proposed instead that Palestine be included "in a united Syria state" for which the United States should hold the mandate. The very nature of the anti-Zionist opposition—American, British, and Arab—its indifference to Palestine except as part of an Arab whole, made the reasoning of pro-Zionists like Lord Balfour plausible. Their psychology may have been faulty; the Arabs did and do "grudge that small notch," but nothing could be more irresponsible than to foster the myth that Arab national feelings were ignored by the promulgators of the Balfour Declaration.

The same holds true for the Zionists. Those who lived to graduate from utopian visions to the hard bargaining tables of diplomacy were foolhardy innocents only in the extent of their hopes for Jewish-Arab cooperation in the Middle East. They were thoroughly aware that Palestine, though denuded and sparsely inhabited, had a native population. They came prepared with agricultural studies and demographic charts demonstrating that soil reclamation in Palestine would make room for more Arabs as well as Jews and would provide a better life for both. They were certain that the Arabs would prosper materially as the result of Jewish settlement, and they did not disregard the more delicate matter of Arab national feelings. Weizmann, a more reliable authority on this subject than romantic predecessors like Herzl, whose idyllic vision of coexistence of Arab and Jew in *Altneuland* bore no relation to the facts of life, declared unequivocally that the Zionists assumed that the

> national sentiments of the Palestinian Arabs would center in Baghdad, Mecca, and Damascus, and find their natural and complete satisfaction in the Arab kingdoms which resulted from the Peace Treaty settlement in the Near East.

The Zionists proved poor prophets with one vital exception. Paradoxically, their coming did make more habitable room in Palestine. I refer of course to the period of Jewish settlement up to the establishment of the state—the period in which the Jews strove unsuccessfully to live in peace with their Arab fellow citizens. If peaceful Jewish colonization, beginning at the turn of the century, had resulted in the dispossession of the local population this would have been a more serious indictment of Zionist policy than the subsequent flight of refugees in later wars. *No such dispossession took place.* Since the current indictments of Israel include not only the urgent troubles of the present but the "historic wrong" done the Arabs through their dispossession by Jewish settlers, this fact must be clearly established. Instead of diminishing, the Arab population increased spectacularly in the three decades after the Balfour Declaration. It grew from 565,000 in 1922 to 1,200,000 in 1947—an increase of 100 percent and striking evidence of the stimulus provided by the agricultural development. During the same period Egypt showed an increase of 25 percent, while Transjordan, lopped off from Palestine in 1922 and also under a British mandate but closed to Jewish immigration, remained static.

Not only the local Arabs prospered because of the better sanitary and economic conditions created by Jewish labor. After the Balfour Declaration Palestine changed from a country of Arab emigration to one of Arab immigration. Arabs from the Hauran in Syria as well as other neighboring lands poured into Palestine to profit from the higher standard of living and fresh opportunities provided by the Zionist development.

All reports agree that prior to the Jewish return Palestine was a dying land. Throughout the nineteenth century the favorite adjectives of travelers describing the Holy Land, beginning with the French Volney who visited the country in 1785, are "ruined" and "desolate." Each successive writer mourns the further decline of the country. A. Keith, writing in *The Land of Israel* some decades after Volney, comments: "In his [Volney's] day the land had not fully reached its last degree of desolation and depopulation," and he estimates that the population had shrunk by half. By 1883, Colonel Condor in *Heath and Moab* calls Palestine bluntly "a ruined land." And, of course, Americans are familiar with Mark Twain's shocked account of the Holy Land's total "desolation" which introduces a somber note into *Innocents Abroad.*

Up to World War I the picture of Palestine is one of a wasteland inhabited by impoverished, disease-ridden peasants in debt to absentee landlords residing in Beirut, Damascus, Cairo, or Kuwait. The transformation of the country comes when the sand dunes and marshes purchased by the Jewish National Fund from absentee landowners at fancy prices are reclaimed at an even greater expenditure of Jewish lives and labor. The Valley of Esdraelon, today one of the most fertile regions of Israel and the location of flourishing kibbutzim, was described by the high commissioner of Palestine for 1920 to 1925 in the following words:

> When I first saw it in 1920, it was a desolation. Four or five small, squalid villages, long distances apart from one another, could be seen on the summits of the low hills here and there. For the rest the country was uninhabitable. There was not a house or tree.

Not to exculpate the Jews but to defend British policy, the not overfriendly British secretary of state for the Colonies, Malcolm MacDonald, declared in the House of Commons (24 November 1938):

> The Arabs cannot say that the Jews are driving them out of the country. If not a single Jew had come to Palestine after 1918, I believe the Arab population of Palestine would still have been around 600,000 at which it had been stable under Turkish rule. . . . It is not only the Jews who have benefited from the Balfour Declaration. They can deny it as much as they like, but materially the Arabs have benefited very greatly from the Balfour Declaration.

In the light of the grim present, a recital of former benefits rings hollow if not downright offensive. But this much emerges from the record. In 1948, the Jewish state, created through partition into one-sixth of the territory originally envisaged by the Balfour Declaration, emerged without dispossessing a single

Arab. Prestate Zionist settlement had brought Arabs into the country instead of driving them out, uninhabited land had been made habitable, and the abstraction from Arab sovereignty of the territory on which the Jewish state arose represented no blow to the goals of Arab nationalism as till then expressed.

Had the account between Arabs and Jews been closed in 1948 with the acceptance by the Arabs of the compromise represented by the Partition Resolution, it would have been difficult to place the Arabs in the loser's column. The Jews had their minuscule, much amputated state. The original area envisaged by the Balfour Declaration in 1917 had been approximately 3 percent of the former Turkish provinces, but by the time of the Mandate in 1922, the Promised Land had been whittled down to less than 1 percent (.8 percent) through the truncation of the territory east of the Jordan for the purpose of establishing Transjordan. The Jewish state that emerged after the Partition Resolution shrank further to one-half of one percent. In other words, while six independent Arab states had emerged to enjoy sovereignty over a million and a quarter square miles, the Jewish state was ready to dwell in peace with its neighbors within its 8,000 square miles. But this balance could not be struck. Arab calculations were different, and the attack of the Arab states on newly declared Israel, with all that followed in its wake, changed the bookkeeping.

Now there were to be dispossessed Arabs who would continue to multiply but without flourishing, while the Jewish state would expend on war and defense the energy and tenacity that had formerly been expended on the desert. From this point on the drama unfolds with the fatality of a self-fulfilling prophecy. The Arabs, who in the thirties had raised the false spectre of dispossessed Arabs, created the reality of the Arab refugees. I have written elsewhere about the refugees and will not rehearse the familiar arguments as to Arab and Jewish responsibility.[4]

4. See Marie Syrkin, "The Arab Refugees," *Commentary* (January 1966)

However, one element of relevance to the present discussion should be noted, particularly as it has escaped the attention it merits.

All kinds of reasons have been offered for the wild flight of the Arabs from Israel in 1948 when hostilities started: they were driven, they were terrified, they acted in obedience to the orders of the Arab High Command, and so forth. Whichever of these explanations is believed or dismissed, none makes adequate allowance for the swiftness and readiness with which the flight took place. People picked themselves up as though they were going from the Bronx to Brooklyn, not as though they were abandoning a homeland. Part of the speed was due to irrational panic, part to the assurance of return after the victory, but it was undoubtedly abetted by the subconscious or conscious feeling that flight to a village on the West Bank or across the Jordan was no exile. The Arab who moved a few miles was in the land he had always known though not in the same house. He arrived as no stranger, and any differences between himself and his neighbors were due to local antagonisms, not national alienation. The West Bank, which had been Palestine till its seizure by Abdullah in 1948, and Jordan, which had been Palestine till 1922, offered the familiar landscape, language, and kin of the abandoned village. No tragic uprooting took place, such as that which befell the Jews in Europe lucky enough to survive or the countless millions shuffled around in World War II by the victors, particularly by the Soviet Union.

TV interviews have familiarized us with the Arab refugee pointing from his hillside barrack toward his native village in Israel. Sometimes a well-dressed young Arab student indignantly claims to behold the house his family left behind. His anger is understandable. Nobody enjoys seeing his property used by others, even if compensation is available. But the very proximity of the abandoned neighborhood, while tantalizing, is the true measure of how little national loss the Arab from Palestine suffered. Even for so slight a cause as a new subway or urban relocation, people are shifted longer distances and to stranger surroundings than the changes endured by the majority of the Arab refugees. Nasser had no qualms about dislodging whole villages for his Aswan Dam despite the objections of the inhabitants, and the impressive ease with which the Soviet Union has repeatedly shifted huge numbers of its people to further some social or political purpose is a matter of record. Only in the case of the Arabs has village patriotism been raised to a sacred cause.

Arab refugees left so readily not because of cowardice but because departure represented no fundamental wrench; they had a choice. I refer to the aftermath of the 1948 fighting. Even in June, 1967, the comparatively small number who crossed into Jordan did so in the inner assurance that both banks of the Jordan were home, regardless of the physical privations endured as a result of the war. The mobility of the Arabs as refugees or guerrillas, within Jordan, Lebanon, and Syria, indicates strikingly the strength of Arab nationalism and the tenuous character of the Palestinian attachment except as a political tactic against Israel.

What bearing has all this on the present? Guerrillas will not be disarmed by documents irrefutably demonstrating that they are really southern Syrians, nor by British census figures which prove just as convincingly that Jewish settlers did not displace their Arab neighbors. The refugee camps, with their potential for violence, continue to exist, and the furies fed by a humiliating defeat show no sign of abating. Under these circumstances is any accommodation short of the destruction of Israel possible? A Fourth Round, whatever its outcome, will provide no solution. Should the Arab states with the active aid of Russia succeed in destroying Israel, a harvest of horror will be reaped for generations, as after the "final solution" of the Germans. Should Israel win again—the probable result unless the Soviet Union openly intervenes in behalf of its clients— Arab rage will not be lessened. The prospect of Fortress Israel, besieged by hostile millions, will become a bitter parody of the vision of the Jewish state which animated its founders.

The answer to the apparent impasse is not a Palestine state in which Jews—if we take at face value the assurances given—will be relegated to the status of a steadily dwindling minority. And any one who has read the fine print of such Arab proposals knows how even the promise that the Jews will be allowed to live is amplified by references to "Zionists," "foreigners," and "imperialist criminals" to whom the amnesty would not extend. A small number of Arabic-speaking Oriental Jews might qualify for citizenship under these generous provisions. (It should be clear that no binational state is intended. The latter, though advocated by some Israeli groups before the declaration of the state, never found a response among Arabs.)

The official statements of the Palestinians leave no illusions as to their view of what constitutes a democratic Palestine. Articles 5 and 6 of the Palestinian National Covenant, formally adopted by the Palestinian National Council in July, 1968, define who is to be considered a Palestinian after the "liberation": any Arab who lived in Palestine until 1947 or anyone born to a Palestinian Arab in or out of Palestine. Article 6 deals with the Jews of Israel: "Jews who were living permanently in Palestine until the beginning of the Zionist invasion will be considered Palestinians." In Arab terminology the "Zionist invasion" starts with the issuance of the Balfour Declaration in 1917. Consequently, by this definition only a handful of Israelis would qualify for citizenship in the new state; over two million Jews would be expelled as aliens.

In the May 1970 declaration of The Unified Command of the Palestinian Resistance Movement, the Arab objective is defined as "the liberation of the whole of Palestine to establish a community in which all citizens will coexist with equal rights and obligations within the context of the Arab nation's aspirations for unity and progress." The "equal rights" of even such few Jews as could remain would be subject to the "Arab nation."

The final paragraph of the declaration promises the annihilation of Israel. "The aim of the Palestinian Revolution is to dismantle this entity [Israel] with its political, military, social, syndical, and cultural institutions and to liberate all of Palestine."

An illuminating footnote to this program is provided by an interview with Ghanassan Kanafani, a leader of the PFLP, the Popular Front for the Liberation of Palestine, and editor of its weekly journal *Al-Hadaf,* which appeared in the French quarterly *Elements.* The interviewer asked how he thought the Israelis would react to their proposed destruction. Kanafani answered: "When we shall have proved to every Israeli citizen that his place is not here, that he would be safe in Jordan, for instance, or in the United States or in the Soviet Union, he will have understood." So much for the pluralistic Palestine which some enthusiasts of the left obdurately claim is within the realm of possibility.

That the Jews of Israel remain sceptical of Al Fatah's soothing syrup may be taken for granted. In any case, even if they believed that they would be neither exterminated nor deported, it would be hard to persuade the Israelis that some moral imperative demands the snuffing out of their country. They cannot understand the tenderness of every variant Arab nationalism allied to a brutal disregard for the sole national hope of the Jews.

As they see it, no development in the contemporary world has weakened the ideological argument for a Jewish state. On the contrary, the wave of romantic internationalism which threatened to swamp Zionism as a form of parochial nationalism has long receded. Emergent nationalisms are burgeoning all over the globe with the full blessing of the anticolonial left, whose latest discovery is Palestinian nationalism. In the midst of this ardor for movements of national liberation, it is difficult to convince survivors of the Hitler era that Jewish nationalism is the only heretical specimen. Remembering not only active persecution but the barred doors and closed immigration quotas of every land during the holocaust, Israelis are unlikely to agree that the only people with no national need are the Jews. Surveying the globe from European Poland to Asian Iraq, they would reverse the order: no people is still in such desperate need of national independence if only to ensure physical, let alone cultural, survival. "They killed us because we had no country," Jewish refugees in Israel repeated over and over again. And they view indifference to the fate of Israel as simply another manifestation of an ineradicable anti-Semitism which interchangeably exploits the slogans bequeathed by Hilter and Stalin, be it the Elders of Zion of mediaeval legend or the "Zionist imperialists" of communist doxology.

Ideology aside, no Israeli of the pioneer generation will take seriously charges that his coming displaced the Arabs. His personal experience in the process of rebuilding the country testifies otherwise. That is why more concern on this score is to be found among some sabras—not because the young are perverse or more ethically aware than their ruggedly idealistic parents but because they have no memory of the country to which their elders came. Golda Meir knows that her toil in malaria-ridden Merhavia made an uninhabited spot livable, just as she knows that her grandchildren in Revivim, a Negev kibbutz, are creating another oasis in the desert. In human terms, is this good or bad? Every farmer and kibbutznik will indignantly echo the question. A scientist at the Weizmann Institute may less rhetorically point out that only a dozen Arabs lived on the waste on which Rehovoth was founded in 1891. Even a city dweller in Tel Aviv will remind you that Jews built this bustling city on a sand dune; the only ones displaced were the camels who used to parade slowly along the beach. All are united in the conviction that their coming enlarged the habitable area for both Arab and Jew.

The post-1948 inhabitant of a former Arab house in Jaffa or Jerusalem must resort to a more modest rationale. He cannot speak grandly of his creative role as a remaker of land and bringer of light. If he is an Oriental Jew he may call to witness the house and possessions of which the Arabs despoiled him when he fled from Iraq, Yemen, or another of the Arab countries from which half a million destitute Oriental Jews escaped to Israel in an informal population exchange. A Western Jew will use the mundane terminology of realpolitik: what morality demands that foiled aggressors escape scot-free? Besides, Israel is prepared to discuss compensation for abandoned Arab property anytime the Arabs want to negotiate a peace settlement.

The Israeli government has repeatedly announced its readiness to negotiate "secure and agreed" borders whenever the Arabs are ready to discuss peace. Though there are differences of opinion in regard to what should be retained or returned, for the overwhelming majority of Israelis the conquered territories, with the exception of Jerusalem, have no value in themselves; barring peace, their occupation makes defense against attack easier. The Sinai Desert, which three times served as the staging ground for Nasser's armies, the fortified ridge of the Golan Heights from which Syrians shelled the Israeli settlements at will, the enclave of *fedayeen* in Gaza—all are cases in point. Neither the empty Sinai nor the Golan Heights presents a human problem. Gaza and the West Bank are another matter. There live the bulk of the Arabs displaced by the fighting of 1948.

The most reasonable solution among the many informally discussed, the one which does least violence to the vital interests of the parties concerned, is the proposal to set up a Palestine entity on the West Bank and the East Bank of the Jordan. To begin with, the East Bank was part of historic Palestine till 1922, as was the West Bank until 1948. The area represents five-sixths of the territory originally set aside for the Jewish home by the Balfour Declaration. It is the place where most Arab refugees already live for the reasons of consanguinity and proximity already indicated. The dominant role of the Palestinians in Jordan is an open secret. Such a Palestinian state could serve to satisfy newborn Palestinian nationalism and, in conditions of peace, could prosper economically in partnership with Israel. The emergence of such a state would mean compromises for both parties to the conflict. Israel, regardless of victory, would have to accept the narrow confines of its much amputated state, and the Arabs would have to come to terms with the reality of Israel.

Since the likelihood of the immediate acceptance of what could be a rational solution is, for the time being, remote, such questions as the role of King Hussein's shaky throne in such an arrangement or whether the state should be known as Jordanian Palestine need not be argued. The proposal, however, serves as a reminder that the Palestine homeland is already basically in Arab hands and that it does not have to be recovered—unless such is the real objective of the agitation—on the corpse of Israel. Given an honest will to peace, the exact delineation of borders and such problems as the compensation for abandoned property lend themselves to negotiation. But such negotiation, to be meaningful, must be preceded by the recognition that the new national need of the Palestinian and the ancient one of the Jew can be satisfied within the confines of historic Palestine without the destruction of either Israel or Arab Palestine.

13   *Why the new left needs Israel*

MENACHEM S. ARNONI

Contemporary Jewish youth shares the malaise of American youth generally and adds to it nuances of its own. A perennial dissenter, Menachem S. Arnoni explores those nuances and puts the revolt of Jewish youth into a comprehensible perspective. Arnoni's personal odyssey of dissent is a moving document in itself and should serve to validate the sincerity of his analysis of the fallacies inherent in equating Israel in the Middle East with the United States in Vietnam.

    Pointing out that Israel is the product of a liberation movement that succeeded, Arnoni insists that its success must not be distorted into an excuse to invalidate the Jewish National Liberation Movement. Sketching the long process of moral deterioration that has been afflicting the New Left movement for a long time, Arnoni sees Israel's progressivism of deed as the answer to the current Crisis of Ideology.

It is not without pain that I write an essay which, in part, will be unflattering to the American New Left. As founder and editor of the now defunct *Minority of One,* a publication which many have come to view as one of the intellectual forerunners of the American New Left, it is least of all satisfying to me to say some of the things which I am about to say. Yet, precisely because I am resolved to remain faithful to the revolutionary principles which have guided me for many years, I see it as my duty to offer criticism of what was once my movement and which has, I now believe, gone astray.

    The *Minority of One* was founded in the southern city of Richmond, Virginia, in 1959—the first post-McCarthy period. America was slowly beginning to awaken from the nightmare of

MENACHEM S. ARNONI *was the founder and editor of the* Minority of One *and is currently living in Israel, where he is a free-lance writer.*

the crusading intolerance led by the infamous senator from Wisconsin, but people were still losing their jobs for relatively slight deviations from conformist "American" opinions. The cold war was still at a high point. As a minimum gesture of "Americanism," one had to open any political statement with a denunciation, if not of the expansionist Soviet Union, at least of the "treacherous" Rosenbergs or Alger Hiss.

But then-prevailing popular standards, the *Minority of One* could at once be seen as an un-American publication. It openly accused the United States of major responsibility for the cold war. It championed the cause of Castro's Cuba. It accused the U.S. press of news slanting and warmongering. Pledged to the "eradication of all restrictions on thought," each of its issues carried, as its legend, an invigorating quotation from George Orwell: "There was truth and there was untruth, and if you clung to the truth even against the whole world, you were not mad."

But the magazine's road was not all that lonely. Embracing the causes of colonial peoples everywhere, and particularly when defense was needed against greedy American interests, the publication soon found grateful response all over the world, especially in the countries of rising expectations. And because its pages had achieved a high intellectual standard without being formalistically academic, prominent American and international personalities volunteered their cooperation.

The Soviet press was not remiss in echoing the criticism of America that was appearing in the pages of an American magazine. Some articles were reprinted or elaborately reported in such prominent Soviet journals as *Pravda, Izvestia, New Times,* and *Komsomolskaya Pravda.* Moreover, there was hardly a major international event on which Radio Moscow would fail to interview the dissenting American editor. Often berated and maligned at home, he was being built up and celebrated by the Soviets.

But Soviet enthusiasm came sharply to an end as soon as the

publication began criticizing the U.S.S.R. for standing by the Vietnamese people half-heartedly, their cause being sacrificed for the sake of Russia's burgeoning flirtation with the United States.

The *Minority of One* was perhaps the first American magazine to put major stress on the issue of Vietnam and to oppose U.S. policy there — even before the U.S. involvement became overt and direct. Its well-documented exposures of the genocidal cruelty with which American and American-supported troops tried to subdue the Vietnamese patriots made an impact far beyond the circle of the magazine's readers. Nor did the editor-publisher confine himself to literary warfare, but helped organize teach-ins, protests, and demonstrations. "An American genocide is not preferable to a German genocide; and the indifference of millions of Americans is as criminal and inhuman as was the indifference of German onlookers," he said to an audience of tens of thousands at the famous and contagious Berkeley teach-in of October, 1965, while donning the uniform the Nazis had made him wear in the concentration camp of Auschwitz. "I cannot wear this concentration camp uniform without remembering my young parents and sister who perished in the gas chamber of Auschwitz. In my memory, I see them on their death march. . . . My concentration camp has not come to an end so long as there are concentration camps for others."

The crisis to which the *Minority of One* succumbed almost ten years after its foundation began in June, 1967, with the outbreak of the Six-Day War. I had struggled for too long on behalf of the weak against the strong, the small against the big, the colonial against the imperial, to remain indifferent to an evolving leftist verbiage that would sanctify what had been recognized as appalling when done by a Hitler. I had spoken out for the Cubans against the Americans; for the Guatemalans and Dominicans against the Americans; for the Puerto Ricans against the Americans; for the Algerians against the French; for the Guianans against the British; for the Angolese against the Portuguese. Was I now to applaud the intention of genocide, just because this time it would suit the interests of the Soviet Union? The wiping out of a nation was the ultimate atrocity when accompanied by a fascist rationale; was it right when couched in Marxist terminology? I was soon to write in an article that eventually grew into a book:

> One conclusion that necessarily follows from this is that Hitler was wrong merely bibliographically. I mean to say that he read, or wrote, the wrong book. If he had read, or written, the right book, then even if he acted precisely as he did, he would have been right. It is not what you do that is decisive, but the words you think of while doing it. Here we are at the base of Existential Mysticism, which provides a philosophical bridge between Nazism and any other ideology that claims absolute paramountcy.[1]

As for an analogy with Vietnam, indeed I found it applicable:

> While one is on sound moral grounds when petitioning the Soviet Union for whatever exertion is needed to effectively save the innocent, valiant, and victimized Vietnamese people, to petition for equally unlimited aid for governments which propose to wipe out another country is least of all of the same moral quality. The only valid analogy between Vietnam and Israel derives from the fact that both are targets of an extermination policy, the former by the Americans, the latter by the Arabs. Aid in the defense of a people against its exterminators is the opposite of aid to would-be exterminators of a people.

My brand of leftism told me that Israel cannot be expendable for the sake of American big-power calculations.

Overnight many of my friends became enemies, partisans of the other side of the barricade. A whole world of associations collapsed around me. My former comrades, had they been pull-

1. Menachem S. Arnoni, *Rights and Wrongs in the Arab-Israeli Conflict: To the Anatomy of the Forces of Progress and Reaction in the Middle East* (Passaic, N.J.: Minority of One Publications, 1967).

ing triggers instead of hitting typewriter keys, would have been shooting at me.

What fervor they displayed in their new role as crusaders denying a small nation the right to exist! What enthusiasm! How much hidden bloodthirstiness suddenly found an outlet, sanctified by the "progressive" equivalent of psalm and prayer! And how much Gentile anti-Semitism and Jewish self-hatred freed themselves from frustration and self-denial.

The position the American New Left adopted towards Israel, following its victory in the Six-Day War, was merely the culmination of a process of moral deterioration that had been afflicting the movement for a long time. The emergence of the New Left had coincided with the emergence of the American youth movement, and since both were protests against the American Establishment, it was merely a matter of time before they would merge. The trouble was that the youth movement was largely made up of beatniks, hippies, and diverse other nihilists who had shed all moral, social, and revolutionary responsibility.

There are sociological facts that can hardly be reflected in statistics. No one, to my knowledge, has researched and established the statistical proportion between the miscellaneous variants of cynics—those in hippie attire and the more coherent radicals who populate the protest amalgam. Nor can there be any doubt that even within the New Left, as composed today, there are thousands of inspired, coherent, socially responsible young men and women, who are thinking and acting within a frame of reference of their own, if nonconformist, morality.

But whatever the uncharted statistical proportions between these components of the American New Left, the spiritual impact of the fusion has been hooliganism, drug addiction, every kind of offense to ethics and esthetics in the name of politics. The age that saw pornography elevated to the status of art, instrumental flatulence accorded the prestige of music, and carnival extravaganzas accepted as fashions of attire, has also had to bestow respectability on hooliganism. What has emerged is a politics by temperament, not by reason—the pop art of politics.

Anything that sounds tougher is superior. It matters not what the toughness is against or whether it is also *for* anything. It matters not whether its consequences are socially desirable; splitting heads is better than not splitting them, and splitting two heads is twice the fun of splitting one head. And long live the Revolution! Whose revolution? What revolution? For whom, revolution? Don't bother me with questions, fink, you're probably a CIA agent!

To such people the right party in any social or political contest is necessarily the one which sounds more extreme, unconventional, outlandish, exotic. Stop cutting and combing your hair, and you have gone a long way to qualify for their affinity. These are the advocates of fanaticism for its own sake.

Perhaps it was unavoidable that radicals rejecting the status quo in a postideology generation would fail to produce their own vision of a corrected world. Perhaps it was unavoidable that they should reject, but not embrace; negate, but not affirm; protest, but not recommend. Thus the New Left, unable to accept the American experience it had known, nevertheless ran into the dead-end street of the Crisis of Ideology.

For several generations, social visionaries could lean on a presumably exact, if intricate, science of progress. Its logical structure was perfect; its sociological depth exhaustive; its conclusions absolute. Here was an all-embracing thought system, on which man's intellect could feed from cradle to grave. Mental exertion was needed to master it; and so universal were the applications that one never needed to end the study of them. It sufficed for understanding ancient times, our own times, and all of society's stages in between. It applied to Europe and American, as well as to every other continent. It applied both to peace and to war; to language and to the price of goods. To matter and spirit. To economics and the humanities. To health and taste. To all men, young and old. It applied to everything. The only intellectual-sociological challenge left after Marx was to chart the yet uncharted or evolving labyrinths of the relevance of his teachings. Marx, despite warnings he himself had issued, was viewed not merely as one of the scientists, but as super-science itself.

Then something went wrong with this supposedly infallible intellectual system. Basic, supposedly foolproof, predictions did not materialize. Surprises occurred. The grammar no longer fitted the language. The road maps were not taking the drivers to their destinations.

The new Mother of the Sciences could no longer suffice to explain all economic developments. Capitalism's social contradictions did not, as was predicted, lead to its catastrophic collapse. The proletarian's place in capitalist society became increasingly comfortable in more and more countries. In peace and war, the proletariat behaved in a spectacularly unproletarian manner. The greatest challenge to imperialism was not proletarian, but nationalist. Even the capitalists proved unpredictable.

Worse, the society which had been built on supposedly scientific socialism was a disappointment. It did not liberate the individual; it could not even feed him. The presumed grammar of humanism proved no less dependent on repression than systems of greed. The socialist state behaved like any other power aggregate. It, too, became an Establishment. And, as if all this did not suffice to undermine the morale of the disciples of the ultimate science, they were soon treated to the sight of socialist weapons poised against each other; the army of one socialist country was invading the territory of another socialist country; war ultimatums were exchanged between the disciples of Lenin.

Against the background of this disillusionment, how could those who were rebelling against current society pin their hopes on ideology or on any theory as to how society might correct its ways? All they could do was to reject. They learned to negate, but not to seek and embrace.

In all this there was little real rebelliousness. The nihilistic hippie-New Leftist is much less of a revolutionary than he pretends. Actually, he is in the worst American tradition. Our generation's distrust of ideology is in keeping with three hundred years of nonideological American civilization. Nor is cynicism and nihilism anything new in American thought. American civilization, ever since its inception, has revolved about power and greed. The New Leftist's rejection was not so extensive after all; all that he rejected were greed and power. In everything else, he was in no way dissimilar from the mainstream of the American civilization. Lack of social responsibility, violence as a way of life, the belief that anything goes that can make itself prevail, orgiastic anarchism—all these are not only the properties of the hippie-New Left, but also of the Wild West, the California gold rush, the Roaring Twenties.

Nor could it really be otherwise. For contrary to prevailing slogans, young people, no matter how much they implore you not to trust anyone over thirty, tend by nature to be more conformist than their elders. All we learn in our youth—eating, talking, walking, and so forth—we learn through conformism and emulation. It takes a long time and much deliberate effort to free oneself from conventional modes of thinking and behaving.

What appears to us as youthful rebelliousness is often the precise opposite. The youngster, while initially accepting inherited values, soon takes his parents to task for their hypocrisy. He is no revolutionary, but he is an excellent psychologist. If he rejects conventional values and notions, he does so because he senses his parents' own insecurity towards them. Essentially, the hippie-New Leftist says to his father: "Look, Pop, you ain't foolin' me. I know what's really going on in your heart, and I'll externalize this by the ostentation of outrage. Don't tell *me* that you believe in democracy, decency, justice, generosity. I know you better than that, Pop, and I won't be taken in. Look closely at me. See the unkempt whiskers, the dirty clothing? That's you,

Pop, that's the protrait of your generation—a generation that produced wars, conquest, racism, and materialism. I refuse to appear as the son of a moral father, for I am *not* the son of a moral father!"

For such a man to identify with Israel and its struggle is virtually impossible. He has come to reject all the conventional standards of coherence, logic, and social responsibility which alone could "sell" Israel to him. He now believes in the phoniness of all the familiar professed principles. He can only identify with something which is unknown, strange, foreign, exotic, unconventional. The Arab *kefiya,* symbolizing an unknown world, has greater attraction than anything that smacks of standard logic and hypocritical morality.

Then there are other radicals, the radicals who still pursue logical symmetry. They are trying to recover the lost entertainment of ideology. If something went awry with Marxism, then a few house repairs are needed. Theory can offer much intellectual entertainment. For them, "scientific" socialism was as much of an artistic-intellectual experience as it was a social science. It engaged intellects and imaginations no less than music and literature did. It fulfilled spiritual and mental needs. Marx, with his perfect logical symmetry, was, by inadvertance, as much of an intellectual entertainer as a great political sociologist. He provided not only recipes for the cure of social ills, but also an intellectual staple for feeding and satisfying the brains of his disciples. All this must be recovered; the table of theoretical equations must once more be brought into repair.

Minds so conditioned do not find personal self-fulfillment in programmatic social realization. Give them the socialism of reality, give them freed, fed, and educated human beings, and they will not be aware that a social dream has in fact been fulfilled. They will be left with personal nostalgia for the dreaming itself.

The successes of the Jewish self-determination movement and of the Israel welfare state have no attraction to these people.

They are not conditioned to welcome imperfect social achievement as even a partial substitute for perfect but unattainable social dreams. Anything that succeeds becomes in their eyes "Establishment," and they draw no line between entrenched establishments based on exploitation and establishments dedicated to the fulfillment of human rights.

To such people the realization of an idea will always be a source of disillusionment. The idea of the Jewish National Liberation Movement, when realized, arouses their hostility. They sympathize with national liberation movements and libertarian trends generally, but failure seems to be a condition for their continued support. Israel represents no such failure.

Just as the beatnik-hippie-New Left movement in America is a typically American phenomenon, so the contemptuous attitude of at least some of the Jewish participants towards their Jewishness is really nothing more than an exposure of the old, hidden contradictions of American Jewry. The origins of the New Left are not in the now-young generation, but in all the American generations. The origins of Jewish self-contempt, as manifested in so much of the New Left, are in all the generations of American Jewry. My thesis about the preeminence of Jewish participation in the fostering of the New Left's hostility towards Israel does not, I hasten to add, apply to all the Jews in the ranks of the New Left, but it nonetheless points up an essential sociological motif.

The Jewish youngster in America grows up in a home where he is admonished to remain faithful to his Jewish inheritance. This admonition comes in a variety of forms, from preaching to the example of synagogue-attending parents. Yet, this is not sufficient to make a positive impression on the youngster. For he has learned something from his own knowledge of his parents' hidden motivations. If he suspects that his parents themselves do not take their Jewishness seriously, he will refuse to appear so naive as to accord his own Jewishness greater seriousness. Who likes to be caught taking a joke seriously? His parents may pretend, they may even give the impression of participating in a Jewish cultural-religious revival in the United States, but that natural psychologist, the child, understands better than anyone else what makes Papa run to the synagogue:

What did make Papa run to the synagogue? The answer is: an inverted manifestation of assimilation that is peculiar to American Jewry—an assimilation that expresses itself in utterly misleading symptoms, an assimilation that gives the impression of being the opposite of what it really is.

Nothing was more important to the Jewish immigrant than to integrate into American society. While crossing the ocean he vowed to himself not to repeat his European mistake. He did not want to enter an American version of a ghetto. Here in the new land, he would make every effort not to put himself in an exceptional status, to be part of the majority. If necessary, he would sacrifice for that goal part, or even all, of his Jewishness. In Europe his record as a person and as a Jew had been within the *shtetel's* public domain. Whether he prayed and even how many times daily he prayed were a matter of public concern. On this depended his social standing, his reputation, his career, even whom he would marry. His life could have been ruined if he were caught eating pork. But in the New World, in an entirely changed environment where no one knew him and where no social conscience followed him, he would be at liberty to live as he pleased or, at any rate, as was expedient.

When a Jew had reached this stage of personal motivation in Europe, his program was clear. He became an assimilationist. He stopped attending synagogue and participating in organized Jewish life. He avoided social encounters with other Jews. He made himself sound and look like those in the Gentile environment. If he followed the process to its ultimate, logical conclusion, he converted.

The act of conversion was not merely one of adopting another religion. The convert also changed his ethnic membership and even his political status. From then on he became a full-fledged German, Pole, or Frenchman. He saw himself as a changed personality, and the Gentile environment accepted him largely without reservations. His escape from Jewishness was complete and effective.

But the same opportunity did not offer itself in America. For here, denominational membership was deprived of doctrinal essence. Although the state and society encouraged church membership, there was little theology involved in the matter. It was rather a question of mental hygiene. "The family that prays together stays together," admonished signs in the subway. "Go to church on Sunday and business will be good on Monday." Good citizenship required church membership, but the state and society promoted it more for the sake of indoctrinating the citizen with obedience to a hierarchy of authorities than for the sake of a God-centered religiousness.

Belonging is a great thing in America; it keeps people out of trouble; it immunizes their minds against unpopular, possibly red and anarchistic, tendencies; it fosters welcome conformism. So *why* you are a member is less important than *whether* you are a member. The good citizen is a member of the church of his denomination, of some ethnic society, of a social order, of the American Legion or its equivalents, of some fan club, of the local PTA. Although membership in the church of one's denomination is important, the man who keeps his mind preoccupied with doctrinal matters is looked upon askance. He seems peculiar, does not know what life is all about, and has not grasped American pragmatism, which weighs people by concrete achievement, not by refinements of belief and thought. The only man who is forgiven theological preoccupation is the professional—the clergyman—for he has a pragmatic reason for his preoccupation, precisely as the dentist has in pulling teeth.

In that kind of pragmatic religiousness no significance can attach to conversion, except to the degree that it comes to serve a practical purpose, such as intermarriage. Tell the American that you have converted because you prefer Jesus to Moses, or

Moses to Mohammed, and he will send you to a psychiatrist or at least consider you a man without an American mentality—a man whose mind floats in heaven instead of serving his land-based feet. Least of all will you have changed your social or political status. No one will suddenly consider you a remade person, once a Jew, today a non-Jew. Those who looked at you askance because of religious or ethnic background will continue to do so. Those to whom it did not matter will remain indifferent.

Hence conversion offered no escape route to the motivational Jewish assimilationist, seeking not a new god, but a place in the ethnic-political majority. Unable to change his status as a member of a minority group—at least not in the first generation—he had to settle for the next best thing, and, paradoxically, he found it in a return to Judaism. The trouble was that in this reversal his motivation was least of all Jewish; he was merely out to make his Americanism more complete by being a member of the church of his denomination. Thus, he sought not to become a more genuine Jew, but a more genuine American. His practiced Jewishness was inspired not by Jews and Jewish fidelity, but by the Gentile environment and its prescription for good citizenship.

The child, that dangerous psychologist, had sensed his parents' motivation. He knew that they were not serious about their Jewishness even while they ran to the synagogue. And precisely because he was a good son, he was willing to follow in his father's footsteps and to adopt his father's real values. But adopting those real values did not mean accepting counterfeit. He would accept what was really important to father but reject what father *pretended* was important to him.

His own, the youngster's, Jewish experience was strictly limited. It was made to preoccupy him for several months prior to his reaching the age of thirteen. He recalls with distaste the long months during which he was being prepared to recite some strange text in an unknown language, without knowing how to relate the whole thing to anything pertinent to his life and interests. There was much ado about nothing. Yet it all sounded so terribly important. Everyone was concerned, and everyone in the family busied himself with preparations for the bar mitzvah.

At long last, the big day came. He still remembers the ceremony in the synagogue, when, after reciting the obscure text, he and his parents were being congratulated on his "splendid *haftarah*" by people who, like himself, hardly knew a word of Hebrew. And he remembers the reception, the contrived ceremonial atmosphere, the pomp. Everyone in evening clothes, everyone smiling and drinking champagne. He seemed the only one not to understand what it was all about, what was the nature of the big event. He knew that, at bottom, Papa was merely trying to impress his friends and relatives with the ease with which he could splash his money about and with his aristocratic, patrician behavior, as if it were natural to him.

But there were consolations. When the guests finally left, he remembers sitting with Papa and totaling up the checks he had received as gifts and Papa exuberantly announcing the balance over the expenses incurred. But the greatest consolation was that, at long last, he was retiring from his practical Jewishness. No more obscure texts, no more contrived theatrical ceremonies.

It is now several years later. He is at college, breathing in the atmosphere of radicalism and political restlessness triggered by the Vietnam war. Then, early in June, 1967, something happens that makes his Jewishness come back to him. But this time it comes as something very pertinent, something related to the world of ideas and politics that has been preoccupying him. The newspapers, the radio, and the television all say that the phenomenon of Jewishness, of which he is a part, is engaged in a war with one of those fascinating peoples from afar—the Arabs. For the first time, his Jewishness comes to him with real meaning and with an address: Israel. And he knows the exact nature of the conflict, for had he not had his own Jewish experience? Doesn't he remember his father's hypocrisy in running to synagogue and the empty ostentation of his own bar mitzvah? So he knows that in that home of his Jewishness called Israel there is a fight going on between the hypocrisy, the falsehood, the ostentation, and the contrivances which he too had experienced and one of those suffering exotic nations which has been kept down for centuries and which is trying to free itself.

The young bar mitzvah Jew turns against Israel—the Judaism with an address—all the bitterness he has accumulated in his heart against the nonmeaning of the Jewishness he has been exposed to. He speaks up against Israel with a vengeance, each time as if laughing at yet another comical guest at his bar mitzvah, each time as if in protest against yet another check received as a gift to drown the hypocrisy of the occasion in an ocean of dollars.

To be sure, the leftist bar mitzvah Jew is not the only, perhaps not even the predominant, type among those young people in whose hatred of Israel are expressed psychological complexes stemming from the minority status of American Jewry. Nor would it be fair to contend that all opposition of Jews to Israel must be psychoanalytically rather than politically explained. But there is truth in the perception. Take, for another example, the "hero Jew."

He has grown up in a generation which has actively confronted the Germans on the issue of their acquiescence in the Nazi regime's criminal adventures. He is convinced that had he been a German and had he lived in those days, he surely would have raised his voice in protest. Contemptuous of his own freedom or even of life itself, he would have acted as the good German should have. It is almost a pity that history has cheated him of an opportunity to practice heroic morality. Or has it? It is one's closest social environment that one must be capable of rebelling against. The object of opposition should be immediate, not safely remote, and it must involve the risk of personal ostracism. The young Jew sharpens and oversharpens his vision until he begins to perceive the products of his own moribund imagination: Israel, object of admiration by his Jewish environment, suddenly emerges as the new Third Reich, and the Israelis as successors to the Nazis. At last he has built an appropriate stage for acting out the heroics on which the Germans so shamelessly defaulted. His imagination raises him to the stature of a Carl von Ossietsky. Sweet self-righteousness emerges in proportion to the horrors projected onto his own environment and everything related to it.

The self-appointed hero acts according to the prescription he had once made out for would-be German anti-Nazi heroes. No, he is not betraying his people, he is betraying nobody, for would not anti-Nazi commitment have been the ultimate in German patriotism? And so, the more clearly he dissociates himself from his own people and the more actively he struggles against their "outrages," the more he upholds universal humanism and thus is bound to be recognized eventually as his own people's faithful son. In the labyrinths of one particular generation's agonies and dilemmas has emerged an utterly unrealistic, diabolic portrait of Israel.

The paradox of all of this is that Israel's fate depends on the support of the New Left less than does the human rehabilitation of many of Israel's critics. The integrity of progressive thinking itself depends on such a reorientation. For Israel, as the product of a uniquely successful national liberation movement, is particularly relevant to our time's Crisis of Ideology. It provides an opportunity for a sound appreciation of the gap between progressive abstraction and progressive reality. It can alert man to the futility of idealism for its own sake and the futility of treating social theory as an intellectual feast. It should dramatize to all those who are concerned with human fate, and not merely with logical symmetry, that it is worth trading the Paradise of Heaven for the Republic of Man. The example of Israel should enable us to bring our libertarianism down to earth and away from the drawing board.

The position of a Peruvian miner living in misery has an

indirect relation to that of the Israeli technician. They are mutually pertinent. The Israeli may himself once have been living in misery and persecution, no more a part of the Establishment than the Andean Indian mining copper ore. The Israeli holds out a hope to the Indian—hope that misery can be ended, progress and dignity gained. The Israeli is not an offspring of a hereditary world elite; what he made of himself he made by himself, and his starting point bears analogy with any human misery. The Israeli youth does not relate to the *campesino* in a Latin American banana republic the way the son of the *latifundista* does. The Israeli is the child of a man who threw off the shackles of deprivation and represssion by whatever exertion was needed. He is *not* a man of a different social class; he is a member of the same class—after it has raised itself by its bootstraps.

No other society provides blueprints and hopes for solving the problems of the oppressed as does Israel. Be they in India, Nigeria, or the Middle East, they can all find encouragement in the example of Israel, which has raised almost all of its population from refugee status to that of respected and constructive citizens. The Israeli soldier at the Suez Canal is not a Junker raised to glory in militaristic adventure, but the offspring of people who decided they would no longer be pogrommed. All who are deprived, repressed, unprotected by law and uprooted share with the Israelis a common history; where their histories part, the Israelis provide a lesson and an example.

But above all else, implicit in Israel's struggle is the principle of universal coexistence. If the Arab cause is to be deemed as justifying the annihilation of Israel, whose cause against whom will be so deemed next? No progressive approach to the world's problems is conceivable if the continued practice of international capital punishment is found acceptable.

These implications, discerned in Israel and its struggle for existence, can lead to a desperately needed reevaluation of progressive ideas. They can lend progressive people a new equilibrium, this time rooted in actual social achievement rather than in overintellectualized formulae. A crisis of progressive ideology so seen is not a crisis at all; it is a catharsis, freeing us from theoretical encumberances. Out of this we can gain new trust in progressivism, a much-needed new confidence that the libertarian struggle continues to have something to offer. If the price of schools and hospitals is lost romanticism, it is not too high. If the self-determination of peoples must be obtained by sacrificing engaging intellectual entertainment, the price involves no real loss at all. There can be more liberty and socialism in a glass of milk for a hungry child than in 500 pages of print, and those disgruntled by the Crisis of Ideology should remember the importance of the milk even after the hungry child has drunk it.

This is not to say that opportunism, or Khrushchev's "goulash-Socialism," should replace ideology. It would be a fatal mistake to replace the Marxist pseudoscience with a philosophy justifying any direct interest of the person, the group, or the state. A consistent ideological frame of reference is indispensable, for without it, it is impossible to find the causative interconnections between social problems. But we must beware that no intellectualization for its own sake color our social ideas, answering to symmetrical needs of the human mind rather than providing solutions for social problems. And if it is social relevance that counts, those who, out of progressive notions, used to bemoan the plight of the Jews before they wrested self-determination for themselves cannot now picture the achievement of Jewish self-determination as regressive or reactionary.

Confused progressive Jews and non-Jews alike can find in the experience of Israel and in its struggle for survival an answer to the Crisis of Ideology. Their rejections of contemporary American society are as just and legitimate as were the rejections of the status quo by many great generations of revolutionaries that preceded them. But the drugs to which they resort—their sexual anarchy, their hooliganism-turned-politics—these are signs of the anguish and frustration of a generation that can no longer look to ideology for salvation. The practical ideology of Israel—the implication of universal coexistence in its struggle, a proud and constructive citizenry of one-time refugees, the proof that deprivation and persecution can be escaped by one's own efforts—can rehabilitate those who are escaping an ugly world without finding the road to a better one.

There *is* a better one, and some people, including those who make up Israel, have found it.

14 The new left: areas of Jewish concern

TOM MILSTEIN

The tug-of-war between those who maintain that the New Left is so diverse as to defy intelligent generalizations and those who see it as a fairly coherent social movement is decided in favor of the latter by Tom Milstein. He sketches the development of the movement, its WASP genesis, and the groups and subgroups into which it has split. The rationale of the movement's elitism is explored, along with the sources of other elements in New Left ideology.

Milstein is particularly concerned with the latent anti-Semitism of the movement and the sociological disguises it assumes, and he analyzes this phenomenon in the movement as a whole and among its black segments. New Left attitudes towards the Jewish community, Jewish participation in the movement, and black nationalism and the Jewish community are carefully scrutinized. The most frightening aspect of New Left activity, according to Milstein, is its success in dividing and demoralizing large sections of the Jewish community. In his view, the rebuilding of the liberal-labor-minorities coalition is the only response that offers any hope of success.

The past five years in American politics have witnessed the reappearance of a type of anti-Semitism long thought to be extinct. For the first time since elements of the Populist movement personified their hated foe, industrial capitalism, as a Jewish banker, the community has encountered a significant threat to its security from the political left. So far, that threat has not assumed the

TOM MILSTEIN *is a Junior Fellow at Columbia University's Research Institute on Communist Affairs, where he is writing a book about the New Left.*

blatant forms long visible in traditional right-wing anti-Semitism. It does not usually manifest itself as clear-cut ideological anti-Semitism. Instead, it has appeared in more subtle dress, disguised sometimes as realistic sociology ("After all, those Jewish shopkeepers do exploit the black ghetto . . ."), on other occasions as the kind of philo-Semitism which bemoans the Jew's militant defense of Israel as a betrayal of his historic mission (to bear passive witness to man's inhumanity). But precisely because the anti-Semitism component in these sentiments is latent and requires analysis to make it manifest, it is in some respects more dangerous than its right-wing cousin. Its very insidiousness tends to disarm opponents, to mark them as overly sensitive to nonexistent dangers, to confuse and divide the Jewish community, and to make the development of countering strategies quite difficult.

THE NEW LEFT: AN OVERVIEW

Commentators on the New Left phenomenon—particularly sympathetic commentators—like to preface their remarks with the caution that the phenomenon is so diverse as to defy intelligent generalizations. They thereby reveal their own inability to squarely face an appalling reality. The New Left is not monolithic, but it is a fairly coherent social movement with a well-defined subculture, more or less clear-cut organizational patterns, distinctive social bases, and an ideology which, beneath the many disputes, is surprisingly consistent and widely shared.

The New Left is a radical youth movement with extensive adult participation. It has two basic components: black nationalist groups located in Negro ghettos and on college campuses, and white radical groups composed of middle- and upper-class college or college dropout youth. Until its recent split, SDS (Students for a Democratic Society) acted as the main organizational focus for the latter group.

The black nationalist groups subdivide into *pork-chop*

and *revolutionary* nationalist sections. The pork-chop nationalist organizations consist of militants who emphasize Afro-American cultural identification, self-help as a means of improving the situation of Negroes, some form of racial separatism (often taking the form of calls for a separate black state), and hostility to the idea of alliances with white radicals (even though considerable behind-the-scenes interchange with white businessmen occurs). Examples of this faction are such organizations as CORE, the Black Muslims, and Ron Karenga's US.

The pork-chops nationalists have recently been eclipsed, at least temporarily, by the revolutionary nationalists, foremost among whom is the Black Panther party. The revolutionary nationalists are disdainful of the "dashiki-Swahili bag," are opposed to all concepts of black capitalism, and seek to build alliances with white New Leftists. Most crucial is their identification with one faction or another of the world communist movement, which currently means one or another communist nation.

Finally, there are the numerous black student organizations which have sprung up on college campuses in the past few years. These groups have no distinctive point of view apart from militant nationalism and are often the arenas for fierce struggles between pork-chops and revolutionary nationalists. The Panthers appear to be winning most of these struggles.

The white New Left is composed of the remains of SDS, various groups which were at work within SDS and are now attempting to scavenge its corpse (in competition with certain old left groups like the Communist party of the United States and the Trotskyist Socialist Workers party), and various groups which arose to oppose American involvement in the Vietnam war. Since most of the New Left antiwar groups are offshoots of SDS or SDS-related groups, they will not be discussed separately.

Students for a Democratic Society, prior to the recent split which smashed it, encompassed three more or less coherent formations. First, there was the indigenous SDS, which traces back to the old SDS of the early 1960s. At that time, its politics were mildly left-liberal but featured certain characteristics which survive even now—among them, a highly personalistic approach to politics, hostility to formal organization and procedures, an obsessive preoccupation with individual morality, and a tendency to view politics as a means for the salvation of souls. With the radicalization of SDS that took place after 1965, this group became steadily more hysterical and extremist. It has culminated in the notorious Weatherman faction of SDS, which believes that by blowing up public buildings it can precipitate a revolution.

The main force instrumental in promoting the radicalization of SDS was the Progressive Labor party, the official Maoist organization in the United States. PLP was also a key force in transforming New Leftism from a nonideological movement with its roots in the American radical tradition into a Marxist-Leninist-Stalinist movement with its roots in the foreign policy needs of various communist nations. By the time of the 1969 split, PLP was operating more or less openly in the SDS through its Worker-Student Alliance caucus. This caucus, composed of PLP members and sympathizers, comprised a majority of the participants in the 1969 convention of SDS and, after the split, presented itself as "the real SDS."

The third group surfaced only briefly in the struggle which led up to the split and existed visibly for only a short time thereafter, but it may be inferred to have played a major role in that struggle. It called itself the Revolutionary Youth Movement II (or RYM-2) faction and was allied to the Weatherman faction against PLP's Worker-Student Alliance caucus. In the struggle leading up to the split, RYM-2 portrayed itself as being to the left of PLP and as being the "real Maoists". It also arranged for the intervention of the Black Panthers on behalf of the Weatherman—RYM-2 side in the dispute. After the split and the effective isolation of PLP, the Maoism of RYM-2 disappeared with remarkable speed. The role played by this faction in SDS, as well as the activities of some of its leading members after the split, suggests that its conduct was inspired by a pro-Soviet orientation in the Sino-Soviet dispute, rather than by the actual issues in dispute at the SDS convention.

The subculture of New Leftism is well known. It stresses the youth culture, psychedelic experience, radical individualism, romantic anarchism, rejection of concepts of rationality and responsibility as "traps," a fascination with violence and the fantasy ritual of heroic sacrifice followed by heroic death, and apocalyptic world views. The New Left's subculture resembles that of a religious revival in the degree to which it relies on ecstatic experiences (induced by chemical or confrontationist means), rejection of worldliness, and cultivation of myths, in order to sustain itself.

The New Left recruits followers from fairly distinctive sections of the population. The black nationalist groups frequently consist of a leadership drawn from middle-class Negro life and a membership from the lumpen proletariat. In the Panthers, however, lumpen elements predominate even at the leadership level. The white New Left recruits almost exclusively from the upper middle and upper classes, particularly on college campuses where large numbers of students from these backgrounds cluster. No New Left group, black or white, has had any success in recruiting from the American working class, black or white.

In addition to the class factor, there is an ethnic dimension to the social base of the New Left. This ethnic dimension has been somewhat obscured by the internationalization of the New Left, that is, by its relatively recent connections with various branches of the world communist movement and the consequent reconstitution of its ideology according to the dogmas of that movement. Since public interest in the New Left developed mostly after this internationalization had taken place, many persons concluded from the number and prominence of Jewish youth in its leadership and ranks that New Leftism was in some sense a disproportionately Jewish phenomenon. Actually, disproportionate Jewish participation in the New Left arose after New Leftism was already well launched as an ideology and a movement—with its own, distinctively non-Jewish, ethnic base.

New Leftism was born as an essentially WASP phenomenon. The early chapters of SDS were concentrated at the more parochial and ingrown academic centers of upper-class WASP life—places like Tufts, Swarthmore, and Antioch. Its earliest heroes were such men as Staughton Lynd, A. J. Muste, and C. Wright Mills, all men who gave expression to particular themes in the radical Protestant tradition. (Lynd concentrated on extolling the moral primacy of the "inner light" of individual conscience over social norms; Muste expounded an apocalyptic and millennialist brand of absolute pacifism; Mills sociologized the conspiracy theories of his rural Populist background.) It is the Protestant radical tradition which gives to New Leftism its most characteristic style, that of politics conducted as a moral crusade, in the fashion of the Abolitionist and Prohibitionist movements. This moralistic style, which is foreign to Marxian radicalism, has survived even the internationalization and Stalinization of the New Left.

The ideology of the New Left is a pastiche drawn from several sources. Contrary to both its critics and its supporters, the most characteristic feature of New Left ideology is not Marxism, about which the vast majority of New Leftists know nothing, but rather elitism. This elitism—noted by Marx as a basic theme of middle-class radicalism in almost all of its forms— is expressed in the New Left's perception of how society works and of how to bring about social change. New Left social theory always emphasizes a fantastically powerful and clever power elite which rules by manipulating the consciousnesses of its subjects, convincing them that what is objectively not in their interests in fact is. From this derives the view that the masses cannot become conscious of their true interests and require the services of an enlightened elite, as opposed to the old power elite, to make the revolution for them.

Elitism helps the New Leftist to account for the persistent unwillingness of the masses to embark on the revolutionary course which seems so obviously correct and moral to him; it also inflates his self-esteem to Nietzschean proportions. As he sees it, revolutionaries must possess special characteristics setting them apart from the ordinary run of humanity—characteristics which enable them to ascertain the "truth" about society and justify them in enforcing that truth on everybody else. Opposition, if it is acknowledged as sincere, is explained away as the product of manipulation by the power elite, the Establishment, or whatever the current terminology is, and if not sincere, as the product of secret deals, sellouts, or CIA gold.

Into this basic elitist social theory has flowed the perverted Marxism of communist totalitarianism, with which it is not at all incompatible. This infusion has served to link the New Left with various branches of the world communist movement, particularly as it appears in the so-called Third World, and although it would be inadequate to view the New Left as merely an arm of that movement, it is true that without this international connection the New Left would have evaporated long ago. The link to communist movements in the Third World enables the New Left to justify to itself and to outsiders the confrontationist tactics which gain it publicity and prestige. Confrontation can be defended on the grounds that, by disrupting the United States, the New Left is weakening the ability of imperialism to control the oppressed revolutionary masses of the Third World. The advantage of this theory is that it permits almost any action, no matter how insane or irrational.

The New Left is therefore the sum of both indigenous American and international communist causes and influences. It is neither the clever band of communist conspirators that the right wing supposes it to be, nor a group of innocent, bright, and sincere youths carrying on the American tradition of radical protest and moral renewal that its apologists describe. It is rather a complex synthesis of both international and national elements which found in the war in Vietnam a common ground. That common ground could slip away as the war ends. But a new common ground could be found to replace it—most likely provided by the race issue in American politics.

NEW LEFT ATTITUDES
TOWARD THE JEWISH COMMUNITY

Relatively little has been explicitly written by the New Left about the American Jewish community. Nonetheless, its attitude may safely be described as contemptuous. First and foremost, the New Leftist is hostile to American society. The relative success of American Jewry's experience in America is therefore evidence to the New Leftist of an immoral accomodation to evil. This attitude is reinforced by the awareness that since Jews are a traditionally oppressed minority, their relative success in America must be evidence either that American society is not the Frankenstein monster of reaction that the New Leftist fancies it to be or else that the American Jew has worked out some special arrangement with the Establishment involving the betrayal of his traditional commitment to social reform. Naturally, it is the latter conclusion to which the New Leftist is driven.

This theme of Jewish betrayal is quite strong in both the black and white branches of the New Left. One finds it in the writings of Harold Cruse, particularly in his recent book *The Crisis of the Negro Intellectual,* where it takes the form first of a denunciation of what he regards as manipulation of Negroes by Jewish communists in the 1930s and then of a generalization from that experience to Jews as a whole and to the present time. In addition, I. F. Stone and David McReynolds both have written tracts bemoaning the defection of Jews to American imperialism, as expressed in their support of Israel. Its most common form, however, is not the reasoned argument but rather the incidental remark, the innuendo, and the unarticulated attitude. The Jew is condemned by his success, his affluence, his political power, and, indeed, his very liberalism, which to the New Left is the subtlest of all forms of reaction. True, he is not condemned by these traits to the status of a diabolical force, at least among white New Leftists. The New Left does *not* embrace ideological anti-Semitism. Rather he is regarded as an obstacle to the revolution, and obstacles to the revolution do not occupy a favored place in the New Left pantheon.

The view that Jews have made it in America also serves to justify another characteristic New Leftist trait: the tendency to apologize for or to explain away incidents of overt anti-Semitism. (Among black nationalist groups, this tendency extends to a willingness to engage in overt anti-Semitism.) One of the most common forms this practice takes is a reference to the lengendary exploitative Jewish shopkeeper in the black ghetto. Whenever a simple denial that anti-Semitism exists at all among the black nationalists fails to convince, the next argument usually resorted to is the alleged prevalence of this infamous character. New Leftists possess an almost biblical faith in his existence, despite the fact that recent studies have shown that his ilk is far less numerous than they suppose. They also believe that his existence explains, if it does not justify, black anti-Semitism. Since the same studies reveal that non-Jewish white, as well as black, shopkeepers exploit ghetto residents every bit as rapaciously as their Jewish colleagues, the question may fairly be asked why the nationalists single the Jew out for special attention. Such questions usually go unanswered, since the Jewish shopkeeper theory neither explains nor justifies black nationalist anti-Semitism. An answer may nonetheless be ventured.

The New Left's equivocation with respect to anti-Semitic incidents goes to the heart of its paradoxical, dualistic attitude toward American Jewry. On the one hand, the movement believes that Jews have made it, that they have "gotten theirs," and that they therefore occupy a privileged position in the American hierarchy—that they are, in a word, secure. From this perception New Leftists conclude that Jews are more or less *invulnerable* to attack and that their privileged position enables them to take the abuse of the nationalists. That is why New Leftists are so contemptuous of expressions of outrage by Jews at such abuse. New Leftists believe that Jews should exercise an attitude of noblesse oblige—there is no other term for it—toward black nationalist anti-Semitism. It is this perception of Jews as particularly invulnerable that underlies the New Left's willingness to apologize for anti-Semitic expressions.

On the other hand, New Leftists also know, or at least sense, that the Jew is peculiarly *vulnerable* in spite of his vaunted success and power. The vulnerability, of course, derives from the unique status of the Jewish minority in America: it is the only minority against which all other minorities have something in common, including even minorities which are currently more oppressed than Jews. The Jewish minority is therefore always exposed to the danger of social isolation, since attacking the Jew as a Jew can become a means of expressing the solidarity of non-Jews. It was precisely this insight into the peculiar vulnerability of Jews that the young girl who authored the notorious introduction to the Metropolitan Museum's "Harlem on my Mind" catalog expressed, and the fact that she cribbed it from Moynihan and Glazer's *Beyond the Melting Pot* does not detract from its significance as a semiconscious or conscious motivation of New Left anti-Semitism and apologies for anti-Semitism.

The Jewish community has thus become a special target of the New Left not because of misconceptions about it, but rather because of a shrewdly accurate appreciation of its ambiguous position in society. New Leftists have discovered how disarming it is to respond to expressions of alarm over black nationalist anti-Semitism with the flip comment, "Oh, come on, now, are you trying to tell me that American Jews are in any real danger? Look how well off they are." Meanwhile, they can enjoy the innuendo that because Jews are well off, they rather deserve what they are getting—their comeuppance, retribution for a betrayal of their historic role as symbols of oppression. And, although it may be a paradox in logic, the notion that the Jewish community is invulnerable accords in practice with the parallel recognition that the Jewish community is also peculiarly vulnerable, the easiest group in America to attack, particularly if the attack comes or appears to come from the most oppressed, that is, from those represented by the left.

JEWISH PARTICIPATION IN THE NEW LEFT

Jewish participation in the New Left falls roughly into three categories. The first consists of Jewish youth who are drawn to the New Left because of the traditional Jewish commitment to progressive social change. Lately, the experience of such young people in the New Left has been short and unhappy. If the New Left's equivocation on the subject of black nationalist anti-Semitism proves insufficient to alienate this type of young person, the movement's anti-Israel bias usually does the rest. The tragedy is that a tendency exists to translate disillusionment with the New Left into general disillusionment with all progressive causes.

The second category includes the so-called red-diaper baby phenomenon. This term refers to the offspring of Communist party members and sympathizers. These young people inherit a number of characteristics from their parents' politics that serve them well in the New Left: most importantly, a contempt for democracy, well-developed organizational skills, and the ability to rationalize away New Left anti-Semitism, gained from long experience at rationalizing away Soviet anti-Semitism. Such young people do not comprise a large number of the New Left rank and file, but their organizational skills do enable them to assume leadership positions out of proportion to their numbers. At the recent Chicago SDS Convention, the author conducted an informal survey of the delegates and found that over half of the sample 15 to 20 delegates fit directly into this red-diaper syndrome. Such communist influence as there is within the New Left is transmitted through these young people. It does not take the form of instructions to a cadre, but rather of a more diffuse conditioning of the New Left mentality to accept uncritically a number of key communist shibboleths: anticommunism of any kind is reactionary; no such thing as totalitarianism exists, only capitalism and socialism; the communist countries may have their defects but they are basically progressive in contrast to the West, which is reactionary; and so forth.

There is nothing specifically Jewish about the behavior of the red-diaper set in the New Left. Offspring of communist non-Jewish parents do not behave in a qualitatively different manner. This group of young people, far from engaging in generational revolt, is in reality carrying on a family tradition. Their behavior is generally viewed benignly by their parents, which may partially account for Kenneth Keniston's finding that many New Left youths are on better terms with their families than are non-New Left youths.

The third category of Jewish youth participation in the New Left may be termed the passing generation. The term has reference to the ability of New Leftism to serve as a medium of assimilation for upper middle-class and lower upper-class youth of Jewish parentage into the dominant culture. The New Left subculture is heavily loaded with the values of radical Protestantism: extreme individualism, moralism, evangelism, and reference to the conscience rather than to the intelligence or the community as the supreme arbiter of what is just. As such, it often becomes a means of resolving the status anxieties of Jewish youth whose economic background exposes them to intense personal anxiety. This anxiety is the internalized reflection of a marginal social situation: the conflict experienced by those who possess a communal Jewish background but who must enter a competitive, Protestant society. The complaint that "American Jews have sold out my birthright," heard from so many young Jewish New Leftists, even when accompanied by the corollary argument that New Leftism constitutes the rekindling of a "purer Judaism (despite the fact that the individualist ethos of New Leftism is the antithesis of Judaism's communal ethos), is simultaneously an expression of self-hatred and a manifesto of capitulation to it. By surrendering to a radical version of the elite's ethic, one can avoid confronting the self-negating significance of the act of assimilation.

These categories do not by any means exhaust the varieties of Jewish participation in the New Left. Individual cases may reflect all three influences, or they may be unique. The categories are generalizations meant to identify and distinguish between those forces at work within the Jewish community which culminate in New Left participation.

BLACK NATIONALISM AND THE JEWISH COMMUNITY

It is important to recall that the slogan of "black power," which was publicized by Stokely Carmichael and which marked the beginning of nationalism's current ascendancy within the Negro movement, was part of a self-conscious attempt by its advocates to wrench the Negro community out of the liberal-labor-minorities coalition. The argument was that Negroes must withdraw from any and all coalitions with white people until such time as they were organized into a cohesive bloc—that is, until they possessed black power. For Negroes to ally themselves to any other group in society was to invite manipulation by outside forces for purposes not in the interests of the Negro community. The argument was often clinched with the provocative question: "After all, hasn't there been Irish power and Jewish power? Why can't there by black power?"

The answer, of course, is that there indeed has been Irish power and Jewish power, but that they were never created by means of appeals to ethnic separatism, but rather through appeals to multiethnic solidarity. Any Irish or Jewish American idiotic enough to raise the inflammatory slogan "Irish power" or "Jewish power" in the political context in which minorities found themselves—in the context, that is, of urban capitalism where minorities of all ethnic backgrounds had to learn to co-operate with each other at least to the extent necessary to capture the Democratic party or else face the most unrestricted and naked exploitation which the laissez-faire Republican party could devise—any such Irishman or Jew would have been treated as an agent provocateur. That is why one has to look far and wide for any sloganizing expressions of Irish power or Jewish power in American political history. By and large, the minorities have avoided nationalism out of a healthy respect for the danger inherent in being pitted against one another by the elite—a danger created by ethnic nationalism.

But two factors have enabled nationalism to gain a foothold in the Negro minority, neither of which had to be faced by minorities in earlier periods. The first is the relatively high level of permanent unemployment among Negroes, which is a dis-organizing factor that renders the community less resistant to demagogic appeals and movements. The second is the influence of the mass media, which early took up the cudgels for black nationalism by giving almost daily coverage to Carmichael, Rap Brown, and other nationalists, despite their initial lack of any following.

Just as the success of black power was inevitably linked to the demand that Negroes withdraw from cooperation with all other groups in society, such a demand required the launching of a fierce attack on precisely the groups to which the Negro had been allied—liberals, labor, and the other ethnic minorities. "Honky," therefore, became the inevitable corollary of "black power." Once race became an issue among the groups comprising the Democratic coalition, that coalition began to fragment, and its conservative opposition, the Republican party, registered corresponding gains. This process initiates a vicious circle, because once in power the Republicans can exacerbate ethnic friction by cutting back on progressive social programs and playing each group off against the others.

Black nationalist anti-Semitism becomes somewhat more explicable in the context of these developments. In the first place, extensive Jewish participation in the civil rights movement had to be eliminated in order for the demand for separatism to subvert the demand for integration. Second, the alliance between American black nationalism and Third World movements, symbolized by Carmichael's tour of a number of totalitarian and semitotalitarian countries, required that an attack be leveled at American Jews as "Middle East murderers of colored peoples." And finally, the peculiar vulnerability of Jews, already referred to, made them easier to attack than other minorities.

The recent rise to prominence of the Black Panther party calls for special attention to be focused on the record of their anti-Semitic beliefs and actions. A typical example is an article by Don Cox, field marshal of the Panthers, in the 30 August 1969 issue of the Panther newspaper. The article's headline was "Zionism (Kosher Nationalism) + Imperialism = Fascism." This example illustrates the Panther practice of disguising anti-Semitism as "anti-Zionism." Sometimes this flimsy disguise is dropped, as, for example, in an article by Connie Mathews, international coordinator of the Black Panther party, in the 25 August 1970 issue of the *Black Panther:*

> . . . The White Left in the U.S.A. is comprised of a large percentage of the Jewish population. Before the Black Panther Party tooks its stand on the Palestinian people's struggle there were problems but the support of the White Left for the Black Panther Party was concrete. However, since our stand the White Left started floundering and became

undecided. This leaves us with no alternative than to believe that a large portion of these people are Zionists and are therefore racists.

It was a Zionist judge, Judge Friedman, who sentenced Huey P. Newton to two to fifteen years in jail. It was a Zionist judge, Judge Hoffman, who allowed the other Zionists to go free but has kept Bobby Seale in jail and sentenced him to four years for contempt charges. . . .

The other Zionists in the Conspiracy 8 trial were willing and did sacrifice Bobby Seale in his role in the conspiracy trial to gain publicity. Once again we condemn Zionism as a racist doctrine. . . .

"Other Zionists" refers to Jerry Rubin, Abbie Hoffman, Willian Kunstler, and so forth!

CONCLUSIONS

The New Left, except for certain black nationalist groups, is not an anti-Semitic movement. It does not advocate ideological anti-Semitism. If it did, there would be very little difference between it and fascism. But it does not. Nonetheless, it is quite definitely a clear and present danger to the security of the Jewish community in the United States. It has succeeded in legitimating anti-Semitism on the left in American politics, something that would have been inconceivable a few years ago. The gravest danger which this development portends is not that of a mass expression of left-wing anti-Semitism; too little fuel exists on the left for that to happen. The danger instead lies on the political right, where the mass base and the hardened ideologues of mass anti-Semitism exist. This potential has been kept bottled up in the past by the fundamental illegitimacy of anti-Semitism in American politics, but it is difficult to envision how that illegitimacy can be maintained in society at large if it cannot be maintained on the left in particular.

An additional danger posed by the New Left lies in the sphere of the defense of Israel. The New Left is overwhelmingly anti-Israel and has willingly served as a vehicle for the propagandizing of pro-Al Fatah positions to the American public.

But perhaps the most frightening aspect of the New Left's activity has been its success in dividing and demoralizing large sections of the Jewish community. Two dangerous trends have developed within the community in response to it, and both have served to reinforce New Leftism. The first is accommodation or outright capitulation, and takes the form of fellow-traveling with the New Left. This course serves only to provide New Leftism's extremist actions with a Jewish cover and has had no noticeable tendency to reduce the level of anti-Semitic and anti-Israel expression. The second trend is blind reaction, taking the form of a shift to the right and a repudiation of the community's traditional identification with progressive social values. This course serves to deprive the community of the political allies it must have to avoid that most dangerous of all situations for minorities—social isolation.

The only effective strategy is the rebuilding of the liberal-labor-minorities coalition, and the development of a movement dedicated to that purpose. These tasks may lack the emotional gratifications and the high drama of other courses, but they remain more vitally important than ever.

15 New left go home

AMOS KENAN

*There is something very strange and monstrous about
the New Left as seen from Israel by one intellectual
who is himself a leftist. Amos Kenan has no patience
with American and European New Leftists who decide
that there is no justification for Israel's existence and
conclude, therefore, that no people constitutes Israel
and hence there is no justification for this nonexistent
people's struggle for existence.*

*In Kenan's view, because the New Left is incapable
of carrying out revolution in the developed countries
is no reason for them to foist their revolution on the
underdeveloped Middle East. He is not prepared to be
the victim of the leftist hunger for excitement and
amusement.*

In the beginning, there were the missionaries.

They came to teach the natives how to wear a fig leaf over
their private parts, and to worship one God, and to brush their
teeth after morning prayers.

After a number of missionaries had been murdered by natives who did not understand the purity of their motives, the
soldiers came to ensure their safety, and that was how the empire
was born.

And after the empire had crawled back into its hole, the
New Left came to give the natives the word.

There is something very strange and monstrous about the
phenomenon known as the New Left. When the New Left talks
about a "proletarian revolution," it is not referring to what the
old left meant by the term. Proletarian revolution? Rome had

AMOS KENAN *writes for* Yediot, *a popular Israeli afternoon newspaper,
and is well known in leftist circles in the United States and Israel.*

its proletariat too, and it demanded just two things of its caesars: bread and circuses. The student proletariat of Europe has bread enough but is short of entertainment. So it looks for entertainment in the catastrophes that beset our planet.

It is a shocking fact that the Vietnam war has cost the Vietnamese people a million casualties, while all it has brought European youth is the new fashion of longer hair. Student demonstrations to the contrary notwithstanding, it is difficult to compare the war for freedom that the Vietnamese are waging with the gay clashes between students and police. The latter war, to put it mildly, is not being fought with comparable strength, scope, or resolve. The cemeteries of Europe are not full of hundreds of thousands of student graves. Nor are the Vietnamese letting their hair grow as a sign of sympathy with the student cause.

The Vietnam war is drawing to a close, because of the fighting ability, unparalleled in history, of this small, brave nation, its historically deep-rooted national unity, and its almost unprecedented resoluteness. In short, the outcome of the war in Vietnam will be determined on real, rather than imaginary, battlefields.

To repeat, the modern proletariat wants to be amused. Having seen the Vietnamese gladiator begin to defeat the American lion in the arena, these charming long-haired boys are now ready for new amusements. Like the proverbial birds of prey, they soar aloft to see where else blood is flowing, and thus they have reached the Middle East.

For the past twenty-one years, the Middle East has been the site of a war between two nations, or rather, between two nations-in-the-making. It may be that war is necessary to the development and ultimate consolidation of these nations. This does not change the fact that the current war is a straightforward exchange between two nations.

Any normal left which endorsed supranationalism and internationalism and for which the class war superseded any national war would simply call the two parties to order. If one of the sides sought left support, the left would reply: first of all, put your house in order, and then we can talk it over. The New Left, however, is not a normal left. So, with a mixture of dogmatism and paternalism, this gay proletariat has taken on the task of distorting terms and concepts.

The distortion of terms and concepts is a purely intellectual craft. The first step is to avoid taking facts into consideration. The second step is to transform reality into a word or a series of words. And the third step is to draw from the lexicon a new word or series of words that will overpower the first words, thereby ensuring verbal victory. Let the good words defeat the bad ones, and reality be damned!

The State of Israel is an established fact, and the Israeli nation is an established fact. A living, breathing fact requires neither proof nor recognition of its existence. The very fact that it *is* is sufficient. Every human group has the right not only to live, but also to choose the manner in which it wishes to express the fact that it is a group of humans. The right to be a nation is likewise self-determined and does not require any outside recognition.

The New Left, however, has investigated and found that, historically, there is no justification for the State of Israel's existence. Since Israel has no justification, it follows that no people constitutes the state. Since the state contains no people, there is a priori no sense or justification for this nonexistent people's struggle for existence and freedom.

In short, as I do not fit somebody's intellectual image, I do not exist. Since I do not exist, I must disappear. Thus, we find Arab Marxists describing Israel as a country where people of the Mosaic faith reside, to whom they are prepared to grant religious freedom as "Arab Jews" within an Arab state.

Similarly, we find international Marxists who have decided that Israel is not a nation, but a class. The Fatah is, therefore, not the fighting arm of one nation against another, but a revolutionary group waging a class war against the Zionist class, a war, incidentally, which serves the interests of international colonialism.

In a third and extreme stage of this war of words, Israel is described as a phantom state. And everybody knows that fighting a phantom is very easy. You merely whistle, and the phantom will retire to the grave from which it came, to the eternity of history.

As even a Marxist beginner must know, a prerequisite for changing a situation is first of all to know it, to recognize it. Israeli tanks are not driven by delegates from some temporary union of members of the Mosaic faith. Israeli air force planes are not flown by a class—they are flown by a people. To change us all into a word, and a dirty word at that, is intellectual corruption and a betrayal of all the lofty principles that have ever led movements toward changing the world for the better. Helping those who seek to annihilate us is beyond corruption; it is complicity in murder.

The aim of any organization of freedom fighters is to make the other side agree to parley, to force the ruling side to recognize the ruled. The Vietcong aim was to force the Americans to parley. The Algerian FLN had similar aims. When, therefore, Yasir Arafat announces that he does not recognize us, he is a fool. When the New Left supports him, that is corruption.

The New Left has lost out on the political front. It is obviously incapable of carrying the revolution to developed countries. Even its real willingness to carry out a revolution is open to doubt. A few heads battered by policemen's clubs are not a very great sacrifice to lay upon the altar of revolution. Six million Jews paid a more honorable price for a different ideal. And neither the Vietcong nor the FLN dispersed and went home after an unsuccessful demonstration.

The New Left is unable to create heroes, though it needs them badly. As parasitic as its imperialist ancestors who plundered the world, it borrows heroes from the world of hunger.

What a paradox it is that young people from the most advanced countries in the world are seeking their heroes among men who fought for an agrarian revolution, as if that were Europe's problem!

There is still another paradox. Che Guevara, a doctor from a relatively advanced country, followed in the footsteps of his missionary antecedents to spread the word to the natives. Instead of teaching them to believe in one God, he set out to teach them revolution. However, for the native of Bolivia, Che was merely another white man—and so he failed.

We, the natives of the underdeveloped Middle East, want the left to makes its revolution in its own territory, if it can. If it can't, it can stay home, go to discothèques, let its hair grow, and leave us alone.

We don't want it to come here to plant its unsuccessful revolution. In fact, we don't want it to plant anything at all here. We'll manage by ourselves, among ourselves, for better or for worse. We are not prepared to be the victims of leftist hunger for excitement and amusement.

We do not want this paternalism. We do not want to be taught what, where, or how from above. We'll learn everything in due time, by ourselves. New Left go home!

We are still in a primitive stage of development; we still wage wars between nations—in Biafra, the Sudan, Iraq, Israel, and many other countries. Incidentally, dear left, what are you doing about the Sudan and Iraq? Why are the Kurds less deserving than the Palestinians? Why shouldn't they have the right of self-determination? Suppose we call our Arabs "Jewish Arabs" and promise them equality?

It is possible that we must take another very serious phenomenon into consideration: the conscience of Europe has gotten tired of beating its breast in regard to the Jewish question and has decided that it has been solved (with Nazi help, by the way). There is no longer any need to be anti-Semitic, just as it is no longer fashionable to be a declared fascist. The fascists of today are subtle and camouflaged.

Shukairy used to say that the Jews should be driven into the sea. After the 1967 defeat, it appeared that a slogan of this sort was not good public relations for the Arab cause. So today, only the Zionists are to be thrown into the sea. The only trouble is that when the Arabs get through pushing all the Zionists into the sea, there won't be a Jew left in Israel. For not a single Jew in Israel will agree to less than political and national sovereignty. We are now a nation that has shaken off the dust of a thousand years. Anyone who deludes himself into believing that he means to drive only the Zionists into the sea should know what he is really talking about.

A word of advice to the Fatah. If you are struggling for recognition of Palestinian rights, you will find allies among us. The Land of Israel has room for two nations, each taking its place within one homeland according to the dictates of both historic and present justice.

But, in contrast to Solomon's judgment, we are prepared to do with half, while you want everything. And the curious thing is that willingness to make do with half is not a sign of weakness, while willingness to accept nothing less than the whole is not a sign of strength. We have proved this three times, and we will prove it again.

You have nobody to appeal to. The world is prepared to give you up for reasons of profit or loss or domestic considerations. And this includes Nixon, Sadat, Hussein, Brezhnev, and everybody else. You are a card that everybody is cynically prepared to play. You must now decide whether you are ready to talk to us.

The New Left will save you as it saved Spain, Greece, Czechoslovakia, and six million Jews.

16 The kibbutz as a revolutionary society

SAADIA GELB

New Left admiration for positive aspects of life in Israel is expressed in—and limited to—approval of the kibbutz, or collective, movement. Indeed, according to Noam Chomsky, Martin Buber's Paths in Utopia *is about the only required reading among the leftists. How relevant this line of thinking is to contemporary Israel and its collective societies may be determined from the fact that Buber deals with utopian socialism generally, traces its history through Proudhon, Kropotkin, Landauer, and their forerunners, analyzes experiments that failed, and then goes on to Marx and Lenin. It is only in the epilogue—the closing ten pages of his book—that Buber even gets to the kibbutz, the "experiment that did not fail." But even in 1945, when* Paths in Utopia *was written, there was surely enough kibbutz history to justify more than Buber's restrained, almost eulogistic evaluation of this struggle over the emergence of a structurally new society as an attempt that "will not be forgotten in the history of mankind's struggle for self-renewal."*

There is a considerable body of much more recent and relevant analysis of the kibbutz, its successes and its failures, which might be put on the New Left reading list. An excellent start might be made with Saadia Gelb's frank evaluation of the kibbutz as seen from the inside: its premises and promises, its fulfillments and failures. Gelb's remarks might also clarify for the New Left the question of whether the State of Israel has indeed stunted the growth of the kibbutz movement and arrested, if not reversed, its progress.

SAADIA GELB—*teacher, social worker, and administrator—is a member of Kibbutz Kfar Blum.*

We see the kibbutz as a revolutionary society because it posits specific goals and shapes itself in the form best calculated to realize those goals. It is not the result of the imposition on reality of esoteric, theoretical concepts, but the reverse: a pragmatic testing of paths which would best lead our kibbutz society to the desired goals. Any analysis of the kibbutz, then, to be valid must be pragmatic rather than theoretic. It must see the kibbutz as a constantly evolving life-style based upon certain fundamental assumptions and striving for commonly accepted goals.

Our first assumption is that man can shape his society. If he could not, if we were all subject to some external fate or will, if we were all simply pawns in some universal game, there would be no point to either plan or struggle — and, of course, no point to a left, New or old, either. We assume, then, that man can change; that he can adapt himself and his life-style to the realization of predetermined goals.

A second assumption is that the larger society will at least tolerate, if not encourage, this effort, an assumption validated by the constant growth of the kibbutz movement from its very inception to the present day. There is, therefore, no validity to the view that the very creation of the State of Israel has led to a decline in our movement. The kibbutz is a totally voluntary society which people join or reject in accordance with their own social and economic orientation and psychological needs. The state does not regulate its growth, nor is the state responsible for its support; the kibbutz is entirely a product of our own needs and desires and the fruit of our own striving. The larger society, of which the state is one expression, will tolerate us if what we do is meaningful to us and at least not inimical to society as a whole.

We must assume, judging from our growth over the years, that our goals are meaningful and satisfying, even when we fall short of their realization. This alone would explain our growth from an initial membership of exactly nine people to well over 90,000 men, women, and children in more than 230 kibbutzim.

There is one final assumption: there must be no dogmas to

hamper our flexibility. Dogma leads to aridity, to sterility, to an inability to react pragmatically to changing conditions.

The question of motivation is something else again. No single motive is adequate to assure a viable kibbutz society; there must be at least two. By and large, our kibbutzim have been built upon a combination of national and social motivations in some instances, religious and social motivations—with perhaps a dash of the national, as well—in others. Social motivation alone will not provide viability.

There have been many attempts to emulate the Israeli kibbutz, and almost all have ended in failure because of the absence of adequate motivation; there is, for instance, a long list of such failures in the United States and in Africa. In Burma, there has been a measure of success because the kibbutzim established there were built on the borders of the country and thus serve national as well as social purposes. There is a vast and growing movement in Japan, with over 7,000 members, and every year some half-dozen groups come to Israel to study our movement; they too combine a variety of motivations. However, the kibbutz idea is not translatable to any society without these motivations. A black kibbutz planted somewhere in Louisiana would not survive; external pressures would be too great. But a black society, combining a social and national or a social and racial striving, is conceivable. In the Soviet Union, where the kibbutz, or *kolkhoz,* to use their term, has none of these motivations and was established by fiat of the government, the movement has failed. To the extent that the *kolkhoz* exists, it does so as a result of government pressure and regulation; it is not a growing, self-regulating society impelled by the idealism of its members, sharing goals and purposes.

Even such a sharing cannot, of course, produce a utopia. With all of its idealism, with all of its motivation, with all of its achievement over the years, the kibbutz cannot be represented as a society which has found all the answers to the problems of life and of society.

The history of the kibbutz in Israel demonstrates that there is need for an awareness of the goals among those individuals who set the pace for its development, as well as among the vast majority of the membership. Perhaps this will explain references to the kibbutz as an elite society. The kibbutz does not consist of an elite, but it is a society of aware people, conscious of what they are doing. Otherwise, the realities of daily life would make the kibbutz impossible. The element of awareness is clearly characteristic of every activity within the kibbutz. Indeed, it would be impossible for people to live in a kibbutz without an understanding of its meaning. The results, which in a sense are permanent and revolutionary, cannot be achieved by external pressure, as we see from the *kolkhoz* experience. Pressure cannot keep the system going.

Furthermore, it is not possible to understand either the development or the meaning of the kibbutz by thinking of it as it is at any given moment—the essential weakness of the latest studies, of which Professor Bruno Bettelheim's *Children of the Dream* is the most significant example. A picture is a view of a particular place at a given time; it cannot portray an evolving society. The kibbutz must be seen as a process. It must be viewed periodically as to both development and trends. It can best be considered from the vantage point of at least thirty years. Although the first kibbutz was actually established some sixty years ago, we may consider the first two decades or so as prehistoric. Examining it over the several decades that followed, we find that it has achieved at least some of its goals. Any critical evaluation must deal with a number of themes.

PERSON-TO-PERSON RELATIONSHIPS

The structure of the kibbutz has led to the creation of a unique person-to-person relationship. All decisions of the kibbutz are taken at a general meeting, where the rule is "one person, one vote," with only those present voting. In other words, one who does not attend a general meeting foregoes his right to vote and is bound by the majority decision. There is no possibility of weighted votes or of undue pressure; it is the individual who counts.

Anyone may bring up any problem at a general meeting — even what may seem to be a matter of slight concern. Of course, he must adhere to established procedure; otherwise there would be chaos and anarchy. But there is a direct person-to-person relationship and, with it, an opportunity for self-expression. Although we are all subject to the will of the majority, self-expression is guaranteed in the sense that every member is entitled to a full hearing at a general meeting and may also appear before all relevant bodies. He may continue with his life and work even though he advocates a minority view, so that the personality of the collective does not alter the personality of the individual. *He has, in fact, become, not a collective individual, but an individual within a collective.* From the viewpoint of human development, this is probably the most significant achievement of the kibbutz.

CHANGING MORES

The mores of the kibbutz society, when examined, show many changes. First, the group is attuned to the trends in society at large. People often refer to changing mores in terms of the sexual problem. We in the kibbutz can predict almost exactly what will happen along these lines in the United States, because we have already lived through our own sexual revolution. We have tried the permissiveness now being demanded in the United States, and we have found that it is not good; the basic family unit seems to meet a more genuine human need than the so-called total freedom now in vogue.

Thus, changing mores have not hampered our development. We are able to survive as a collective and as a society with a wide variety of mores, including those of the Orthodox kibbutzim which, from the beginning, accepted the strict Orthodox guidelines and survived, too. The kibbutz has not suffered thereby. It is possible to conduct this collective, idealistic, or "socially migrant" society, irrespective of mores. The question is, are we accepted?

CAN WE CONDUCT OUR AFFAIRS?

Without going into detailed statistics, it is significant that the kibbutz produces the bulk of the country's cereals, much of the vegetables, and a large proportion of the poultry and eggs. We represent 10 percent of the industry and, all in all, constitute a significant part of the economy. An examination of the exact statistics will show that the kibbutz sector is a completely integrated and essential part of the economy of the country. We have learned, despite our collective approach and our concern for the individual, to be effective.

Granted that from the standpoint of efficiency something has been sacrificed to democracy. Undoubtedly, greater efficiency would be possible with a managerial type of administration, in which each individual would be trained in a very narrow field. But that would weaken our democratic fabric because our society would then be under the rule or under the tyranny — certainly under the guidance — of "experts." We have our experts, but we keep them in their place.

When we examine the relationship of our stated goals to our actual development, we find that we have done very well in some instances, not so well in others. This, too, is an indication of a living society.

We are not quite satisfied with our influence on the youth of Israel. In the last fifteen or twenty years, in particular, we would have liked to attract more of them to our way of life and deflect them from the forms of individual expression which obtain in the United States and the Western world as a whole.

However, since the Six-Day War of June, 1967, there has

been an upsurge in young people's interest in the kibbutz. Although our ability to attract city-born youth fluctuates, we have had an influence on education. The kibbutz ideal of national service has permeated all of Israeli society and has contributed to the tone of the country, so that when people speak of the epitome of the goals of Israel, Zionism, and the labor movement, they often refer to the kibbutz. That, too, reflects a certain kind of achievement.

A detailed critical evaluation of the kibbutz would indicate that our society has not found the answers to all problems. For example, our political influence, at one time predominant, is now simply "important." Americans seem to be skeptical of that importance. One newspaper reporter commented that since we are such a small group of people—less than 4 percent of the total population—we should have no influence at all. But our influence flows from our origins; at one time we were probably the most influential single factor because the total society was geared to our specific goals. Under present developmental circumstances, the university is important and so are technology, capitalism, and the wide world. If, despite these, the kibbutz is still at least important—witness the number of kibbutz members in the Knesset, in the labor leadership, and in all kinds of public bodies—I think we have more than proportionately achieved our objectives.

THE END OF THE CRISIS

Some years ago people were concerned over a crisis in the kibbutz, a development which appeared serious at the time. It arose shortly after many of the services previously performed by the kibbutz were preempted by other elements—when the army took over defense of the country, the government assumed responsibility for immigration and other specific, functional integration activities, and the Histadrut grew into a big industrial complex. Many in the kibbutz felt that perhaps the goal of national service had been realized and all that were left were selfish personal goals. Now it is a mark of our structure that self-satisfaction alone does not suffice. If we were merely enjoying a benign society, the majority of kibbutz members would have been dissatisfied. There was a minor crisis then, and there were those who wrote brilliant eulogies to the effect that within five years the kibbutz would be finished. But the eulogies were premature.

Ample testimony to the good health of the kibbutz is to be found at any kibbutz association conference, where hundreds and sometimes thousands of young people, very much alive, congregate. As to how it will all end, we kibbutzniks leave prophecy to others. We try to deal with reality, with our daily tasks, and are content to let history record what ultimately happened.

The educational and cultural patterns we have developed and which have evoked such serious study and comment grew out of our efforts to shape our own future. Although we have no *new* educational methods as such, we have been able to adapt normal educational instruments to the development of a wholesome personality attuned to the kibbutz aims. Having achieved that, we draw attention to the fact that it is possible to realize educational goals on a voluntary basis through peer-group participation, through experimentation and flexibility, utilizing both the old and the new. As a result, the kibbutz has been able to develop and change without fear that its essential goals will be lost.

NO CONFLICTS OF INTERESTS

There is no conflict between our national, socialist, and individual interests. We have learned how to reconcile them, giving each its weight and its place after a thoroughgoing, honest evaluation. We do not set ourselves theoretical priorities, but rather take each issue as it arises. At times, the entire kibbutz movement may be preoccupied with one issue, because it seems to be the pertinent, the most pressing, issue. By such allocation of priorities we respond to real-life situations. And it is that attunement to life which characterizes the entire kibbutz structure. Do we fulfill the group's inner strivings? I think we do; otherwise people would not remain in the kibbutz.

What about the young people? Roughly 60 percent of the young people of the kibbutzim remain. Perhaps it seems dreadful that 40 percent leave. But current trends show that any rural area loses about 80 percent or more of its populations. Under circumstances of modern technology and conditions, the kibbutz record, with 60 percent continuing the basic revolution of their parents—and sometimes of their grandparents—is impressive indeed. Inevitably, the conclusion is that the kibbutz *does* serve the group's strivings.

On the other hand, kibbutz meetings and kibbutz literature are full of endless discussions of problems plaguing the community. Obviously, we are not at a stage where we can say that we have found the formula and now we can relax. We know we are a long way from finding it, or we would not be a true kibbutz, reacting pragmatically to life.

Although, statistically, we may retain more of our youth than nonkibbutz rural areas do, any loss represents a measure of failure. However, we feel that our failures do not parallel those in other societies, where the generation gap has come to loom so large. Rebellion, when it occurs, is not against parents or authority, as such, because the kibbutz structure is simply not authoritarian; it generally centers on issues, goals, or motivations. We meet such rebellion—or such challenges—by open discussion—endless hours of wrestling with the issues until they are resolved. We invoke no punishment, we utilize no pressures; we talk—with understanding and sympathy, of course, because otherwise talk is useless. Most often, talk will resolve an issue. Where talk fails, the youth leaves.

Objectively and subjectively, therefore, the kibbutz has stood the test; it is as close to that so-called permanent revolution as a human society can be. I should, however, qualify this statement by saying that any society, to go on functioning, must in one way or another be institutionalized. The kibbutz, too, has its Establishment; it, too, has a certain amount of conservatism; it, too, is subject to stress. So, within the kibbutz there are individual and sometimes group feelings of restraint and frustration, and our young people sometimes find they are dissatisfied. There is, therefore, constant criticism and reevaluation.

There is constant experimentation, too, not only to improve the present framework of the kibbutz, but to develop new forms altogether. The kibbutz was originally conceived of as a rural, agricultural society. It is still rural, but a progressively larger share of its economy is becoming industrial and may now be classified as an agro-industrial economy. So far, the kibbutz movement has suffered no ill effects from this transformation, perhaps because basic kibbutz goals and motivations have been retained. There have been attempts to break out of the rural setting, but these have not been successful so far. The possibility of a viable urban kibbutz is still to be demonstrated; previous attempts, made some years ago, failed. Perhaps this is because a measure of isolation and some distance from the daily lure of the larger society is needed. There are further attempts being made at present: perhaps they will be more successful.

CONTINUING CONTRIBUTION

In brief, and to sum up, the kibbutz is a revolutionary phenomenon that has found ways of inner rejuvenation. Were it not so, it would be a passing phenomenon. Because it is constantly being rejuvenated, it has become an important function of Israeli society. Sometimes it is more a focus of world-wide attention than of Israeli attention. Sometimes Israel as a whole is completely immersed in its own specific and special local problems; there are probably still some Israelis who have never stepped inside a kibbutz. Yet, it is a society worthy of study, and in any serious discussion of the influence of the left, New or old, on the development of society, the kibbutz has a particular contribution to offer. After all, it has successfully applied socialist thought to daily life and demonstrated the possibility of its realization.

It has a further contribution to make, too. Because the kibbutz is a revolutionary society, because it is pragmatic and unhampered by dogma, it is in an excellent position to carry on a dialogue with the New Left in the United States and with progressive elements anywhere in the world, including the Arab world. The nonexploitative, revolutionary society of the kibbutz may yet find that its greatest contribution to Israel is still to be made.